# GERTRUDE
# AND
# ALICE

Diana Souhami is the author of many widely acclaimed books. Her *The Trials of Radclyffe Hall* was shortlisted for the James Tait Prize for Biography.

# GERTRUDE
# AND
# ALICE

Diana Souhami

PHOENIX
PRESS

5 UPPER SAINT MARTIN'S LANE
LONDON
WC2H 9EA

A PHOENIX PRESS PAPERBACK

First published in Great Britain
by Pandora Press, HarperCollins, London in 1991
This paperback edition published in 2000
by Phoenix Press,
a division of The Orion Publishing Group Ltd,
Orion House, 5 Upper St Martin's Lane,
London WC2H 9EA

Jacket design © Peter Campbell

A CIP catalogue record for this book
is available from the British Library.

Printed and bound in Great Britain by
Butler & Tanner Ltd, Frome and London

ISBN 1 84212 033 6

*Gertrude Stein and Alice Babette Toklas first met on Sunday 8 September 1907, in Paris. From that day on they were together, until Gertrude's death on Saturday 27 July 1946.*

# Contents

# FOREWORD

I have drawn from archive material in the Yale Collection of
American Literature and in the Bancroft Library in Berkeley, from
published memoirs, collected editions of letters and from books
and articles by and about Gertrude Stein and Alice B. Toklas.

I have no more than touched the surface of what are described
as Gertrude's resistant or hermetic writings, and I offer no new
insights into her work.

My focus is the story of the relationship between Gertrude and
Alice – a devoted marriage, funny, quietly eventful, orderly,
domestic, intimate and happy. I was beguiled by the fact that this
marriage, of the sort that eludes so many heroes and heroines,
should be achieved by two odd-looking, strong-minded women,
who followed the creed of being true to themselves.

First publication of this book was in 1991. I remain indebted to
Philippa Brewster, my original editor. All thanks too to Rebecca
Wilson, Publishing Director at Weidenfeld, Georgina Capel, my
agent at Simpson Fox Associates and to Peter Campbell who
designed the jacket.

To avoid cluttering the text with footnotes, sources of quoted
material are cited, at the end of the book, by page number and
opening phrase. Credits and copyright permissions appear on
page 291.

# ILLUSTRATIONS

Yale University refers to Collection of American Literature, The Beinecke Rare Book and Manuscript Library, Yale University

*Dedicated by request to N.N.*

*Gertrude and Alice in 1935. Photograph by Cecil Beaton.*

# 1

## GERTRUDE AND ALICE

*'In me meeney miney mo.*
*You are my love and I tell you so'*

Gertrude and Alice made a strange-looking pair. In photographs they look like a double act of pontiff and acolyte, or Little and Large, or a mountain and its shadow. Alice is always carrying the bags and umbrellas, or sitting in the lesser chair, or walking behind Gertrude, or is scarcely visible at all. But she fostered this image of the self-effacing maidservant, and it belied her force of character and true role in the relationship.

She had a cyst between her eyebrows which Picasso said made her look like a unicorn. To hide it, she combed her hair forward to the bridge of her nose and pulled her hats down to her eyes. She was under five feet tall and, when sitting, her feet seldom reached the ground. She loved expensive gloves and took great care of her hands and nails, which she manicured daily, and she had a moustache which the food editor of *House Beautiful*, Poppy Cannon, in 1958 said made other faces seem nude by comparison. She had grey-green eyes, a large, hooked nose and an acute sense of smell and taste, even though she was a heavy smoker.

Gertrude was large in girth, though not in height. In her prime she weighed 200 pounds. She liked loose, comfortable clothes, with deep pockets. Pierre Balmain was a friend, and he made clothes for her and Alice in the late 1930s while he was still a student. He lined Gertrude's baggy tweeds with mauve taffeta. She wore sandals even in winter with fronts like the prows of gondolas, had a collection of waistcoats embroidered with flowers, birds and the like and, for hats, she wore an assortment of felt caps, straw lids, a cloche, modelled on one that had belonged to Louis XIII which Alice thought would suit her, and a flower-bedecked one for high summer.

When Ernest Hemingway first met Gertrude in 1922, she reminded him of a northern Italian peasant woman, with strong features, beautiful eyes, a mobile face and 'lovely, thick, alive immigrant hair', which she wore up in the same way she had probably worn it in college'. But in 1926 Gertrude asked Alice to give her a haircut. Alice did not know how to go about it, so the style became shorter and shorter, and the shorter it became, the better Gertrude liked it. By the end of the session, Gertrude did not have much hair left. Hemingway then thought she looked like a Roman emperor: 'That was fine if you liked your women to look like Roman emperors.'

Though neither Gertrude nor Alice ever wore trousers, their appearance could confuse. Gertrude, particularly in evening dress, was sometimes mistaken for something ecumenical - a bishop, or a cardinal. At Christmas 1934, when they were staying with Gertrude's cousin, Julian Stein, in Baltimore, one of his children, aged three, said of them that she liked the man, but why did the lady have a moustache.

They first met in Paris on 8 September 1907. Alice heard bells ringing in her head when she saw Gertrude and thought that was proof she was in the presence of genius. She described Gertrude as 'a golden presence burned by the Tuscan sun and with a golden glint in her warm brown hair'. She thought her beautiful, with a wonderful, velvety contralto voice, an enormous sense of life, and deep experience.

On Gertrude's suggestion they walked alone together the next day in the Luxembourg Gardens and ate cakes in a patisserie off the boulevard St Michel. From then on, until Gertrude's death thirty-nine years later, they were never apart. They never travelled without each other, or entertained separately, or worked on independent projects. Gertrude felt low in her mind if she was away from Alice for long. And Alice, writing about their relationship, at the end of her own long life, said that from the moment they met, 'it was Gertrude Stein who held my complete attention, as she did for all the many years I knew her until her death, and all these empty ones since then'.

They became intractably related to each other, a classic duo, as inseparable as Romeo and Juliet, or Laurel and Hardy, or Napoleon and Josephine, perhaps. They called each other Pussy and Lovey in front of strangers. (Alice was Pussy.) They wrote notes to each other inscribed DD (Darling Darling) and YD (Your Darling). They regarded themselves as married. Alice often called Gertrude, he, or her husband, or her Baby Woojums. She gave her a cut-out, hand-coloured paper Annunciation in a golf-leaf frame, inscribed 'MON EPOUX EST A MOY ET JE SUI A LUY' (My husband is mine and I am his). Gertrude, on occasion, signed letters from them both 'Gertrude and Alice Stein'. And in her love poems she made many a reference to the joys of conjugal life with Alice. 'Little Alice B. is the wife for me,' she wrote. Or

Tiny dish of delicious which
Is my wife and all
And a perfect ball.

Or

You are my honey honey suckle.
I am your bee.

Friends liked Gertrude's pleasant handshake, huge personality, conversation, repose and easy laughter. Alice was sharp, and more exacting company. Basket, their giant poodle, became a famous additional member of the family. Strangers commented on him. Mostly they said he looked like a sheep. Children called him Monsieur Basket, or the dog in pyjamas. Gertrude said that of his ABCs he knew only the Bs: Basket, bread and ball.

There was a moral base to the tryst between Gertrude and Alice. As a student at Harvard, Gertrude had been entangled in a fraught, triangular relationship with another woman. She wrote about the experience in her first novel *QED*. She described herself in the affair as trapped in 'unillumined' immorality, and observed:

> If you dont begin with some theory of obligation, anything is possible and no rule of right and wrong holds. One must either accept some theory or else believe one's instinct or follow the world's opinion.

Gertrude and Alice's relationship accepted the 'theory of obligation' and, apart from the fact that they were both women, fulfilled the codes and expectations of conventional romantic love. Their life together became a paradigm of a good relationship. They fell in love, saw life from the same point of view, and lived as a couple, with much emphasis on domestic harmony, until parted by death. They were happy and they said so. Alice said Gertrude was the happiest person she had ever known. They were acerbic about the more fraught, or varied, private lives of many of their friends - Hemingway, who had three wives, Picasso's succession of women, Natalie Barney's spirited affairs with lots of ladies.

They had much to unite them. Both were brought up in the San Francisco Bay area of California. Both were the daughters of European Jews who were first-generation immigrants to America. Both travelled in Europe when they were children and were in their teens when their mothers died. They had a Californian openness and hospitality, a cultural interest in Europe, a kind of pioneer courage. Though they lived in Paris, they had little to do with the indigenous French. Sylvia Beach, who ran the bookshop Shakespeare and Company, said she never met French people at their apartment at 27 rue de Fleurus. They were staunchly patriotic about being American: 'Americanism is born in me,' Gertrude said. They liked waving American flags at the end of the the two World Wars. Though they left the States in the early 1900s, and only once returned for a visit thirty years later, they regarded France as their adopted country and America as their native land.

Their deepest point of agreement, and the focus of much of their shared life, was that Gertrude was a genius ('Twentieth-century literature is Gertrude Stein,' Gertrude said) and that she and her genius must be served. This made for a perfect symbiosis, a harmonious division of labour. Gertrude liked to write, talk to people, drive the car, stay in bed until midday, lie in the sun, walk the dog, look at paintings and meditate about herself and life. Anything else made her nervous. Alice did the rest.

Alice was always fiercely busy. She could knit and read at the same time. She typed Gertrude's manuscripts, dealt with household affairs, embroidered chair covers and handkerchiefs, dusted the pictures and ornaments, planned the menus, instructed the cook and the maid, washed the paintwork, arranged the flowers. In the country, she did the digging, planting and sowing. When she came to her own writing, after Gertrude's death, it was reminiscences, menus and letters, in a crisp, acerbic style.

'Alice B. Toklas is always forethoughtful,' Gertrude wrote, 'which is what is pleasant for me'. A friend, Mabel Dodge, said to Alice in Italy in 1912, 'I can't understand you. What makes you contented? What keeps you going?' Alice replied, 'Why I suppose it's my feeling for Gertrude.' More than twenty years later, when Gertrude, as a celebrity, toured America with Alice, Alice said that Gertrude was at home in America through her writing, whereas she, Alice, was at home through Gertrude.

There was nothing demeaning in Alice's servitude. She was the power behind the throne. Those who wanted to see Gertrude were first checked out by Alice, and if Alice did not approve they were turned away. She believed herself to be descended from Polish nobility. As a girl, she was taught to open a bottle of champagne cleanly at the neck and, when sweeping up the day after a party, to watch out for diamonds in the dust.

Visitors to their Paris apartment found her frightening. Most of them wanted to see Gertrude. But behind Alice's imperious façade was a streak of romantic daring. She left her home in San Francisco when she was thirty and took a chance on life in Paris. She had a passion for clothes, dangling jewels and hats adorned with flowers and feathers. On a train journey to Florence in the summer of 1908, troubled by the heat, she took off her cherry-coloured corset and threw it out of the window. She had wanted to be a pianist, and studied music at Washington University, but thought her own talent fifth rate. So she promoted Gertrude's talent instead. She was an excellent impresario. She managed and organised both their lives, shaped their fame and promoted their public image. It was she who selected the motto 'Rose is a rose is a rose is a rose' to appear in a circle on Gertrude's stationery. Gertrude first used the words in a poem called *Sacred Emily*. Alice polished anecdotes about themselves until they became legend. Above everything, she ensured that the quality of their daily life was orderly and agreeable.

Inherited money from the Stein estate allowed them to live in freedom and comfort. They chose to live in France when the cost of living was low. They never owned property. They rented their apartment in Paris and, for fifteen years, a large house in the Rhône valley. They ran a car from 1916 on and always had one or more servants. Their lifestyle was hospitable and extremely comfortable, but not grandly affluent.

Gertrude's true fortune was acquired through love - her collection of modern art, bought, for the most part, before the First World War, for not much money and before the success of the artists was established. The paintings, by Picasso, Matisse, Cézanne and others, were the treasures of her youth. She sold one or two of them reluctantly in later life to finance the publishing of her work or to buy food on the black market in the Second World War. She never adequately insured them, or made an inventory of them. After she died, Alice suffered financial hardship to avoid selling any of them. She wanted them to go *en bloc* to a museum as Gertrude's collection.

They were both well-settled in Paris long before the international literary community arrived there in the twenties and thirties. They were at the cultural heart of Paris life for four decades: through the revolutionary exhibitions of the Fauves and the cubists, the struggles of the innovative magazines of the twenties, the aspirations of the expatriate writers between the two World Wars. They were intrinsic to Paris at that time and became famous by virtue of being themselves. They attracted an audience wherever they went - in Charleston, Oxford or Avila. They were indomitable and a sight to be seen. They loved driving around in 'Auntie', their Ford car, looking at paintings and Roman ruins, eating delicious food, talking to everyone, making the best of where they were. For much of the time they seemed like two biddies on a spree. They took great delight in Gertrude's success, when it happened late in their lives, and in spending the money she earned. They practised the art of enjoyable living in an unpretentious way. And they were so emphatically and uncompromisingly themselves, that the world could do nothing less than accept them as they were.

*The Stein family in Oakland, California in 1880. From left to right:*
*Simon, Daniel, Gertrude sitting on a pouf, Amelia, Leo and Bertha.*

# 2

## GERTRUDE'S EARLY YEARS

*'Laying an egg this is the*
*Occupation of a horse'*

I guess you know my life history well enough, that I was in
Vienna from six months of age to four years, that I was in Paris
from four years of age to five, that I was in California from six
years of age to seventeen, primary & grammar school East
Oakland, and that I was born in Allegheny, Pennsylvania.

Allegheny was a problem to Gertrude when she lived in France with Alice:
'French authorities always threw up their hands imploring "Would you mind
spelling that?" Imagine expecting a Frenchman to spell Allegheny,
Pennsylvania.'

The bones of biography - what happened when and where - did not concern
Gertrude. Cosmic issues interested her: existence, identity and descriptions
of what she believed to be fundamental aspects of human character. 'Bottom
nature', she called it.

She was the youngest of five children. 'One should always be the youngest
member of the family. It saves you a lot of bother, everybody takes care
of you.' Her eldest brother Michael was born in 1865, Simon in 1867, Bertha
her only sister in 1870, Leo her favourite brother in 1872 and Gertrude at
eight o'clock on a snowy morning on 3 February 1874.

Her parents, Daniel and Amelia, had resolved to have five children and
no more. Gertrude and Leo were only conceived because two previous
babies died. It made them 'feel funny' and they did not like talking about
it: 'If anyone is the youngest of seven children and likes it he does not care
to hear about birth control because supposing he had not been born.'

Grandma Stein came from Weikergrubben, a Bavarian village. She was
a mountain of a woman and she married a butcher. One of her sons died
of obesity. Most of the Steins were large and keen on food. Gertrude's

third brother Simon would eat a family-size rice pudding at one sitting and was by any standards huge. Grandma Stein was of tough stock. Even in old age, said Gertrude, her back was straight and firm. She inspired her sons with the courage to emigrate as pioneers. 'She led her family out of the old world into the new one.'

Gertrude's father, Daniel and his four brothers set up a large clothing store, dealing in imported textiles, in Baltimore, Maryland. Business was good but they all quarrelled. In 1862 Daniel left the firm with his younger brother Solomon to open another branch in Pennsylvania, trading in wholesale clothing and fabrics. They built identical adjacent houses on Western Avenue, 'the most high-hat street in Allegheny' and it was there that Gertrude was born. She was, said her father, a 'perfect baby', a fact with which he reproached her in later years if ever she was ill.

Alice B. Toklas described Daniel Stein as 'a man of brilliant ideas and no patience to carry any of them through'. Gertrude said of him, 'he liked to buy things and have big undertakings'. He had rapid mood swings and was uncertain whether to live in Maryland, Pennsylvania, California, or Europe. He was big with little brown eyes, 'sharp and piercing and sometimes dancing with laughing and often angry with irritation'. He liked eating, worried about his digestion and could be terrifying. He would pound the table and say he was the father, they were his children and they must obey him. In the street he walked with his hat on the back of his head, so that it looked as if it was falling off, muttered to himself, threw his body from side to side and forgot about his children if he was with them. He quarrelled with Solomon over business and with many of the clients too, and Solomon spent much time wooing back the customers driven away by Daniel's bad temper.

He married Amelia Keyser, a 'sweet gentle little woman', in 1864, soon after their first meeting. She was twenty-one, he was ten years older. One of his brothers more or less arranged the marriage. Sometimes, said Gertrude, her father thought his wife was a flower, usually he forgot she existed. She called him 'Darling Dan', or 'Dear Dan', in her diaries and worried about his moods, his travels away from home and his bowels.

Amelia's parents were German immigrants too. English was the second language for both her and Daniel. The Keysers settled in Baltimore, had a large family and, according to Gertrude, were 'cheerful pleasant little people.' Amelia's father was hard-working and religious. He first worked as a tanner, then he became a rubber merchant.

Despite her mild, compliant disposition, Amelia had a 'fiery little temper'. She disliked her sister-in-law Pauline and by the time Gertrude was born had stopped speaking to her. As Daniel quarrelled constantly with his brother, living in adjacent houses was not a success. He dissolved the partnership,

*Amelia and Daniel Stein.*

moved his family to the next street, then in 1875 took them all to live in Vienna.

There, Gertrude remembered picture books, the taste of beer and walks in the public gardens where she once saw the Emperor Franz Joseph, 'a natural figure to have in a formal garden'. Her father had business interests in property, investment and mining and travelled a lot, often sailing back to the States. 'Oh God send him a safe return', Amelia wrote in her diary. The family lived comfortably – good food, simple, expensive clothes, a cook, a governess and servants. There were music lessons for the children – the violin for Mikey and Leo, the piano for Bertha and Gertrude. In adult life Gertrude liked playing on the white keys only.

For her first four years Gertrude heard 'Austrian German and French French', then, when she was five, 'American English'. 'Our little Gertie is a little Schnatterer,' her Hungarian governess wrote in 1875. 'She talks all day long and so plainly. She outdoes them all. She's such a round little pudding, toddles around the whole day and repeats everything that is said or done.'

Amelia's diary for 1878, their last year in Vienna, has survived. She recorded the weather, 'it was lovely untill about 6 o'clock it commensed to rain', the day the cook Betty arrived and the day seven months later when she left to get married, the cost of corsets, dress lining, beer, wine, 'gurgle water', matzos and sausages, the purchase of leggings for the children, the loss of Mikey's new slippers, money received for returned wine bottles and Simey and Leo's visits to the dentist, each to have a tooth drawn. 'All well' was her usual refrain. For Gertrude's fourth birthday, she gave her a three-year-old canary and Mikey made a cage for it. The week before, Gertrude had 'diaorhea' and Dr Steines prescribed powders. 'Thank God Gertrude is better', Amelia wrote on 26 and 27 January 1878. And then again on 29 January, 'Thank God the Baby is all right again.'

Amelia was an efficient housekeeper, the wife of a wealthy man, the mother of nice children. She wore Paris furs and 'pleasant stuffs for children to rub against'. Her son Leo said she only ever read two books in her life: light novels by Grace Aguilar, a Jewish writer, *Home Influences* and its sequel, *A Mother's Recompense*. Leo never saw his father read a book of any sort.

Gertrude felt her mother to be unimaginative and unaware of the individual characters of her children. Amelia treated each of them with remorseless fairness, buying presents for their birthdays and thanking God with the same scrupulous and laconic courtesy when He cured Bertha of a sore foot, Leo of the measles or Gertrude of diarrhoea. She showed interest if Gertrude was unwell, or getting dressed up for some special do, but she 'had never a very lively realisation of her children'. She had no time for what was singular in them:

She was never important to her children excepting to begin them. She was a sweet contented little woman who lived in her husband and children, who could only know well to do middle class living, who never knew what it was her husband and her children were working out inside them and around them.

When Gertrude was four-and-a-half her mother suddenly moved with the children to Passy, near Paris, to be near her husband. Gertrude and Bertha went to boarding school. Gertrude remembered talking French, having her photograph taken, eating soup for breakfast and leg of mutton and spinach for lunch. She always liked spinach. She remembered a black cat jumping on her mother, and the gloves and sealskin caps and muffs her mother wore that came in special boxes. 'There was the smell of Paris in that', she said. Amelia kept her diary:

Rented a place for 150 francs a month. Dear Dan not feeling well having a slight attack of diorhea ... Took a walk in the Boulevards. Cold and clear. The children enjoyed themselves hugely. They visited the exposition five times.

She and Dan went to occasional concerts at the Hippodrome, to the ballet and the 'Grand Opera'. She took the children to the Louvre, walked with them in the Bois de Boulogne, picked flowers, went boating, played ball, got caught in heavy showers. For her birthday, in 1878, Gertrude was given a box of toy furniture. On 29 March, 'Dear Dan left at 7.45 pm for London on his way to America.' He sailed on the SS *Republic*. Amelia and Mikey saw him off from the Gare du Nord. In June, Mikey took driving lessons and Amelia tried horse-riding. It 'went splendidly'. On 2 July she had an impression taken for a new set of teeth. 'Mine are broken,' she recorded.

She organised her children's daily life in Paris, but she was isolated. Her sisters were all in Baltimore, her husband travelled a lot on business and she did not speak French. She put up with it for a year then, in 1879, took the children on a huge spending spree. Gertrude said they all 'bought everything that pleased their fancy' - seal skin coats, caps and muffs, dozens of gloves, extravagant hats, riding costumes, a microscope and all the volumes of a French history of zoology. Thus laden, Amelia and the five children sailed for America.

For a while they all stayed with the Keyser family in Baltimore and, for Gertrude, 'emotions began to feel themselves in English'. But Daniel did not like living with his in-laws and was as ever restless. He went west, decided that business opportunities were good in San Francisco, invested in the street railroads and real estate and took his family to live in Oakland, across the bay from San Francisco.

Of the journey across America, from Maryland to California, Gertrude remembered a sense of landscape and the moving train, eating a turkey lunch from a hamper, Bertha's hat flying out of the train window and their father pulling the communication cord to retrieve it. She was told she saw some Indians.

In Oakland they lived for a year at the Tubb's Hotel, then rented for $50 a month a ten-acre farm called Old Stratton House. They moved there early in 1881. This was to be the only memorable family home for Gertrude and it was where her 'half city half country living began'. It was a wooden house, medium sized, with a winding avenue of eucalyptus and blue gum trees as the drive. The front lawns were never green because the trees sucked all the moisture. Summers were long with a dry heat. 'In the winter there was rain and the north wind and the owls in the walls.' The ten acres were used for hay and there was a vegetable garden and an orchard with a hedge of roses all around.

Amelia chronicled their daily life in the style she learned from her housekeeping classes. 'I receive 300 dollars per month from my Husband from which I pay rent all Household expenditures including my own and Childrens Clothing except Mikeys.' On 31 March 1881 she bought a cow from Mrs Jorden, 'the lady who lived in the House that we have rented. Paid 50 dollars for her.' Ten days later she was making her own butter. She went with Gertrude to Oakland to buy the 'sundry articles' needed for its manufacture and some new shoes for her. Herman the gardener was hired for $25 a month, Louise the cook and housekeeper received $20 a month and the new governess was called Fraulein Wiedersheim.

The children went skating and fishing, but seldom caught any fish. Mikey went hunting, Gertrude was given a tricycle and another canary which she named Dick. He cost $2.50 and his cage, $3.25. Bertha's canary was called Billy. Simey fell off his bicycle and bent one of the peddles badly. 'Thank God he did not hurt himself more than a little bruise on his knee', Amelia wrote. On 5 August 1881 Bertha had a ring clipped from her finger, 'it being too small to take off'.

The regular Friday night supper was sweet-and-sour fish. On the Jewish New Year and some Saturdays Amelia and Mikey went to synagogue. The children helped Herman cut the hay and on 29 October 1881, 'Dear Dan bought two Horses, that is Mares Topsy and Lucy'. Then he went to San Francisco and bought a single and double harness. And then they went out driving in the buggy – to the cemetery, to the fish market, to visit Mrs Levy and her children, Mrs Schlessinger and her sister and Henrietta Greenblat. Dan became Vice-President of the Union Street municipal railway in San

Francisco and travelled daily across the bay. Amelia drove him to the ferry in the buggy.

Gertrude caught the measles, 'not being able to use my eyes was the hardship otherwise it was all comfortable'. She sprained her foot and had a rash on her face which Dr Fine diagnosed as 'poison oak'. He prescribed 'sugar of Lead to be dissolved and applied to it with linen cloths'. She took drawing lessons with Leo, was given castor oil and birthday parties. Amelia made monthly investments of money for the children and occasionally went to meetings of the Ladies Society or to the Tivoli Opera House, 'the most beloved theatre in the United States', to see such shows as 'Women's Whims'. Most days she stayed at home and did routine household things. She sewed, swept the store room and the bed-rooms, exchanged recipes with neighbours, had chocolate cake or butter cake for tea. On 30 January 1884 she cooked hare for dinner, 'the first I ever cooked'. The butcher's bill was $21 a month and the coal bill was $25 a month.

In a way, Gertrude championed her mother's bourgeois values and her preoccupation with the details of daily life. She liked ordinary people, chat, and the day-to-day business of living. It was at the root of her social charm. 'I have it, this interest in ordinary middle class existence,' she wrote in her long autobiographical book *The Making of Americans*:

> in simple firm ordinary middle class traditions, in sordid material
> unaspiring visions, in a repeating, common, decent enough kind
> of living, with no fine kind of fancy ways inside us, no
> excitements to surprise us, no new ways of being bad or good to
> win us.

If mother represented domestic comfort, father was an increasing problem as the children grew up. At first he was proud of them and encouraged their interests and disputes but, as time passed, he became ever more irritable and took to pounding the table a great deal saying he was the father, they were the children, they must obey him, or he would know how to make them.

They were ashamed of him because he was so peculiar. He wandered around muttering, jingling the money in his pockets, brushing people away from him or domineering them. In the street he swept the air with his cane and held forth about the weather or the fruit and made his children feel unhappy, uncomfortable and embarrassed. 'Come on papa all those people are looking,' they would say. He took fruit or cake from street stalls and gave it to them, leaving them uncertain whether he would pay the vendor. But he always did pay. He was eccentric and even a little mad: 'His children never could lose, until they grew up to be queer themselves, each one inside him, the uncomfortable feeling that his queer ways gave them.'

They were all afraid of him and confused by him. They never knew, if they were playing with him, when play would change to an outburst and how far that would go. He would dragoon them into card games then, after a few minutes, get his impatient feeling and say, 'here you just finish it up I haven't time to go on playing'. Then he made the governess take his hand and left them to play a game none of them was interested in and none of them would have thought of beginning. Nor could they abandon it because he would keep coming in to see who was winning.

Leo in particular disliked his father, harboured resentment towards him and felt afflicted by him with an unshakeable neurosis. He described him as stocky, dominant, aggressive and ill-educated. 'He had three winters of schooling in his youth,' Leo said of him. On one occasion his father took Leo to the dentist in Oakland and told him if he behaved well he would get a present. Leo behaved impeccably. On the way home they saw a dead man in the square. This distracted Leo and he did not ask for his reward until he was home. His father then said he had intended a cake or chocolate, but Leo had not asked for anything. 'I felt irreparably injured', Leo wrote in his autobiographical book *Journey Into the Self*.

Gertrude conceded that her father was in 'some ways a splendid kind of person . . . big in the size of him and in his way of thinking' who, in his strange way, encouraged all his children to have a sense of freedom, but she never cared for him, though she looked like him and felt that there were similarities in their temperaments. He was not particularly nice to her. He felt she was not the kind of daughter he wanted. 'She was not very interesting ever to her father,' Gertrude wrote of herself. He was critical of the way she looked and said she was never thorough in anything. He wanted her to do housekeeping, cooking and dressmaking. But nothing Gertrude ever cooked turned out right. Not that she made many attempts. Sometimes he asked her to do some domestic thing for him and she could not: 'And then he would be full up with impatient feeling that she could not do that thing, that always she was not, as he put it, ever thorough in anything.'

Mostly he took no notice of her. Usually she went her own way in the evenings and the days. Then capriciously he would decide that she could not go out that evening, that she should stay in the house and be with her mother. And he would lecture Leo for not taking better care of Gertrude and impress upon him that Gertrude was his responsibility: 'You have to take care of her sometime and you might as well begin, the sooner the better. You will have to do it sooner or later I tell you'.

The Steins were the only rich people in East Oakland. Nor were there many other Jews in this rural suburb of San Francisco. Sometimes Daniel

Stein was angry if he saw Gertrude talking in the small houses of poorer neighbours and would say that she should be at home studying. At other times he felt she should be more like ordinary people. Perhaps unsurprisingly, in her adult years Gertrude had little praise for fathers:

father Mussolini and father Hitler and father Roosevelt and father Stalin and father Lewis and father Blum and father France . . . There is too much fathering going on just now and there is no doubt about it fathers are depressing.

He had faddish ideas about food, medicine and education. On one occasion, to impress dinner guests with his discipline over his children, he forced Leo to eat carrots and turnips which Leo hated and which made him sick. Leo then made himself get over his aversion by pulling up young carrots and turnips from the vegetable garden and nibbling them. Throughout his life he had digestive problems which he blamed on his father. He went on terrible fasts and regimes of raw vegetables and did not know when he was hungry.

Gertrude, whose appetite was hearty, said of her father and food:

He always liked to think about what was good for him in eating. He liked to think about what was good for every one around him in their eating eating. He liked to buy all kinds of eating, he liked all kinds of thinking about eating, eating was living to him.

Daniel Stein was all caprice, impulse and unpredictability, and he lacked credibility in his children's eyes. Sometimes he thought they should all have castor oil. Sometimes he thought a Chinese doctor would be good for them. Sometimes he brought a 'queer blind man to examine one of them'. 'Sometimes their father would be strong in religion and then this would make for the children complications in their daily living.' For the most part they had ordinary schooling at the nearby school. Then suddenly he would decide that they should be fluent in French and German and he would hire tutors to teach them at home.

In the strange atmosphere generated by their father's capriciousness and their mother's passivity, Gertrude and Leo turned to each other for a sense of relationship. Leo was Gertrude's best friend and the only one in the family to whom she felt close. But Leo said even though they were always together, they never confided in each other about their inner life. He directed her learning, was a mine of information, helped her and gained such confidence as he had from her. The arrangement suited her:

It is better if you are the youngest girl in a family to have a brother two years older, because that makes everything a pleasure to you, you go everywhere and do everything while he does it all for you and with you which is a pleasant way to have everything happen to you.

They went on long walks, swam in the rivers and pools and helped the neighbouring farmers at harvest time. They read widely and unselectively - Wordsworth, Scott, Bunyan's *Pilgrim's Progress*, all of Shakespeare, Congressional Records, encyclopaedias, Mark Twain, Jules Verne, George Eliot, science books and history plays. Gertrude read the Bible to find out about eternity. 'There was nothing there. There was God of course and he spoke but there was nothing about eternity.' Her favourite things were books and food:

Evolution was all over my childhood . . . with music as a background for emotion and books as a reality and a great deal of fresh air as a necessity, and a great deal of eating as an excitement and as an orgy . . . Most of all there were books and food, food and books, both excellent things.

She went to primary school in East Oakland. She recalled the 'Lend a Hand Society' where pupils were asked to recount their good deeds of the day. Neither she nor Leo ever could think of a deed they had done that was good. Her essay about a sunset in East Oakland was chosen to represent her class at the school's open day. She then went to the Oakwood High School and was thought bright enough to jump a class and go from the lower second to the high third.

A painting of the Battle of Waterloo impressed her when she saw it in San Francisco at the age of eight. She said it made her realise the difference between a painting and out of doors:

out of doors is made up of air and a painting has no air, the air is replaced by a flat surface and anything in a painting that imitates air is illustration and not art.

A few years later, in 1886, she saw Millet's *Man with the Hoe*, also at a 'loan show' in San Francisco. She bought a photograph of it and her eldest brother Michael commented that it 'was the hell of a hoe'. Gertrude said she saw from the painting that France was 'made of ground, of earth'. Alice B. Toklas, who was three years younger than Gertrude and who spent most of her childhood in San Francisco, saw the same exhibition when she was nine. Fifty years later, as a married couple, Gertrude and Alice saw the picture again, when Gertrude was on a lecture tour of the States. Both felt startled at how much smaller it was than they remembered.

Despite her colourless mother and fearsome father, Gertrude felt her childhood, up to the time of adolescence, to be happy. Leo, on the other hand, had enough unhappy memories 'to make a dozen neuroses'. Apart from his extremely disagreeable recollections of his father, he remembered a girl at school who had a piece of sticky tape pasted over her mouth for giggling and whispering, and a maid who said she would give him to a witch if he did not behave. He suffered from what he called a 'pariah complex': 'The pariah is one from whom love and participation are not desired. The pariah complex is the fantastic belief that such is the case.' He was shy, awkward about being Jewish and bad at making friends. If anyone paid attention to him he 'blushed so hard as to give me a headache'. If girls interested him he ran away from them. At a party where kissing games were being played, he jumped out of the window to avoid his turn.

He thought that he must have had a traumatic time at birth and weaning, for when adult he could not be chivalrous or romantic towards women and found it difficult even to be polite:

> All sex expression toward them was rigorously suppressed and
> was reserved in later years for prostitutes who are for the most
> part regarded not as belonging to the real world but to the world
> of fantasy, since none of the ordinary obligations of the sex
> relation obtain in intercourse with them.

His early sexual feelings towards girls terrified him. At school there was a bright girl called Anna who always got top marks. Leo would go round the block to avoid meeting her because he wanted to meet her so much. The only subject he was good at was general knowledge. He knew all the answers. Once he had to partner with Anna for a spelling test on words that ended in '-ible' or '-able'. He got them all wrong, she got them all right. 'I still recall the faint smile with which she handed me back my wretched performance,' he wrote decades later. Gertrude's adult successes were a similar humiliation to him.

Neither he nor Gertrude felt close to their brothers and sister. They liked and respected Michael, but he was older and had the demeanour of the responsible eldest son. As for Bertha, 'she was not a pleasant person', said Gertrude. 'Naturally she did not like anything.' Gertrude slept in the same room with her. 'It is natural not to care about a sister, certainly not when she is four years older and grinds her teeth at night.' In the end Bertha 'married a man who well they married', and one of her sons became a biologist in Russia. Leo's only adult recollection of her was as a little girl on a chamber pot. In October 1941, when nearly seventy, he dreamed that he was married to her, a condition which he found intolerable. In his dream she wanted to sleep with him but he insisted on going to another bed.

Simon, the very fat brother, was 'a little simple minded'. He had, said Gertrude, 'a very good nose and foolish but not silly eyes and he loved eating'. She tried, when she was eleven, to teach him that Columbus discovered America in 1492. She asked him every morning and evening, but he could never remember. He disliked Leo so he used to take Leo's violin into the barn and get it to smell of horses. When he left school he had difficulty in getting or keeping a job. He fancied being a farmer. His father thought him beyond the pale and wrote to him on 13 June 1890 with a Gertrudian scorn for the conventions of syntax, grammar and punctuation:

Dear Simon

You may rest assured that unless you improve your mind by observation, reading, studying & learn to think for yourself, keep yourself tidy, be prompt in everything you wish to do, be temperate in Eating and drinking, in one word your mind must be educated and trained and strengthened to control the body, otherwise a man is very little higher than the lowest of animals, to be a common farm hand is certainly not very desirable, in this country successful farmers are among the brightest and best men we have, many of our Presidents, Senators, Members of Congress & other noted Men in all branches of life have been raised on farms, but they were and are brainy men, it is the mind and will power that makes the man, I have endeavoured for years to impress this fact on your mind without success, I hope you will change yet, you are still young, the world is before you - your destiny is in your own hands, every person in this country has the same and equal chance with every one else, so if you fail you have no one to blame but yourself, You have plenty of time and opportunities to improve yourself, you must remember, if you wish to associate with respectable and intelligent men and women, you must be so yourself.

Your Father

D. Stein

Simon did not take up farmwork, nor did he much improve his mind or body. For a while he worked in a cigar shop in San Francisco. He always kept candy and cigars in his pockets to give to strangers. After their father's death Michael protected him financially. Simon would write laconic letters: 'I must have the mony without fail this time. I want about $500 dollars five hundred dollars. Your affectone Bros. SDStein'. Sometimes, though rarely, he was more loquacious. A year after the San Francisco earthquake of 1906, when Gertrude, Leo, Michael and his wife Sarah and child Allan were living in Paris, he wrote:

> My dear Allan, Mike, Sara, Gertrude and Leo
> Owing you a Long letter I tell you what I have been doing, after the fire I took up the old sport of going fishing I found it a very lonsom sport as I had to go alone, the boy that used to go with me went Ogden, doing all the baiting myself I found it was doing my legs no good, so one fryday I cought thrity nice smelt, I gave them to Bulotti, I told him that I was tiard of doing nothing and next to Nothing going fishing. I said why cant I run the cigar Store. He said the cigar Store is yours if you want it I came around Saturday morning at 5 o'clock and took posession and took Stock Since I have somthing on My mind my leg's are better I sleep like a babby and my time does not drag at all. Mike it is very cold here It must be snowing over in East Oakland, remember when we kids came hom from Sunday school and when we were driving up near the house you and Our Dear Mama threw snow balls at us? I am sending Allan a few dollars to have a good time on as usual, I earned it out of my store this time, and I often think of what you used to try to drum throught that Dick Copth of Mine, Now I can see it All in one Glance. Expience is the best teacher. What Brand of cigars do you smoke over in that country, I sell a good may of you old bran, the Americans.
> Mrs Moffitt is fine and dandy she keeps my books every night and no munky business eather.
> I sepose this letter is a littl bit late but is better late than never.
> Mike, I have no troubles, But if there is a Surplice in my account, why as the New Year is coming a check would suit me very much.
> Well Mike I see a custermur coming across the street, so I will close, sending my love to you all. I remain you Loving. Simon

The cigar retail trade did not work out for him. Michael then found him a job as a gripman on the street cablecars. This suited him better, and he stayed a gripman almost to the end of his life, 'to be sure most of the time only on Sunday or when they were very busy and finally he was too heavy to stand so long and then he stopped.'

Amelia Stein became ill in 1884, when Gertrude was ten. At first she complained only of tiredness and 'diorhea', but otherwise recorded the usual

Simon Stein by the seaside. A postcard to his brother Michael in 1912.

'all well' or 'a lovely day' in her diary. But in the summer she stayed with her sisters in Baltimore, was delirious in the night and could not sleep. Cancer was diagnosed. She tried to continue mothering her children and running her house, but without energy. Never a particularly controlling woman, she went on recording the daily events of her children's lives - their days off school, purchases and achievements, but as if from the other side of a glass. She did not complain and they took little notice of her, absorbed in their own affairs.

Their lives went on unsupervised. Gertrude sprained her foot and stayed at home, had a little party on her birthday, was given roller skates, took picnic lunches into the mountains with Leo, had violin lessons on Saturdays after skating, went to Oakland with Leo to get herself a pair of shoes. They had their teeth filled, sorted their books, went to the Grand Canyon, to the Oakland Theatre to see *Around the World in Eighty Days*, to the Coliseum for *Uncle Tom's Cabin* and to the Tivoli Opera House for *Daughters of the Regiment*. On their mother's birthday Bertha gave her a 'sideboard scarf' of felt and satin adorned with 'lovely pompoms', the others gave her a cake with her name on it.

Bertha caught the mumps and, ill though she herself was, Amelia treated her with hot red flannel cloths 'dipped in hops water'. The $50 cow had a calf on Saturday 14 January 1885, but by Sunday Amelia recorded 'our cow is not getting along nicely' and the next day the cow died at 2.30 pm. 'She left a fine calf. She had inflammation of the second stomach she was a lovely cow we had her three years.' Leo and Simey went to the butcher's to see the carcass dissected, but Gertrude stayed at home with a headache. Amelia sold the calf for $15 and gave the money to Simey.

The house became too much for her to manage. Repeatedly she wrote in her diary 'not quite well'. She visited Dr Fine or Dr Richter every day. They gave her the 'galvanic battery and thermal baths'. Bertha always went with her. 'I do not trust myself to walk alone,' Amelia wrote. The family moved to a house in Oakland that was near to the surgery and easy to run.

Amelia's diary became a chronicle of salt baths, electric treatments, massage and weight loss. By 14 January 1886 she weighed 108 pounds and Gertrude, who was nearly thirteen, weighed 135. More and more the children fended for themselves. Gertrude and Leo spent their pocket money on books and disappeared for days at a time, camping alone in the hills. They 'dragged a little wagon and slept closely huddled together'. They had a gun and shot birds and rabbits. 'We were heartless youngsters then and were so fond of our shooting that we had no sympathy for our victims', Gertrude wrote. Nights were beautiful. 'In other lands the heavens appear as a surface; here every star hangs down out of the blue behind it.'

In 1888, when Gertrude was fourteen, her mother died. Gertrude did not seem to grieve. 'We had all already had the habit of doing without her', she wrote. None the less, their mother had been the linchpin of their domestic lives and after her death, family life disintegrated. Michael was at the Johns Hopkins University. Bertha took over the housekeeping, but could not manage. Simey was not up to·much. Meals were irregular, the dining table was no longer laid and after a while each of them ate when and what they pleased. Gertrude and Leo sometimes talked or walked all night and slept in the day. Father 'was more a bother than he had been . . . Hitherto we had naturally not had to remember him most of the time and now remembering him had begun.' He became entirely eccentric, shut himself up for days at a time, was irritable and dissatisfied and took out his frustrations on his family. His business affairs became erratic. He speculated with money and lost it. Leo and Gertrude bought books as a security in case of financial ruin – Shelley in a green Moroccan leather binding, an illustrated set of Thackeray.

This chaotic insecure home life caused Gertrude an 'agony of adolescence'. She had panic attacks and thought she was going mad. She was afraid not so much of death as of dissolution, of breaking down. She experienced childhood as a civilised time of evolution and order. Adolescence was medieval:

> Mediaeval means that life and place and the crops you plant and your wife and children, all are uncertain. They can be driven away or taken away, or burned away, or left behind . . .
>
> Fifteen is really mediaeval and pioneer and nothing is clear and nothing is sure, and nothing is safe and nothing is come and nothing is gone. But all might be.

Years later Alice B. Toklas heard of the pain of Gertrude's adolescence:

> I was shocked with those bad years she'd had when she told me. I'd never heard of anything like that. I said so. I said, 'How horrible.' She said, 'Didn't you have that period too?' I said, 'Not I' and she said, looking at me, 'Lucky you.'

Gertrude dropped out of high school and was uncertain as to what she wanted to do. Michael thought she should become a musician. Leo 'hastily did three years high school work in seven months' and went to the University of California at Berkeley, and father

> naturally was not satisfied with anything. That was natural enough . . . Then one morning we could not wake up our father. Leo climbed in by the window and called out to us that he was dead in his bed and he was . . . Then our life without a father began. A very pleasant one.

It was 1891 when Daniel Stein died - three years after his wife. Michael, who was twenty-six, took over as head of the family. Gertrude was seventeen and Leo was nineteen. They were both minors so Michael became their legal guardian. 'I remember', wrote Gertrude, 'going to court for the only time I was ever in one, to say that we would have him'. His sense of responsibility towards his brothers and sisters was keen. As Alice put it:

> He saw not any one of them would ever earn any money. None
> of them were made for a business career. And he didnt think of
> any profession in which they would succeed.

Daniel Stein's financial affairs were in disarray. 'There were so many debts it was frightening,' wrote Gertrude:

> and then I found out that profit and loss is always loss . . . and it
> was discouraging because we always had a habit in the family
> never to owe anybody any money.

Shambolic though Daniel Stein's affairs were, his will showed that he owned 480 acres of land, property in Baltimore and California, shares in cable, railroad and mining companies and, most valuable of all, the franchise for an unrealised project to consolidate the various street railroad systems in San Francisco. Michael Stein sold this franchise to the railroad tycoon Collis P. Huntington and took a job with the new consolidated company.

His acumen in dealing with his father's affairs secured for Gertrude and the others a moderate income for life. 'They all had very simple tastes,' said Alice, 'so that they lived in considerable luxury.' Gertrude described their income as enough to keep them 'reasonably poor'. It allowed them to travel, buy books and pictures and be free for ever of the burden of work.

For a year they all lived together in a house in San Francisco. 'Then we all went somewhere.' Gertrude and Bertha went to Baltimore to stay with their mother's sister Fannie Bachrach. Leo transferred from Berkeley to Harvard University. Michael and Simon stayed on in San Francisco working on the railroads: Michael as divisional superintendent of the combined Market Street Railway Company, Simon as a part-time gripman. Simon was the only one to spend the rest of his life in California. He died there in middle age, 'still fat and fishing'.

# 3

―――――――

# ALICE'S EARLY YEARS

*'Her tender nose is between her eyes*
*which close and are very lovely'*

Alice Babette Toklas spent her childhood in San Francisco, across the Bay
from Oakland and from Gertrude. She was born at 922 O'Farrell Street,
the house of her maternal grandparents, Louis and Hanchen Levinsky, on
30 April 1877, three years after Gertrude. (When she lived in France all official
documents gave her birthday as 30 June 1877. There was some confusion
with the authorities when she arrived.)

She was the first child and only daughter of Ferdinand and Emma Levinsky
Toklas. She arrived a day later than due and her father, given to making
weak jokes, liked to tell her that she never found a way to catch up. 'I led
in my childhood and youth', said Alice, 'the gently bred existence of my
class and kind.' Gertrude was raised in the rough and tumble of a large
odd-minded family. Alice was always the little lady.

The O'Farrell Street block, built on sand dunes, was a dream of prosperity
come true - solid bourgeois housing in a fashionable part of town. 'At nine
o'clock every morning the men of O'Farrell Street left their homes for their
places of business downtown dressed in brushed broadcloth and polished
high hats,' - the Levinskys, the Levys, the Nathans. They were self-made men,
immigrants from towns and villages in central Europe, who had worked
their way through casual trade and entrepreneurial risk, to solid business
achievement.

'I was the child who was raised by women, and influenced by women,'
said Alice. While the men went off to earn the money she stayed in the
company of her mother, maiden aunts, great aunts and her grandmother,
Hanchen Levinsky, whom she particularly adored. Hanchen Levinsky was
educated, 'had delightful ways of smelling flowers and eating dates and sugar',
liked all things cultural and played the piano. 'She made that sort of life
normal to me,' said Alice. She was so short in the leg she had to have something

special done to the piano pedals. 'All the sisters were short and swarthy and sitting, their feet scarcely touched the floor.' One of them became a professional pianist, was disinherited for the transgression and married an army officer.

Alice remembered 'quartets and trios at my grandmother's house from the days of my mother's youth'. A French doctor played the violin, an American architect the cello. There was, said Alice, no social occasion to equal it in San Francisco. Alice too had musical talent. A Frenchwoman gave her piano lessons every Saturday and her grandmother took her to the Tivoli Opera House to hear *Aïda, Lohengrin*, Gilbert and Sullivan, and the first American performance of *Cavalleria Rusticana*. Alice heard Luisa Tetrazzini and admired her cadenzas. Until her mid-twenties Alice wanted to be a concert pianist, 'then I found that everything I did was absolutely fifth rate and so I gave it up.' She served Gertrude's talent and ambition instead.

Hanchen Levinsky was a linguist too. Alice remembered her sitting in the parlour with French and German books and newspapers and ringing for a servant to remove them when she was through. She taught Alice French and German. 'I could read German aloud but I didn't know what I was saying. I read French plays and novels, the classics,' said Alice.

Harriet Levy, Alice's close childhood friend, lived next door to the Levinskys and Toklases. (Through her, Alice eventually met Gertrude.) She was not overly impressed by the cultural and intellectual achievements of Hanchen and her sisters. From her bed she could hear Hanchen's rendering of the 'Polish Dance' by Scharwenka and the singing of Alice's Aunt Foffie: 'She had but to strike the first chord of "When the Tide Comes In" and the beach was strewn with the dead', Harriet Levy wrote. 'On calm nights in summer I would be puzzled by the moaning of the winter's wind until I recognized the voice of Flora wailing the tipsy drinking song from *Girofle Girofla*.'

The Levinskys felt the weight of their superior breeding. When Hanchen visited her neighbours, she made it clear she could not stay. 'More letters from Hamburg. Must answer them,' she would say. Or 'Viel Besuch, viel Besuch' (much company). She 'did not bend in social intercourse', wrote Harriet, 'but brought to each encounter an awareness that the uneducated was the negligible'.

Harriet Levy aspired to be a writer and liked the theatre. When adult, she wrote drama reviews for a weekly called *The Wave* and she belonged to 'The Spinners', a literary group. As a girl she wrote to the Italian actor Ernesto Rossi, praising him for his Othello. Knowing Hanchen's reputation as a linguist, she took his reply to her for translation:

To the name of Rossi she nodded soberly as if consenting to his existence. Then she slowly adjusted her spectacles and read the letter. '*Amore*' she said as if that was the only word on the page, 'means love. *Mio*' she pointed to the word, 'means my'. With that she returned the letter in dismissal and resumed her position at the bay window at which she sat for hours each day, from time to time tapping the pane.

The Levinskys were further set apart from their neighbours by the frequency of their funerals. Distant cousins were always dying and Louis Levinsky's patriarchal instinct 'demanded that they should be interred in the family plot'.

Louis Levinsky, Alice's maternal grandfather, left Exin, in Prussia, for America in 1848, worked briefly as a builder in New Orleans, then headed west and joined the gold rush. He and two brothers bought a gold-mine in Amador County. It was near Mokelumne Hill between Happy Valley, Chili Gulch and Big Bar on the Mokelumne River. It was an 'absolutely no good' mine, said Alice. It yielded very little gold and made no one rich. But the Levinskys were on the immigrant trail, so they set up a general store selling flannel shirts, boots, bowie knives and all things useful to those prospecting for gold. They did well enough to open three more stores at Sutter Creek, Dry Town and Rancheria. They lived in Botellas, an unremarkable town near the mine, so called because of all the empty bottles that littered it. It was later renamed Jackson.

By 1854 Louis was prosperous enough to return to Hamburg to marry his cousin, the culture-conscious Hanchen Lewig. After the marriage they sailed for America, spent a year in Brooklyn 'to accommodate her to all that she was about to encounter' - Alice's mother, Emma, was born there - then in 1856 the three of them travelled west. They arrived in San Francisco on the day of a public hanging. 'My grandmother asked why the bells were ringing . . . She thought she had come to a wilderness.'

Nor was Hanchen Levinsky comforted when she got to Jackson, with its bottles, heat and fortune seekers. She missed Europe and lamented the scarcity of schools, concert halls and theatres. The family stayed there for a decade and Louis Levinsky's business prospered. He then bought land in the San Joaquin Valley and would happily have spent the rest of his life ranching, but Hanchen insisted they return to the relative civilisation of San Francisco. He rented out his land and supervised the building of the O'Farrell block.

Emma, Alice's mother, inherited neither Hanchen's cultural pretensions nor the pioneer daring of her father. Alice had streaks of both. Alice described her mother as 'a serious person with no particularly serious interests . . . a stoic without volition', but with more force of character than Gertrude's mother. She liked cooking, sewing, gardening and experimental flower arrangements. Alice remembered her arrangements of hops and sweet peas and the house smelling of lilac, sweet grasses and roses.

'She was a little thing and she had a great deal of presence in spite of that, and violet eyes. I remember the violet eyes.' (On other occasions Alice remembered them as periwinkle blue.) Alice, when little, called them lovely and watery and her mother said, 'I think that you mean liquid'. Emma Toklas dressed charmingly, liked the latest culinary gadgets – she had an automatic ice-cream freezer – encouraged Alice with her button collection and kept a handwritten recipe book. 'Alice's cookies' were vanilla wafers dusted with icing sugar. Capon braised in port was Alice's favourite birthday lunch.

Her father, Ferdinand Toklas, left Poland for America in 1865 when he was twenty. He began as a bookkeeper at the Oregon Woolen Mills in New York, then, ambitious to start his own business, went west. He met Emma Levinsky in San Francisco, married her in 1875 and set up as a wholesaler in Seattle. He sold 'dry goods, fancy goods, clothing, carpets, boots, shoes, hats, gents' furnishings, notions, trunks and valises'. By the 1880s he was 'one of the most prominent and successful merchants on the coast'. Alice described him as a 'minister without portfolio', a distinguished looking man who gave the appearance of being indifferent to everything. He was hard-working, dependable and a staunch Republican. Occasionally he liked to hunt and to drink a glass of beer.

Alice, as a child, saw little of him. He was away on business, shuttling back and forth between Seattle and San Francisco. At home he was 'a quiet man who took things quietly'. He was of no particular significance to Alice, who stayed in the genteel environment of the ladies, where music, cooking, flower arranging and a good book were the virtues of the day. She had a nurse called Maggie and there was a cook called Nora. Alice liked cracked wheat with sugar and cream, corn meal with molasses, and ice-cream made with raspberry jelly, whipped cream and egg whites.

When she was eight, Alice and her parents went for a year on a grand tour of Europe. They stopped first in Kempen, Silesia, to celebrate the golden wedding anniversary of her father's parents. Her paternal grandfather was a Polish patriot, 'always flying the flag' and venomous towards Germans and Russians. He gave the family a painting he had done of Polish cavalrymen slaying Russian soldiers, and frightened Alice by reading *Grimm's Fairy Tales* to her. His wife 'was a large, handsome, imperious woman who wore very long diamond earrings. In her white hair, piled very high, were artificial lilacs.' Both lived to be over eighty and died within a day of each other.

Alice was assigned a Polish governess for the tour who taught her 'The Lord's Prayer' in Polish and a hymn called 'God Save Poland' which she quickly forgot. She became attached to the woman and was tearful when they had to part. In France they saw Victor Hugo's funeral together, while sitting in armchairs in the rue de Rivoli, though 'it may have been the Champs Elysées'.

The family visited relatives in England, Austria, Hungary and Germany. Alice drank her first glass of champagne, danced the cachucha in Pest and 'waltzed with the daughters of our host, Stephanie and Melanie, becoming quite dizzy as they did not reverse'. In Hamburg, at the home of her mother's uncle, a doctor who lived with his wife and widowed daughter, she was served her first frozen puddings: 'I remember a Nesselrode and a Himalaya.' Two black poodles sat on their haunches watching her as she ate. In London she was anxious when a cousin sleepwalked on a balcony without railings. The year's tour was, Alice said, the great influence of her childhood years.

On their return to San Francisco, the Toklases moved from 922 O'Farrell Street to a furnished house nearby. One August night, when she was nine, Alice's father took her to stay alone with her grandparents. He collected her next day and said, 'I have a surprise for you, there is a baby brother for you to see.' 'Is it Tommie?' asked Alice. Tommie was a marble Renaissance head belonging to her mother for which Alice had a 'passionate attachment'. 'No I don't think so,' her father replied. 'You will see.'

> When I did see the small red-faced thing [Clarence], I was ready
> to burst into tears. I wanted to kiss my mother and confide my
> horror to her. He is red like a lobster, I said, are you going to love
> him? Taking me in her arms she said Not like you darling, you
> will always come first.

After Clarence's intrusion into her world, Alice went to Miss Lake's school for girls. 'At once I formed a close friendship with a radiant, resilient brilliant little girl, Clara Moore.' They swore 'eternal friendship'. The Moores' house backed on to the Toklases and from her bedroom Alice sent notes to Clara in a basket on pulleys. They read books together – *Little Women*, 'a sordid dull English novel', *The Lamplighter* by Miss Cummins, a story called *Honor Bright*, which years later Alice tried unsuccessfully to find for Gertrude, and *Great Expectations*. Like Gertrude, Alice was a member of the Mercantile and Mechanics Library in San Francisco.

Alice's childhood world was of governesses and girlie things. She kept Clarence at arm's length, and preferred her girlfriends. There was Nellie Joseph who had a 'caustic wit', Lilyanna Hansen who played the piano and Annette Rosenshine, a distant cousin, who was crucial in bringing Alice to Gertrude. Annette had a cleft palate and nasal speech. Her mother was ashamed at having given birth to an imperfect child and thought the cleft palate due to her own 'youthful ignorance of sex and marital relations'. Annette felt unloved:

> I realize how much it affected me and accounted for all the stress and nervous tensions I had suffered. It was responsible for all the psychosomatic illnesses in childhood as well as over the years, and for my continued dissatisfaction in any achievement.

The boys called her 'split lip', and her mother gave her a glass of sherry each day for her nerves. Annette revered Alice who was three years her senior: 'everything she did impressed me, especially her clothes'. In her fantasies Annette saw herself as a beautiful princess called Alice, admired and loved by her own father.

In 1890, when Alice was thirteen, her grandmother Hanchen died. The year before, fire swept Seattle's commercial district and Ferdinand Toklas lost $600,000 worth of stock from his warehouses. After Hanchen's death, Emma Toklas agreed to leave San Francisco and live in Seattle so that Ferdinand could rebuild his business. He found a house in the rich part of the town, overlooking Elliott Bay and the Olympic Mountains, reconstructed his store on a grand scale and hired a hundred salesmen and an advertising manager. 'It is undoubtedly the busiest and most profitable acre and one third in the northwest,' wrote a trade paper.

Alice was sent to a private girls' school run by Miss Mary Cochrane. She flourished in music but was bad at maths. 'I had a good time in school . . . we were very gay. We learnt our lessons and got some education without too much difficulty.' She spent her vacations in San Francisco with her aunts and grandfather. In the summer of 1892 he took her on a trip to Southern California. They travelled by buckboard, horse, mule and buggy. 'It was amusing but fatiguing. My grandfather however was never fatigued.' He wanted to meet up with his old cronies from the gold-rush days, some of whom were Spanish. Alice was passionate about things Spanish. Gertrude used say to her, 'The only blind spot you show is in connection with Spain and Spaniards.' Alice said, 'I can sit anywhere out of doors in Spain and be thrilled, thrilled . . . The light does something to you – then speaking Spanish – that beautiful guttural Spanish – and moving as they move.'

In 1893, to satisfy university entrance regulations, Alice took private coaching in trigonometry and algebra with a suffragette called Sarah Hamlin, and in the autumn went to Washington University to study music.

Viola Startup was her special friend there. She was the daughter of a rich farmer and wanted a university education so that she could teach at high school. Her father thought her ambitions unorthodox, so she had to pay her own way:

> She had plenty of courage. She was about twenty three or twenty four and I was eighteen and she was very beautiful in rather a coarse way. She was the most glorious blonde you could imagine and she had a high color and dark eyes and she was an experienced woman from the country. You wouldn't think country people would be experienced, but she was - she had earned her living. And so I was enamoured of this - I thought this was a wonderful adventure. My mother wasn't much interested in Viola Startup.

Alice tried to confide her feelings for women - for Lily, for Nellie, for Viola - but her mother became too upset to hear.

She stayed at University only for a year. 'It would have been a happy year if my mother's health had not worried us,' she said. Like Gertrude's mother, Emma Toklas developed cancer. She was operated on, but with limited success. Ferdinand Toklas decided that all the family should return to San Francisco:

> The furniture was packed, my mother, my father and I and my little brother, my mother's trained nurse and my father's hunting dog took the train. We found a house, a simple home where we were comfortable.

Alice got a 'parchment certifying me as a bachelor of music', but her mother's ill health denied her a formal education and a social life. 'I never "came out" at all. I never had any social experience at all, because of my mother's health and then her death. So all that I escaped.' Her first bid for independence ended when she was eighteen.

When Alice returned to San Francisco, Annette Rosenshine thought her 'glamorous, sophisticated and efficient', with her grey-green wide-set eyes and glossy black hair. In the house she wore a grey dress with a 'prim white chiffon *fichu*'. When she went to the opera with her father, the suit and sailor hat she wore were commented on in the morning *Chronicle*. She took on the role of nursing her mother and keeping house for her father and nine-year-old brother Clarence. 'He was never so charming again as he was at that age,' Alice said. 'Between nine and fourteen he was adorable.' In adult life, long after Alice had moved to France and was living with Gertrude, she and Clarence quarrelled over their father's will and stopped all contact. He killed himself in 1937 when he was fifty.

Alice's mother died on 10 March 1897. Both the Toklas and Levinsky households were then without women to run them, but it was inconceivable that this should mean a slip into anarchy, as in the Stein household. At 922 O'Farrell Street, Alice's widowed grandfather, Louis, lived with his brother and various cousins. Ferdinand Toklas continued to run his business 'quietly and methodically . . . like the stroke of a perfect engine'. Louis Levinsky persuaded the Toklases to move in with him. Alice became, at the age of twenty, 'the responsible grand-daughter' in a house filled with men. A lot was expected of her and she hated it. Standards of housewifery were high. 'If you do a thing do it graciously,' her father told her. 'A hostess should never apologise for any failure in her household arrangements. If there is a hostess there is insofar as there is a hostess, no failure.' Annette said that when Alice went to keep house for her grandfather her 'light was dimmed'.

Alice was the only woman at 922 O'Farrell Street and there was always a procession of visiting male cousins, many of them very old. Cousin Eugene, an attorney from Stockton, held particular authority. Alice was given a fixed allowance to cover all household expenses. She had to plan menus and order all the food and she was expected to provide meals at a moment's notice:

> I made the menu and I had to learn what was suitable, what
> went with other things as I remembered them in my mother's
> better days . . . and then I remembered my grandmother's menus,
> and then further than that I went to the provision people who
> supplied my grandmother and they said 'Oh miss, you don't need
> to tell us what to do, we know.' And I knew very well they didn't
> because I wasn't living on that scale at all. I couldn't afford to
> have the things they had at all. And so I said, 'I'll let you know,
> I'll telephone you.' Stevens, the fishman down California Street
> market said to me 'Oh Miss don't you bother about coming in.
> How many are there of you in your family. You just let me know
> and I'll send it to you.' And then the poulterer said the same
> thing 'I know what your grandmother had.' That was just what I
> couldn't have, so I had to come to some understanding.

At table, Alice kept quiet while the men talked about politics and economics and occasionally commended her on her housekeeping. 'When I went to dine', wrote Annette Rosenshine,

> I felt most keenly the stultifying pall that hung over the dining
> room; the stale smell from the chain of after-dinner cigars that
> were smoked during these discussions, clung tenaciously to
> drapes and carpet and seemed to saturate the wooden frames of
> the chairs. Alice and I sat meekly swallowing our food never

attempting to venture an opinion, nor were we encouraged to do so; quickly we fled at the first opportunity to Alice's room to reestablish our lost identities.

In her room, on top of a black writing desk, Alice had a lifesize plaster cast, which she called 'The Unknown', of the head of a woman. She and Annette talked and smoked illicit cigarettes. 'Very commendable,' her father commented when he found them smoking.

The men of 922 O'Farrell Street saw Alice only as a housekeeper, a provider of food and comfort. They thought her odd. She avoided conversation with them, slipped out of the house through the side basement door and ducked away from their friends in the street. She asked nothing from the house. In her grey dresses and long coats buttoned from collar to hem, Harriet Levy, next door at 920, thought she looked like a furtive nun.

Harriet felt stifled in her house too. Her mother had false teeth with a gold plate which she kept in the jewellery box, and her father slept in a red flannel shirt and drawers. Her mother maintained that 'no girl with self-respect would enter a restaurant with a man', called French restaurants brothels, and every summer took Harriet, despite her perfect digestion, to drink the waters of some medicinal spring. She called Harriet's arms 'pipestems' and her shoulder blades 'hatchets', and 'by the withdrawal of her sanction excluded from reality certain areas of the body'.

Neither sex nor love proceeded well for Harriet. Like Annette and Alice she was troubled by her desires. The family physician, Dr Brownell, made a pass at her when she went to pay her father's bill. He told her that he did not want any money, that life was rich with joy and that he would teach her. 'And his powerful arms were about me and his warm cheek pressed against my face', said Harriet, who got out fast, feeling afraid.

Worse than the doctor's advances were her own desires. One late Saturday afternoon, when taking the obligatory promenade down Market Street in San Francisco with her mother and father, she saw a young girl known to them. They often spoke of how problematic she was:

> She roamed the city with an older woman who had a bad
> reputation - a tall swarthy woman with a loping walk and a
> heavy bosom. Nobody could keep them apart. Because of the
> exaggerated difference in height, Mother called them the palm
> leaf and the lemon, symbols carried down the aisle of the
> synagogue on the Feast of Tabernacles.
>   The girl was slender and beautiful. The exquisite line of her
> nose, I felt, singled her out for romantic experience. Her hair
> was of a pale gold, and incredibly large blue eyes sent out

*Annette Rosenshine in 1897. Photograph by Arnold Genthe.*
Inset: *Harriet Levy in 1886.*

exploring glances as she walked down the street. She was dressed in pale grey that never changed to a warmer color . . . She walked fast and I tried to overtake her, but before I succeeded she turned into Dupont Street and quickly disappeared into the narrow street. Why I was so shaken I could not have told.

Annette Rosenshine had problems too. She felt herself too unsightly for love - 'crippled and incapable of responding to any love gesture'. She went to Paris before Alice and confided her problems to Gertrude:

I turned myself over to her as years later I learned one turns oneself over to an analyst. Sex was an uncharted sea . . . Marriage was considered the most important step . . . When this was accomplished one 'lived happily ever after'. The difficulties of adjustment either psychologically or sexually were unknown in the tragic confusion of both women and men.

As for Alice, rebellion bubbled. She longed for experience but it was not on offer. Ostensibly she was the demure housekeeper, making the menus, ordering provisions, caring for her brother. But when she could, she escaped - to Chinatown to buy clothes, ornaments and exotic food and to such parties as there were. Annette studied art at the Mark Hopkins Institute. She invited Alice to the Mardi Gras party. Alice went dressed as Carmen with dangling earrings and a fiery dress. She drank at a table with a group of artists and confounded Annette with the sense of her own 'childish nibbling at the edges of Bohemia'.

Each Spring Alice went to Monterey, a village by the bay, popular with artists and writers. To finance the trips she sold bits of clothing belonging to her decrepit relatives. 'One overcoat, three pairs of woolen underwear and a cracked kitchen stove secured a week's holiday.' She stayed as a paying guest with Senorita Bonifacio, an elderly Spanish woman who lived in an adobe house with a golden rose trailing across the door. Senorita Bonifacio said that she and General Sherman, hero of the American Civil War, planted it when he was a young lieutenant, with the promise that when he returned they would marry when it was in bloom. It was known as the Sherman rose, and visitors gave her half a dollar to have a look at it.

At Senorita Bonifacio's, Alice discarded her nun's attire, wore a red mandarin coat, silk or batik dresses and elaborate jewellery, and lunched alone at the fashionable Del Monte hotel. She rode 'madly' on horseback along the Seventeen Mile Drive to Carmel Beach, and hired a four-wheeled stanhope for an afternoon's drive round the ocean shore and through the pine forest. One year she went to Monterey with Harriet, who was at the University of California. On their last night they went to Louis' French Restaurant, had porterhouse steak and champagne and Alice stood on the table and drank, said Harriet,

> to the eternal damnation of the Crackerjack of the San Joaquin
> Valley . . . grandfathers, uncles, German cousins, and all the
> impedimenta of life, liberty and the pursuit of happiness. But the
> following day she returned to San Francisco, re-entered her
> monastic livery, and gave faultless service . . . for another year.

Grandfather Levinsky caught a cold in 1902. It turned to influenza and within a week he died. With her father and brother, Alice moved out of O'Farrell Street into a smaller house. She was still a housekeeper, but on a less demanding scale. She had more time for herself. With Harriet Levy she ate in Chinatown and went to the Bohemian Club, to drink 'sherry cobblers' and fancy liqueurs:

> We went to theatres, we went automobiling, we went to the
> Little Palace Café and Hotel which had become a fashionable
> shopping district where one could buy Paris clothes and perfume
> if one could afford it and even if one could not.

She bought a silver fox fur coat and Aztec art from a shop in Santa Barbara and she ran up debts. Harriet, who had been to Europe, regaled her with descriptions of a world Alice knew only from the novels of Henry James. Alice longed to be there: 'At worst it would be more diverting to sit behind a window in Paris and see life go by than to observe it from an apartment in San Francisco.'

Harriet Levy's friend, Sarah Samuels, was another of the San Francisco Jewish girls who studied art at the Mark Hopkins Institute and aspired to the creative life. She wore elaborate clothes and jewellery and was very emphatic in manner, so people pretended to agree with her for a quiet life. She said that a fortune teller told her she would meet a man from Baltimore 'in wheels' and marry him. The man she married in 1895, director of the Omnibus Cable Company railway and financial provider to his brothers and sisters, was Michael Stein. By this connection - Alice's friend Harriet was a friend of the sister-in-law of Gertrude Stein - Alice would come to meet the woman who, on first meeting, held her complete attention, 'as she did for all the many years I knew her until her death, and all these empty ones since then'.

*Gertrude and Leo in 1897.*

# 4

## FIRST LOVE FOR GERTRUDE

*'I love things that go round - the world, whirling*
*grouse, gramophone records and all the rest,*
*anything that goes in a circle'*

After the turmoil of her adolescence, Gertrude liked living with her amiable aunts in 'Baltimore, sunny Baltimore'. She went there in 1892 when she was eighteen. She 'began to lose her lonesomeness', but was vague as to what her life's work might be:

> I was interested in biology and I was interested in psychology and philosophy and history, that was all natural enough, I came out of the nineteenth century you had to be interested in evolution and biology, I liked thinking so I had to be interested in philosophy and I liked looking at every one and talking and listening so I had to be interested in history and psychology.

An incident before she left Oakland - to do with what she called 'bottom nature' - made her want to study psychology. On her way to a singing lesson she saw a man hitting a woman with an umbrella. He wanted her to leave him alone. The woman had gone red in the face from anger and pleading. The scene stuck in Gertrude's mind. She felt the need for scientific explanation of such behaviour.

Leo went to Harvard in 1892 to study philosophy but soon got distracted. He described his problem:

> there would be that same quite irresistible tendency to find out one day the truth about the Battle of Vicksburg, another the most recent determination for the date of the second Isaiah, then perhaps Hertwig's answer to Jennings' paper and on a fourth the relation of recalled future time to the possibility of a logically complete induction ... I'm all too easily distracted. If somebody asks me about the habits of giraffes I'm strongly inclined to look

up their anatomy, physiology and embryology. The amount of
time I've wasted because foolish people asking foolish questions
have started my mind off on things it hadn't any business to
monkey with.

Gertrude applied to Radcliffe, known as the Harvard annexe, to be near
Leo. She had no formal qualifications and could not pass the entrance exam
in Latin, so she enrolled as a special student in 1893 (the same year that
Alice enrolled at Washington University to study music). She studied
philosophy and metaphysics with George Santayana, English with William
Vaughn Moody, a poet, who told her, 'I wish you might overcome your disdain
for the more necessary marks of punctuation', and psychology with William
James.

William James was a larky man and fond of Gertrude. He stayed interested
in her career and visited her when she lived in Paris. She sent him her book
*Three Lives* in 1910. He 'read 30 or 40 pages. You know how hard it is for
me to read novels . . . I will go at it carefully when just the right mood
comes.' He died that year before finishing it.

Gertrude said he was a great teacher and her big influence at college.
'Is life worth living?' she wrote in an English essay. 'Yes, a thousand times
yes when the world still holds such spirits as Prof. James.' His ideas of the
'continuous present' and of the 'stream of consciousness', helped form her
subsequent writing. 'Never reject anything,' he said. He wrote in *Principles
of Psychology*:

> Consciousness is nothing jointed it flows . . . so called
> interruptions no more break the flow of the thought that thinks
> them than they break the time and space in which they lie.

Gertrude researched into automatic writing as a special project for him.
She strapped her subjects into a sort of apparatus, reduced them to a state
of fatigue and distraction, then prompted them to let the pencils in their
hands write what they would. The idea was to see what the unconscious
mind proclaimed. She took a sample of fifty women and forty-one men:

> A large number of my subjects were New Englanders and the
> habit of self-repression, the intense self-consciousness, the morbid
> fear of 'letting oneself go' that is so prominent an element in the
> New England character, was a constant stumbling block.

Her findings, 'Normal Motor Automatism' and 'Cultivated Motor Automatism:
A Study of Character in its Relation to Attention', were published in two
articles in the Harvard *Psychological Review*.

Gertrude was a gregarious student. She lived in a boarding-house with 'a very good boarding house keeper' whose husband

> sat at the end of the table and he did not like low lights ... He did not say funny things ... I think he kept an employment agency, we did not know it then but still we must have or perhaps not.

She joined the 'Idler's Club' drama society and was secretary of the Radcliffe Philosophy Club. She and Leo went on group picnics, bicycle rides, boat trips and outings to the opera. She went to concerts by the Boston Symphony Orchestra with her co-researcher Leon Solomons, and walking with girlfriends in the country on Saturday nights. 'We said if we have any trouble with a man, Gertrude will climb out on the furthest limb of a tree and drop on him,' one of them is supposed to have said. She wore her hair piled up on her head, was indifferent to her size - she weighed more than 200 pounds - and wore loose-fitting, comfortable clothes. She could not draw, sew, or do domestic things, but she was regarded as a wonderful conversationalist.

But something was missing from this student life. 'Books, books,' she wrote in one of her essays,

> is there no end to it. Nothing but myself to feed my own eager nature. Nothing given me but musty books ... she felt that she must have some human sympathy. Her passionate yearnings made her fear for the endurance of her own reason ... Her longings and desires had become morbid. She felt that she must have an outlet. Some change must come into her life, or she would no longer be able to struggle with the wild moods that now so often possessed her.

Leo switched studies from philosophy to history then went round the world in 1895 with his cousin Fred Stein, whose father financed the trip. Gertrude, for the first time parted from him for a long period, arranged to meet him in Europe the following summer for a holiday.

In Japan Leo delighted in 'the first view of Fujiyama after nine days of storm at sea with all hatches closed; the wonder ride on the first evening ashore through the paper-lantern-lighted streets of Yokohama.' He spent two months in Kyoto studying and collecting Japanese prints. He went to Canton with 'its mysterious, keenly, almost ferociously intelligent looking crowds', sat under a upas tree in Ceylon and thought the streets of Colombo 'Kiplingesque'. But from Egypt to Italy he tired of Fred and wrote to Gertrude in March 1896 from the Mena House Hotel, Cairo:

> Never in my life have I felt so completely dulled, so intolerably
> stupid so inanely played out . . . I'm glad this thing will soon be
> over . . . I rather thought I was more completely bore proof than
> I have proved to be.

Sarah Stein said that she would send his brother Simon to him so that he
might know the true meaning of boredom.

Gertrude was unsettled too. She did not know what career to pursue.
William James advised philosophy or psychology. For philosophy she needed
higher mathematics, for which she had no aptitude, and for psychology she
needed a medical degree. 'A medical education opens all doors, as Oliver
Wendell Holmes told me and as I tell you,' she wrote. She thought she might
specialise in nervous diseases of women. She was accepted at the newly-
opened Johns Hopkins Medical School in Baltimore. Funds for it had been
raised by four daughters of trustees. They insisted that women should have
equal rights to study medicine there. Alice, in later years, spoke of Gertrude's
mistaken choice of career:

> William James intended she qualify in abnormal psychology – if
> there was one thing she loathed it was the abnormal – she never
> could bear insane women around her . . . we had two mad
> landladies.

Before going to the Johns Hopkins, Gertrude met up with Leo in Europe
in the summer of 1896. It was her first trip abroad since her childhood.
As she prepared for the trip, Michael wrote:

> Let me know at once what drafts you want for use before
> starting. Also see that all your & Leo's bills (room, rent etc.) are
> settled before you go, so as to have everything in ship-shape . . .
> So long
> Your aff Bro
> Mike

She sailed to Antwerp on the ship the *Red Star*. She had not seen Leo
for a year:

> I remember being very worried as the boat came nearer the
> shore lest I should not know him when I saw him. After all one
> never can remember . . . how anybody anybody really knows
> looks like . . . Well when I saw my brother it was a surprise to
> me but I knew quite certainly that it was my brother.

They spent their vacation looking at paintings and walking, then Leo
returned to the Johns Hopkins with Gertrude. He felt at a loose end after

his 'world encircling', so he 'tried biology for a while'. He had stomach trouble, and Gertrude wrote to Michael and Sarah, early in 1897, saying that she was 'going to keep house and nurse him according to all the latest medical school theories'. Sarah Stein replied:

> [Michael] wishes that you could make your mind up to board with the Bachrachs or some other congenial people while in Baltimore as he can't quite see who will run the house when you are at college and Leo reading, and he in particular wonders at your investing in house furnishings before you are sure that you will enjoy house keeping.
>
> Your financial condition after the August allowance, which you will need to pay for your course of study, will be about $300.00 on hand with $150 - on Sept. 1st from Mk't Str. 5%s and $300 - on Oct. 1st from Omnibus 6%s then nothing until Jan. 10th.

She rather wished that Gertrude would stop her liberated life, settle down and be, like her, a mother and wife:

> There certainly is nothing in the line of happiness to compare with that which a mother derives from the contemplation of her first-born and even the agony which she endures from the moment of its birth does not seem to mar it, therefore my dear and beloved sister in law go and get married, for there is nothing in this whole wide world like babies - Leo to the contrary notwithstanding.

Gertrude and Leo found a house at 215 East Biddle Street. They hung Leo's Japanese prints and etchings on the walls, employed a housekeeper called Lena Lebeder, who had two dogs Jack and Rags, and went on 'junking' trips together. They bought prints, books, cabinets, tables, chairs, boxes, bronze mortars, brass lamps, wooden saints, terracotta saints, satin hangings, venetian glasses, ivory daggers and 'a greco Roman Dyonysus (where do the ys belong?) head in marble'.

Gertrude's grades were good for her first two years at medical school: 1 for anatomy, 1.5 for normal histology, pathology and bacteriology, 2 for physiology, pharmacology and toxicology. A chemistry student friend, Arthur Lachman, said she got into a mess with whatever dye she was using in the laboratory and, when asked to make a model of an embryo human brain, turned in a fantastic construction with the spinal cord twisted under the head of the embryo. He described her as big and floppy and sandalled, and with 'a laugh like a beefsteak'.

Leo got sidetracked from biology into art history and philosophy and spent much of his time in the Walters Art Gallery. On Saturday evenings he and Gertrude attended the salons of two rich American sisters, Claribel and Etta Cone, whose family owned most of the southern American textile mills. The talk at these salons was largely of art. Gertrude and Leo held the same sort of social gatherings when, in 1903, they set up home together in Paris in the rue de Fleurus.

The Cone sisters became lifelong collectors. They collected paintings, fabrics, sculpture, antique furniture, boxes, prints and jewellery. Claribel, ten years older than Gertrude, was a research pathologist at the Johns Hopkins. She qualified as one of the first women doctors in America, but disliked physical contact so she gave up general practice after treating her first patient. She weighed 270 pounds and had double-jointed thumbs.

Etta kept house and looked after her sister. When they travelled, Claribel booked a stateroom just for herself. 'Etta, one night is as important as any other night in my life and I must be comfortable,' she said. When they went to the theatre, Claribel occupied two front-row aisle seats - one for herself and one for her packages. Etta sat further back. Etta admired Gertrude's 'magnificent head and features, her appealing voice, her elementally refreshing laugh, her prodigious and largely good humored will to power'. She typed Gertrude's early works and felt *de trop* when all such tasks went to Alice.

Gertrude wrote a portrait of Claribel and Etta called *Two Women*, in 1908, which nobody wanted to publish. It began:

> There are often two of them, both women. There were two of them, two women. There were two of them, both women. There were two women and they were sisters. They both went on living. They were very often together then when they were living. They were very often not together when they were living. One was the elder and one was the younger . . .
>
> They did some things. The elder did some things. The older one went on being living. She did some things. She did go on being living. She was more something than any other one. She did some things. She went on being living. She did this thing, she went on being living. She went on being living. She did this thing, she went on being living.

Before long Leo realised that he

> could do nothing in a laboratory and one day got a great idea in aesthetics - something along the lines of what (Benedetto) Croce later published - I dropped biology and decided to go to Florence for a few years.

*Etta Cone (centre), Claribel Cone (right) and a friend on board ship, May 1903.*

For two years he 'became really intimate with quattrocento Italian art – the art of Piero della Francesca, Paolo Uccello, Domenico Veneziano, Andrea de Castagno and the early Sienese'. He met often in Florence with the art historian Bernard Berenson and used his magnificent art library. 'He's a good man even if he does think there's no one else in Italy that knows anything about Italian painting,' Leo wrote. Leo then decided to write a biography of Mantegna, there being 'no recent book on him in English'. But he soon found that two other books on Mantegna were being written. Then he 'discovered pragmatism' and wanted to find an intelligible meaning for identity and to read the scriptures.

After Leo left Baltimore, Gertrude became involved in a fraught triangle of love and went off the academic rails. She moved into a little red-bricked terraced house, two storeys high with wide white steps. 'One of a whole row of all the same kind that made a close pile like a row of dominoes that a child knocks over.' She shared it with a student, Emma Lootz, who had the downstairs room. Gertrude's living room was the large one over it. According to Gertrude's early biographer, Elizabeth Sprigge, in conversation Emma Lootz said:

> In the other house Leo had been the master, in this one
> Gertrude was. She had more money than I and everything was
> arranged to her liking . . . Once Gertrude got alarmed about her
> health. She thought there was something the matter with her
> blood so she hired a welterweight to box with her. The
> chandelier in my room used to swing . . .

Gertrude met regularly for tea and talk in the Baltimore apartment of two Bryn Mawr college graduates, Mabel Haynes and Grace Lounsbery. They were practical, athletic women, 'activity and no dreaminess'. Mabel Haynes was having an affair with another Bryn Mawr graduate, May Bookstaver, whom Gertrude described as a tall 'American version of the handsome English girl . . . upright and a trifle brutal'. After a while, Gertrude was having an affair with May Bookstaver too, which caused Gertrude confusion and anxiety and disrupted her work. To exorcise the pain of it all, when she settled in Paris with Leo in 1903, she wrote about this triangle of love in her first book, *QED*. She finished it on 24 October 1903, wrote 'FINIS' at the end and put the manuscript away in a cupboard. She said that she forgot about it for thirty years and told no one of it. Certainly she did not tell Alice. In 1932 she unearthed it and showed it to her agent William Bradley and to the writer Louis Bromfield. There was talk of publication, but they advised against this because the book was about lesbian love. Alice B. Toklas read the manuscript and then, 'in a passion', destroyed all of May Bookstaver's letters to Gertrude, for Gertrude had included these verbatim in her book.

The novel was a faithful portrayal of the affair. Only the names were changed. The affair began with attraction and a great deal of talk, on Gertrude's part, about middle-class morality, virtue and passion. Gertrude explained to May that 'the middle class ideal which demands that people be affectionate, respectable, honest and content, that they avoid excitements and cultivate serenity is the ideal that appeals to me'. She believed that physical passion, to be worth anything, must involve idealising another. May told her, 'You are so afraid of losing your moral sense that you are not willing to take it through anything more dangerous than a mud puddle.'

Gertrude confessed to May that she feared 'passion in its many disguised forms', that she did not understand it and that it had no reality for her. 'That is what makes it possible for a face as thoughtful and strongly built as yours to be almost annoyingly unlived,' May told her. Gertrude admitted that she was a 'hopeless coward. I hate to risk hurting myself or anybody else. All I want to do is to meditate endlessly and think and talk.' But then May 'let her fingers flutter vaguely' near Gertrude's lips and, at a point when Gertrude was looking at the stars and talking of honesty, she found herself 'intensely kissed on the eyes and lips'. She was unresponsive, not knowing if she saw the point or not. 'I was just thinking . . .', she said. 'Haven't you ever stopped thinking long enough to feel?' May replied. From that point on, Gertrude was in an affair and neither thinking nor talking helped her.

Mabel Haynes had a prior claim to May Bookstaver and a financial hold over her too. She settled her debts and bills and paid for her trips to Europe. She treated May with an implied ownership that Gertrude resented and disliked. Though Gertrude knew she had to keep her relationship with May secret from Mabel, she did not quite know why. They met secretly in restaurants, museums and for walks through the city. When Gertrude visited May in New York they called at the apartment of a friend who was out. For the first time in Gertrude's experience 'something happened in which she had no definite consciousness of beginnings. She found herself at the end of a passionate embrace.'

Morally, Gertrude had much to ponder. As the affair wore on, she felt herself trapped in 'unillumined' immorality. 'I never wanted to be a hero, but on the other hand . . . I am not anxious to cultivate cowardice,' she wrote. She hoped some day to find a morality 'that can stand the wear and tear of real desire'. That day came, in 1907, when she met Alice. She found no useful models of morality from her family. Leo wrote to her of nights that 'cost me a hundred and fifty francs for champagne, eats, and the lady between midnight and six o'clock'. Sarah wrote to her of the joys of motherhood and of her doctor whom, she said, Gertrude would have 'adored meeting', who treated girls for 'self-abuse' by giving them lectures and '*very strong medicine to dissipate their sensations*'. He said that in cases of very long practice, the only recourse was removal of the ovaries. She wanted Gertrude to marry this doctor 'were you willing and if you have not formed any prior attachment'.

When May Bookstaver visited Baltimore, she stayed with Mabel Haynes. When the three of them were together, May and Gertrude gave no sign of their involvement. When Gertrude quarrelled with May about Mabel, May told her that she trampled on everything without being changed or influenced by what she brutally destroyed. Gertrude asked for patience:

> It is hardly to be expected that such a changed estimate of
> values, such a complete departure from established convictions as
> I have lately undergone could take place without many revulsions.

Gertrude came to hate the 'turgid and complex world' of divided emotions and longed

> for obvious, superficial, clean simplicity . . . no amount of
> reasoning will help in deciding what is right and possible for one
> to do. If you don't begin with some theory of obligation, anything
> is possible and no rule of right and wrong holds. One must
> either accept some theory or else believe one's instinct or follow
> the world's opinion.

Eventually she confronted Mabel and learned the truth about her relationship with May. Gertrude went home angry and hurt, wanting to end the affair but unable to do so. May in her turn was angry when she heard of the meeting: 'If you weren't wholly selfish you'd have exercised self-restraint to spare me this,' she wrote to Gertrude.

In the summer of 1901 Mabel and May went on holiday to Europe, leaving Gertrude waiting for infrequent letters. 'The pain of passionate longing was very hard to bear.' She found consolation in the 'blue of the sky and the green of the countryside. Again and again she would bury her face in the cool grass to recover the sense of life in the midst of her sick despondency.' She wrote to May: 'I am now convinced my feeling for you is genuine and loyal . . . I dread you giving me up . . . I dread more being the cause of serious annoyance to you . . .' May replied:

> Hush little one. Oh you stupid child, don't you realise that you
> are the only thing in the world that makes anything seem real or
> worthwhile to me. I have had a dreadful time this summer.
> [Mabel read a letter of hers to Gertrude and it 'upset her

completely.'] She said she found it but I can hardly believe that.
She asked me if you care for me and I told her that I didn't
know and I really don't dearest. She did not ask me if I cared
for you. The thing upset her completely and she was jealous of
my every thought and I could not find a moment even to feel
alone with you. But don't please don't say any more about giving
you up. You are not any trouble to me if you will only not leave
me.

Gertrude tried not to see May, but when they did, inevitably, remeet they
spent a lot of time in May's room 'in the habit of silent intimacy', and with
kisses 'that seemed to scale the very walls of chastity'. Gertrude wrote trying
to end it all: 'we are more completely unsympathetic and understand each
other less than at any time in our whole acquaintance,' she wrote. May fainted
when she received the letter. Gertrude then saw her by chance in the street
and realised how much she cared for her.

The situation manipulated them all and became an elaborate game.
There were quarrels, reconciliations and desperation. Gertrude felt 'sad
with longing and sick with desire'. Mabel saw Gertrude and May kissing
under a lamppost and made a jealous scene. Gertrude saw that May could
not or would not choose between them:

Hasn't she yet learned that things do happen and she isn't big
enough to stave them off . . . Can't she see things as they are and
not as she would make them if she were strong enough as she
plainly isn't . . . dead-lock.

The affair dragged on for three years and its repercussions affected Gertrude
until 1907 when she met Alice. She did no academic work. Her teachers

would ask her questions although as she said to her friends it was
foolish of them to ask her, when there were so many eager and
anxious to answer. However they did question her from time to time
and as she said, what could she do she did not know the answer.

The medical school graded its students work numerically. One was the top
grade, 4 was to fail. In her final year Gertrude, who had been a star pupil,
was the only one in her class of fifty-four to get a grade lower than a 3.
She got 4 in Opthamology, Otology and Dermatology and 5 in Laryngology,
Rhinology and Obstetrics.
She said that she thanked the Professor of Obstetrics for failing her:

you have no idea how grateful I am to you. I have so much
inertia and so little initiative that very possibly if you had not
kept me from taking my degree I would have, well, not taken to
the practice of medicine, but at any rate to pathological
psychology and you don't know how little I like pathological
psychology and how all medicine bores me.

Other women students thought she 'had done harm to their sex'. 'But Gertrude
Gertrude remember the cause of women and Gertrude Stein said, you don't
know what it is to be bored.'

Her claim to be pleased at being spared from practising medicine came
in the 1930s when she was sure of herself as a writer. At the time, the failure
coincided with her emotional confusion and unhappiness, and infected her
with the same rootlessness and uncertainty as Leo.

In the summer of 1902 she and Leo met in Italy, then travelled to London
and rented rooms at 20 Bloomsbury Square. Leo bought his first oil painting.
It was by William Steer. He felt a bit like a desperado, 'oil paintings were
for the rich'. They visited Bernard and Mary Berenson in their Surrey cottage
and met Bertrand Russell, 'a young mathematician of genius' Leo called
him, who was married to Mrs Berenson's sister, Alys. Berenson said Gertrude's
'apparently seamless garments make her look like the proto-Semite, a statue
from Ur of the Chaldees'. He was fearful she might topple over because
of her size and he noticed she sweated a lot in the sun. They all argued
about America: 'We have American versus England disputes all the time',
Leo wrote. 'The general theme is why in the name of all that's reasonable
do you think of going back to America.' For Gertrude, the discussions set
her thinking about *The Making of Americans*, her thousand-page book, which
Alice was painstakingly to transcribe, about herself, identity, 'bottom nature'
and 'every kind of men and women and all the kind of being in them'.

Gertrude planned to stay in Europe for a year and to communicate with
May only by letters. But in December 1902 Leo went to Paris and she
became lonely and depressed. She spent her days in the Reading Room of
the British Museum. She wanted to read English literature from the sixteenth
century to the present. She bought small grey notebooks in which she listed
books to read and buy, and passages from them that she liked. She read
novels, diaries, collected letters, biographies, autobiographies and weighty
historical tomes like Gibbon's *Decline and Fall of the Roman Empire*. She never
read poetry or books about books.

She arrived at the Museum early in the morning and read until evening,
leaving only when she was hungry. For the rest, she wandered the streets
of London and felt homesick, lonely and afraid:

Anything can frighten her and London when it was like Dickens certainly did . . . The time comes when nothing in the world is so important as a breath of one's own particular climate. If it were one's last penny it would be used for that return passage.

An American in the winter fogs of London can realise this passionate need this desperate longing in all its completeness. The dead weight of that fog and smoke laden air, the sky that never suggests for a moment the clean blue distance that has been the accustomed daily comrade, the dreary sun, moon and stars that look like painted imitations on the ceiling of a smoke-filled room, the soggy, damp, miserable streets, and the women with bedraggled, frayed-out skirts, their faces swollen and pimply with sordid dirt ground into them until it has become a natural part of their ugly surface all become day after day a more dreary weight of hopeless oppression.

She stuck London and its gloomy isolation for five months, then went back to America in February 1903, to New York, wanting cleanness, openness and friendliness, and not the double meanings and need to be on guard that she had found in London. But she was quickly enmeshed again in the trap of her affair with May. She despaired about it and felt that they were incompatible, that 'their pulses were differently timed' and that the incompatibility had been there from the very beginning. She lived in 'The White House' at 100th Street and Riverside Drive - a colonial building with a garden full of roses. She shared an apartment there with three Johns Hopkins friends - Mabel Weeks, Harriet Clark and Estelle Rumbold Kohn. She walked, read, wrote notes for books and letters to friends, bought a landscape by Schilling, bits of porcelain and etchings, and analysed herself and friends.

Then, in spring, again to get away from the tangle of her affair, she sailed to join Leo in Paris. She intended it to be a holiday, but from that time on, Paris became her permanent home.

*The studio at 27 rue de Fleurus in 1913.*

# 5

# THE RUE DE FLEURUS

*'The earth keeps turning around but
you have to sit somewhere'*

When Leo went to Paris in the winter of 1902, leaving Gertrude in London, he had no particular intention of staying there. He wanted to look at paintings. He was thirty-one, had roamed the world in an interested but dissatisfied way and had tried and discarded history, philosophy, biology, art history and biography. He had found no one to take the place of Gertrude and thought that eventually they would live together in America. He wrote to their friend Mabel Weeks:

> If America only were not so far away and if the climate in the possible parts were not so chilly. Those I think are my chief grievances against the land of my birth, though I suppose that they are not very profound ones. Someday I'll make up my mind that I can stand them and then Gertrude and I will retire to Connecticut or Duxbury or somewhere and live happily ever after.

Inevitably, in Paris he thought that he had found a new vocation. It occurred to him when dining with Pablo Casals who was on a concert tour. (The previous year Casals had met Sarah and Michael Stein in San Francisco. He hurt his hand before a recital and Sarah helped his manager, Isadora Duncan's brother Raymond, find a masseur. Casals then met up with Leo in Paris. They ate together once a week and went for walks.) Leo told Casals that he felt himself 'growing into an artist' and that 'the leaven of pictorial vision was working'. 'When I got back to the hotel, I made a rousing fire, took off my clothes and began to draw from the nude,' Leo said. He then spent a week drawing statues in the Louvre, felt that he had found his true way, decided to stay in Paris and enrolled at the Académie Julian, where many Americans studied art.

He needed a studio. His uncle Ephraim Keyser, who had a moustache, was going bald, and who sculpted busts and cherubs, had just finished studio hunting for himself. He told Leo of a good place, for a moderate rent, at 27 rue de Fleurus.

Rue de Fleurus is a short street off the boulevard Raspail on the Left Bank near the Luxembourg Gardens. Number 27, a stone building designed by G. Pasquier, was then seven years old. A central archway led to a small paved courtyard. On the left was the concierge's office. To the right was a two-storey apartment. A small entrance hall separated the kitchen from the dining room. The two bedrooms and bathroom were on the upper floor. The studio, adjacent to the apartment, was angled to catch the north light. By spring, Leo was writing to Mabel Weeks:

> What are your plans for the summer? I am fortunate in not needing to make a choice. I've got my house, my atelier and my fencing school all engaged for the summer, as likewise a cook lady who didn't want to give me any eggs for breakfast this morning because it was Good Friday.

The cook, Hélène, served very good roast chicken, and mutton in madeira sauce.

Leo set out to learn the art market. He bought prints and a little picture 'of a woman in white with a white dog on a green lawn' by Raoul du Gardier. But the contemporary work he saw did not particularly interest him and the older paintings were too expensive and not what he wanted. 'I wanted an adventure,' he told Mabel Weeks.

He wrote to Gertrude and asked her to come and live with him. They spent the summer of 1903 together in Rome, Florence, Fiesole and Siena looking at paintings. They met up with the Cone sisters, Claribel and Etta, and had a good time. 'Gertrude and Sister C came,' wrote Etta in her travel diary. 'Had a table d'hôte dinner at Fiesole and all got drunk . . . Gertrude and I lay there and smoked . . . Gertrude is great fun.' Then Gertrude went back with Leo to the rue de Fleurus and wrote her novel *QED*, about her affair with May Bookstaver.

She wrote in the studio. Leo never did paint there. 'I sat down in there', said Gertrude, 'and pretty soon I was writing, and then he took a studio elsewhere and we lived together there until nineteen fourteen.' Leo went to art school in the mornings, then did life drawings at an afternoon class.

In 1904 Gertrude was still uncertain about leaving the States. She told Leo that if she was to live with him in Paris it was essential for her to visit America at least once a year:

I said she'd probably get used to it but Gertrude is naturally dogmatic and said no, she was like that, and that was like her, and so it must be. That year she went to America for a visit and thirty-one years later she went again. No one really knows what is essential.

Not until Alice arrived did 27 rue de Fleurus smell of beeswax and lavender. But Gertrude and Leo set up a home that became a legend. Gertrude's drifting days were done. 'In our American life', she wrote in her second novel *Fernhurst*,

> where there is no coercion in custom and it is our right to change our vocation so often as we have desire and opportunity, it is a common experience that our youth extends through the whole first twenty-nine years of our life and it is not till we reach thirty that we find at last that vocation for which we feel ourselves fit and to which we willingly devote continued labor.

In 1904 she was thirty and writing was her fit vocation and willing labor.

She got into the habit of writing at night. She sat at a long Florentine table. Light came from incandescent gas lamps hung overhead and heat from a cast-iron stove. She wrote in children's exercise books, or on scraps of paper, in spidery writing, usually in pencil. In her early works, which were short and uncertain in style, to exorcise the pain and confusion she felt, she wrote around the themes of the stalemate and disappointment of her love affair with May Bookstaver. Her style was singular, strangely rhythmic, short on narrative and dialogue, but not as opaque and daring as it was to become. In *Fernhurst* she again wrote of a triangle of involvement, but made the character most like herself into a man. She carried the pessimism she felt about the muddle of human relationships into her third 'early work', *Three Lives* – three psychological portraits of Baltimore women who find life hard.

Gertrude wanted the mental processes of the people in the stories to shape her prose. She wanted to do new things with prose and for her writing to be 'at the front edge of time'. And she also wanted definitively to analyse human character. She took as an epigraph for the book. 'Donc je suis un malheureux et ce n'est ni ma faute ni celle de la vie.' (So I am unhappy and it is neither my fault nor that of life.)

Years later she said that one of the stories, *Melanctha*, was 'the first definite step away from the nineteenth century and into the twentieth century in literature'. It was about a black woman who was rejected as a child and who had a love affair with a doctor who rejected her too. At the time of writing it, Gertrude was not particularly self-confident and Leo did not offer a word of praise. She wrote to Mabel Weeks in the tone of the story:

> I am afraid that I can never write the great American novel. I
> don't know how to sell on a margin or do anything with shorts
> or longs, so I have to content myself with niggers and servant
> girls and the foreign population generally. Leo he said there
> wasn't no art in Lovett's book [an American friend who was at
> Harvard with Gertrude and Leo] and then was bad and wouldn't
> tell me that there was in mine so I went to bed very miserable
> but I don't care there ain't any Tschaikowsky Pathetique or Omar
> Kayam or Wagner or Whistler or White Man's Burden or green
> burlap in mine at least not in the present ones. Dey is very
> simple and very vulgar and I don't think they will interest the
> great American public. I am very sad Mamie.

Gertrude would get up at noon and Hélène would give her breakfast. Leo
painted in the day and in the evenings read, or wrote letters to friends in the
ground floor study which was filled from floor to ceiling with books. He and
Gertrude bought large, heavy, dark, Renaissance furniture. They bought a
Henry IV buffet with eagles carved on it, seventeenth-century terracotta figures
of women, pieces of Italian pottery, prints, paintings – above all paintings –
and quite a lot of junk. Gertrude liked collecting. Mabel Dodge said:

> she didn't care whether a thing was *bon gout* or not, unless it
> affected her pleasantly, and if it did please her she loved it for
> that reason. It made her daring in a snobbish period of art. She
> adored those miniature alabaster fountains, with two tiny white
> doves poised on the brink that tourists bought and she had a
> penchant for forget me not mosaic brooches.

Over the years, she collected glass globes, apocalyptic compositions of saints
and animals in shells and feathers, Biedermeier paper ladies sprinkled with
Christmas frost, a gold-mine in a bottle, horseshoe nails, pebbles, pipe-shaped
cigarette holders, seashells, pieces of bone, buttons, matchboxes.

'Paris was where the twentieth century was,' said Gertrude, 'the place that
suited those of us who were to create the twentieth-century art and literature
naturally enough'. Writers and painters were treated like lords, rents were
cheap and food was good. 'We despised luxury except when someone else
paid for it, and got what we most wanted. That made a satisfactory living,'
Leo wrote. A fixed income went much further than in America. Gertrude
and Leo were rich enough to buy what they wanted, but not so rich as
to interest the tax authorities.

Gertrude liked being encapsulated with the English language and having

French spoken all around her. She made no particular effort to learn French and seldom read it:

> One of the things I have liked all these years is to be surrounded by people who know no english. It has left me more intensely alone with my eyes and my english. I do not know if it would have been possible to have english be so all in all to me otherwise. And they none of them could read a word I wrote, most of them did not even know that I did write. No, I like living with so very many people and being all alone with english and myself.

She also liked to doze in the Louvre and wake up in front of paintings.

Relatives and American friends gravitated to the city. Michael and Sarah Stein and their young son Allan arrived in December 1903. Sarah Stein wanted to be part of the salon life of Europe. In San Francisco, when her son was three, she had returned to college to study art and comparative literature. She was a large, opinionated woman and she was often unwell. Her uterus was torn when her son was born, so she had operations under chloroform, which made her sick, and left her with backache and depression. She often spent half the day in bed. She gave Gertrude a detailed diary of her child's wrinkles, whims and little sayings, sent snippets of his hair, and charted his progress in a captioned photograph album.

Her husband, Michael, was known as Mr Sarah Stein. He gave up working for the railroad company when he found that he had enough money to live in style in Europe on the dividends from his various property investments. Like Gertrude, he had difficulty in getting out of bed in the mornings and came to life late in the day. Sarah said that she grew to appreciate him and not think him weak and negative. 'Mike, the infant, the sleepy, lazy, inconsiderate, irritating Mike . . . he needs me every minute he can spare for me', she told Gertrude.

Sarah and Michael Stein rented an apartment at 58 rue Madame, near to the rue de Fleurus, in a converted Protestant church. Their living room, which had been the schoolroom, measured forty by forty-five feet. Like Leo and Gertrude, Sarah Stein was a spirited collector. She bought oriental art, Chinese bronzes and Japanese prints in San Francisco then, at the rue Madame, Persian rugs and after the trend had been set by Leo, works by Cézanne, Renoir, Picasso and, overwhelmingly, Matisse.

In 1905 Etta Cone also rented an apartment in rue Madame. She took piano lessons from the landlady, Madame Vernot, walked with Allan Stein in the Luxembourg Gardens and in the afternoons went shopping with Gertrude, or visited the Louvre, the small galleries, or the dressmakers. Etta

*Michael and Sarah Stein's apartment at rue Madame in 1907.*
*Left to right: Michael and Sarah Stein, Henri Matisse,*
*Allan Stein and Hans Purrmann.*

noted in her diaries Gertrude's 'exquisite qualities': '. . .talked with Gertrude on her pet subject of human intercourse of the sexes. She is truly interesting.'

Gertrude could not type, so Etta volunteered to transcribe *Three Lives*. When Gertrude visited her she said she found Etta 'faithfully copying the manuscript letter by letter so that she might not by any indiscretion become conscious of the meaning. Permission to read the text having been given the typewriting went on.' Gertrude put this scrupulousness down to the fact that Etta came from Baltimore, 'famous for the delicate sensibilities and conscientiousness of its inhabitants'.

Leo was the first of the Steins seriously to buy modern paintings. In Spring 1904 Bernard Berenson was in Paris. '"Do you know Cézanne?" he asked [Leo]. "I said no." "Well look him up." "Where?" "At Vollards on the rue Lafitte."' Leo and Gertrude went straight to Ambroise Vollard's musty little shop, crammed with pictures. Vollard got out paintings by Cézanne of an apple, then a nude, then a large canvas with a fragment of landscape on it and then a small landscape of Aix-en-Provence that they both liked. Gertrude wrote to Mabel Weeks, again in her *Melanctha* style:

> We is doin business. We are selling Jap prints to buy a Cezanne
> at least we are that is Leo is trying. He dont like it a bit and
> makes a awful fuss about asking enough money but I guess we'll
> get the Cezanne . . . That is Leo's connoisership. Its a bully
> picture all right.

Also on the rue Lafitte was a confectioner's called Fouquet, 'where one could console oneself with delicious honey cakes and nut candies and once in a while instead of a picture buy oneself strawberry jam in a glass bowl'.

Berenson told them of a wealthy American in Florence, Charles Loeser, who had a collection of Cézannes which he kept in rooms separate from his other paintings. That summer Gertrude and Leo went to see them. Leo was so affected by them that he said he went back to Paris, 'a Columbus setting sail for a world beyond the world'.

In October 1904 the second of the Autumn Salons opened at the Grand Palais. The Autumn Salons aimed to encourage the work of new and innovative artists in contrast to the more staid Spring Salons. Leo 'looked again and again at every single picture, just as a botanist might at the flora of an unknown land'. He said the pictures made clear to him the aesthetic foundations of modern art. He saw Toulouse Lautrec's work for the first time and bought a painting of his, *Le Divan*. Then he and Gertrude bought Delacroix's *Perseus and Andromeda*. As a rule, they seldom spent more than 300 francs on a picture.

That same autumn, Michael told them they had an unexpected windfall of 8,000 francs between them in their accounts. 'As this was regarded as criminal waste we went at once to Vollard's,' said Leo. They rummaged through the stacks of canvases and chose two Gauguins, *Three Tahitians* for Leo and *Sunflowers* for Gertrude. 'They were rather awful but finally we liked them,' she said. They bought two versions of Cézanne's *Bathers* and two more Renoirs. Gertrude claimed they bought in twos because they could not quite agree about which they liked. 'Vollard threw in a Maurice Denis, *Virgin and Child* for good measure', said Leo.

They still had money left over and wondered about buying a Bonnard and a Vuillard but, while eating his lunch, Leo felt thrilled at the thought of buying a big Cézanne figure. Gertrude agreed. They were much taken by a portrait of Cézanne's wife, Hortense. They discussed it over honey cakes at Fouquet's, then took it home in a cab. They hung it in the studio where Gertrude worked at night. She said it influenced the way she wrote *Three Lives*, that Cézanne built up the portrait by planes of colour and that she built up her characters by her repetitive sentences.

Gertrude arrived later to modern art than Leo, but stayed with it longer. She was collector, connoisseur, friend and fellow artist to many of the great modernists. Leo judged their work by formal standards. He approached Cézanne through Italian quattrocento painting. Mantegna's *Crucifixion* was his favourite painting in the Louvre. He thought it 'a sort of Cézanne precursor with the colour running all through it . . . I was quite ready for Cézanne', he wrote. He thought the *Portrait of Madame Cézanne* a natural progression from the nineteenth century, with colour, form and content subordinated to composition. For Gertrude, the portrait was revolutionary. She saw in it what she herself wanted to do. She said she wanted to smash the significance of nineteenth-century order and structure, to shuck off old habits of seeing and describing and to let a new art emerge. She said there was no centre to Cézanne's picture to give it an organising principle. The composition *was* the picture:

> Cézanne gave me a new feeling about composition. I was
> obsessed by this idea of composition . . . It was not solely the
> realism of characters but the realism of the composition which
> was the important thing. This had not been conceived as a reality
> until I came along, but I got it largely from Cézanne. Flaubert
> too had a little of the feeling about this thing but they none of
> them conceived it as an entity no more than any painter had
> done other than Cézanne.

Gertrude wrote *Melanctha* at night with Madame Cézanne on the wall in front of her. There was no significant beginning, middle, or end to her

*Paul Cézanne*, Portrait of Madame Cézanne, 1877.

story. She thought this closer to people's true experience of reality, a multi-facetedness, a 'continuous present'. 'Always and always. Must write the hymn of repetition,' she said.

The following year, Gertrude, Leo, Sarah and Michael Stein, and Claribel and Etta Cone all went to the Autumn Salon. 'The walls were covered with canvases,' said Claribel,

> presenting what seemed to me then a riot of colour - sharp and startling, drawing crude and uneven, distortions and exaggerations - composition primitive and simple as though done by a child. We stood in front of a portrait - it was that of a man bearded, brooding, tense, fiercely elemental in color with green eyes ... blue beard, pink and yellow complexion. It seemed to me grotesque. We asked ourselves are these things to be taken seriously ... As we looked across the room we found our friends earnestly contemplating a canvas - of a woman with a hat tilted jauntily at an angle on the top of her head - the drawing crude, the color bizarre.

The art critic for *Gil Blas*, Louis Vauxcelles, seeing a traditional bronze statue among it all, said, 'Tiens ... Donatello au milieu des fauves!'

Matisse was the king of the Fauves, the wild beasts. The painting the Steins were earnestly contemplating was his *Woman with a Hat*, a portrait of his wife who worked as a milliner to keep him and their children from penury. Gertrude wanted to buy it. It seemed to her 'perfectly natural and she could not understand why it infuriated everybody'. For Leo, 'It was what I was unknowingly waiting for . . . a thing brilliant and powerful, but the nastiest smear of paint I had ever seen', and Sarah Stein wanted to buy it because it looked like her mother.

Matisse was asking 500 francs for the painting. Gertrude and Leo offered 450. Madame Matisse told her husband to hold out for the extra fifty francs which would mean winter clothes for their daughter. Madame Matisse was posing with an old guitar in their studio when the Steins *petit bleu* arrived saying 500 francs was all right.

The Steins patronage came at a crucial time in Matisse's career, for he had no money. Within a short space Gertrude and Leo bought *Joy of Life*, *Blue Nude*, a cast of his sculpture *The Slave*, *Portrait of Margot*, *Landscape Collioure*. The walls of the rue de Fleurus began to crowd up with his work. And the Steins were friends as well as patrons. Gertrude liked Madame Matisse's jugged hare and choice in regional wines. As for Matisse, he worked, she said, 'every day and every day and every day and he worked terribly hard'.

Sarah Stein was Matisse's most loyal admirer though. 'She knows more about my paintings than I do,' he said of her. She went on buying his work long after Gertrude and Leo lost interest. She bought a self-portrait, a portrait of Madame Matisse, a still life called *Pink Onions*, *Blue Still Life*, *The Young Sailor*. Her apartment at the rue Madame became a shrine to Matisse. Annette Rosenshine, who went to Paris before Alice and rented a little room at the top of the same house as Sarah, said that Matisse

> found solace in unburdening his latest problems and uncertainties
> to Sarah Stein knowing he would receive sensitive, sympathetic
> understanding . . . In later years, after the Steins' return to
> America, he corresponded with Sarah, telling her of his work and
> over the years his loyalty to her never flagged.

He gave Sarah Stein painting lessons and, in the winter of 1907, she helped him start up a short-lived art class. She was the principal pupil, but when it became clear to her that she had little talent, she gave up painting and became a Christian Scientist.

A few weeks after buying Matisse's *Woman with a Hat*, Gertrude and Leo bought their first Picasso. Clovis Sagot, a dealer with a goatee beard, who liked scandal and a sort of liquorice called Zan, had a little gallery on the rue Lafitte. 'He would interrupt the talk on modern art to put a bit of Zan between his teeth and commend its virtues,' said Leo. 'Then we were back again on the latest show, the latest artistic scandal, the prospects for the future.' Sagot described Picasso as 'the real thing' and gave him an exhibition. Picasso was twenty-four and, like Matisse, hard up. Gertrude and Leo bought a 'picture of a mountebank with wife and child and ape'. It was later called *The Acrobat's Family with a Monkey*. Sagot also showed them a picture of a naked girl holding a basket of red flowers. Leo liked it but Gertrude hated it. She thought the girl had feet like a monkey, so Sagot offered to cut the head off and sell them just that. Gertrude and Leo quarrelled about the picture. 'He wanted it and she did not want it in the house.' Leo brought it home while she was eating her dinner. 'Now you've spoiled my appetite', she said.

Matisse was a frequent visitor at the rue de Fleurus. Gertrude said that was why the formal Saturday evening salons began, because so many people wanted to see these pictures: 'Matisse brought people, everybody brought somebody and they came at any time and it began to be a nuisance and it was in this way that Saturday evenings began.'

All kinds of people went to the evening salons: young painters, writers, collectors, dealers, assorted friends, relatives and acquaintances. Vollard called the Steins 'the most hospitable people in the world': 'People who came there out of snobbery soon felt a sort of discomfort at being allowed so much liberty in another man's house. Only those who really cared for painting continued to visit.'

Americans were a novelty in Paris and the Steins reputation as eccentric personalities and collectors of strange modern paintings quickly grew. People wanted to see the works by Renoir, Gauguin, Degas, Matisse and Cézanne that filled up the walls one above the other. After a while Gertrude started taking the paintings out of their frames, because she thought frames constrained them.

Sarah Stein copied the salon idea. She held hers on Saturday afternoons so that visitors could go from one house to the other to see the latest acquisitions. Harriet Levy said: 'Beautifully gowned in original costumes and antique jewelry Sarah sat on the couch in the corner explaining to everybody the greatness of Matisse.'

Both Gertrude and Leo smoked cigars at that time, and wore brown corduroy and sandals with toes like the prows of gondolas designed by Isadora Duncan's brother, Raymond. Gertrude dyed her sandals black and in winter wore them with thick wool stockings. She liked pongee waistcoats, a felt hat for winter and a straw one for summer. She and Leo were turned out of the Café de la Paix because of their appearance. They both had hearty laughs. Leo could do a very good imitation of Isadora Duncan. Mabel Weeks described it as 'too beautiful to be burlesque':

> He was very playful, very personal, something of a flirt. Both men and women liked him and he was pleasant company . . . He was not particularly gentle – indeed sometimes almost cruel in showing up people whose arguments he disliked. He felt that a very important element in affection and comradeship was tenderness, yet he understood tenderness only in a limited way and admitted a lack of it in himself . . . With people he didn't know he often assumed an *ex cathedra* lecturing manner. With people whose intellectual capacities were not stimulating, he was impatient.

'I expounded and explained,' Leo said of the salon evenings. 'People came and so I explained because it was my nature to explain.' He sat with his feet high up on a bookcase because of his troublesome digestion. He told them about Renoir's feeling for absolute colour, colour 'as the stuff of art', about Degas' distinctive intellect and control, and Cézanne's treatment of mass. While he expounded and explained, Gertrude watched. People were struck by her stillness, composure and sudden laughter. She was making observations of people's characters and behaviour, and fitting them into formal schemes and a 'characterological system' for her novel, which was to be about everybody that ever lived, called *The Making of Americans*. In later years Alice said, 'Gertrude's work at that time on what she called the "bottom nature of people" was profound. It was one of comparison and of likeness and difference every minute of the day.'

Gertrude liked Picasso when he visited. She thought he was like 'a good-looking bootblack . . . thin, dark, alive with big pools of eyes and a violent but not rough way'. When he first went to supper he sat next to Gertrude who unwittingly picked up his piece of bread. 'This piece of bread is mine,' he said and took it back. 'She laughed and he looked sheepish. That was the beginning of their intimacy.' After dinner Leo started showing Picasso all his Japanese prints. Gertrude wrote that Picasso

> said under his breath to Gertrude Stein, he is very nice, your brother, but like all americans . . . he shows you japanese prints. Moi j'aime pas ça no I don't care for it. As I say Gertrude Stein and Pablo Picasso immediately understood each other.

Gertrude, more than Leo, bought Picasso's work. Her favourite early purchase was *Boy Leading a Horse*, a large picture of a nude figure against a pink background. She encouraged friends like Claribel and Etta Cone and Mabel Weeks and Mabel Luhan Dodge, who lived in the Villa Curonia in Fiesole, to buy too.

Gertrude and Picasso became very close. They quarrelled when she varnished two of his pictures without asking him, or when she disliked his lovers, but in the early days such quarrels passed. Gertrude said, 'When a human being exists more in relation to the world than to himself he approaches genius.' She thought that she and Picasso represented the best example of this that she knew. She felt that she perceived his weaknesses. She said that he followed any impulse because he could not say no to anything, that he was childish in his fantasies and in his response to success, that he did not have an 'extremely passionate nature' and that he was indifferent to his lover, Fernande Olivier, as a woman: 'He has a weak character and he allowed others to make decisions, that is the way it is, it was enough that he should do his work, decisions are never important, why make them.'

Picasso lived in the Bateau Lavoir, a studio in the rue de Ravignan in Montmartre. He took many of his friends to Gertrude's evenings at the rue de Fleurus: his lover Fernande Olivier, his best friend the poet Max Jacob, and Apollinaire who would read out his latest poems. 'Oh how badly he spoke his own verse and how he loved to recite it . . .' said Fernande. 'He certainly rendered his poems with staggering inadequacy though he managed to move us none the less.'

Apollinaire's lover, Marie Laurençin, was the only woman artist in the

*Pablo Picasso*, Portrait of Gertrude Stein, 1905-6.

group. She went back to her mother whenever she quarrelled with Apollinaire. Her mother's apartment was white, sparse and convent-like. After her one affair with Marie's father, Madame Laurençin would not entertain men there. Marie Laurençin was training as a painter at the Sèvre porcelain works when she met Braque and, through him, Picasso and Apollinaire. She felt pushed into the shade by them all. 'If the genius of men intimidates me,' she wrote, 'I feel perfectly at ease with everything that is feminine.' After the First World War she became successful in her own right as a painter, designer and illustrator.

Gertrude's Baltimore women friends also went to her salons. Picasso said of them, 'ils sont pas des hommes, ils sont pas des femmes, ils sont des Américains'. He called Claribel Cone 'the Empress'. There was a couple there called Miss Mars and Miss Squire who painted watercolours and went to the local cafés. Miss Mars sometimes dyed her hair purple and both of them wore a lot of make up. Gertrude wrote a story about them called *Miss Furr and Miss Skeene*.

Picasso asked to paint Gertrude's portrait. It took eighty to ninety sittings from winter to spring 1905-6. Most days she walked across Paris to his studio in the Bateau Lavoir where he lived in chaos. She posed sitting in an old broken armchair, with one of its legs missing, wearing brown corduroy and her coral brooch. The studio was cold enough to make the previous night's tea dregs freeze in the cups. Fernande Olivier read aloud from the fables of La Fontaine. Gertrude talked of killing the nineteenth century and of art where composition was the content. The Cone sisters visited and bought Picasso's discarded sketches and a watercolour and an etching, all for $20.

In the spring, Picasso painted out Gertrude's head. 'I can't see you any longer when I look,' he told her. He then went to Gosol in Spain for the summer with Fernande. Gertrude and Leo went to Fiesole in Italy. When Picasso got back to Paris, he painted Gertrude's face from memory, as a mask, with her eyes looking out from behind the mask. Gertrude liked the portrait throughout her life. 'For me it is I and it is the only reproduction of me which is always I for me.'

When friends said that Gertrude did not look like his picture, Picasso would say 'she will'. Leo did not approve of it at all. He thought Picasso's failure to modify the rest of the painting to take account of the newly-painted face, made the whole thing stylistically incoherent. The portrait marked the beginning of Leo's total disaffection with the work of Picasso and Gertrude. Before very long he was calling both their efforts 'Godalmighty rubbish' and 'haemorrhoids', and complaining about 'cubico futuristic tommy-rotting', and rejecting Gertrude's work so roundly that she, in turn, totally rejected him.

*Gertrude outside her studio at rue de Fleurus in 1907.*

# 6

## ALICE MEETS GERTRUDE

*'single mingle bait and wet'*

Alice's father, Ferdinand, slept through the San Francisco earthquake of 1906. She called to him, 'Do get up, the city is on fire'. The quake happened at 5.13 in the morning, on Wednesday 18 April and lasted for forty-eight seconds. Alice saw the chandeliers 'dangling about' and bits of masonry falling off houses. The Toklas house was not badly damaged, though the chimneys came down and the water pipes broke. The house was built of Vermont stone and situated on one of the safe rocky hills, known as the Western addition.

Shifting sand under the pavements snapped the city's gas and water pipes. Three hundred water mains broke and 2,300 service pipes. 'Father didn't care about the gas escaping,' said Alice. Fires started because of cracked or broken chimneys and fifty-seven alarm calls were made to the Fire Department within the first half-hour.

Alice buried the family silver in the garden for safe-keeping against looters and went out to look for food and cigarettes. She saw people cooking from stoves on the sidewalks. At about nine in the morning she called on Annette Rosenshine. They tried to take a cab to Montgomery Street to see how Annette's studio had fared. The stableman told them all cabs were commandeered for hospitals and casualties. Three hundred people were known to have been killed and three hundred were missing.

The city was put under martial law, the army dynamited burning blocks in the downtown area to control the fires, and water was brought in from San Andreas and Sausalito. People piled their possessions and pets on to chairs and barrows and dragged them from the burning areas through the streets to Golden Gate Park and the public squares. The Metropolitan Opera Company was in San Francisco for the first time and Caruso was seen wandering in the street in a bathrobe.

Three days after the quake, Alice and Annette went to visit friends across the Bay, in Oakland and Berkeley. Alice wanted a hot bath and to see Sarah Bernhardt in Racine's *Phèdre*. She took bunches of carnations for her friends (the heat from the fires had made them bloom early) and went on a ferry from a makeshift wharf. From the ferry she saw the demolished city, the destroyed waterfront and the obliterated landmarks. It confirmed her desire to leave San Francisco. 'It was going to be a different place,' she said.

Sarah and Michael Stein went back to San Francisco from Paris to inspect the damage to their properties. They owned a block of shingled duplex houses on Lyon Street, in the same district where Alice lived, and rents from these houses formed the basis of the family's income. 'Our houses are practically all right,' wrote Sarah to Gertrude, 'but the chimneys are gone and will have to be rebuilt perhaps all the way down necessitating tearing open the walls to reach them.' To impress her San Franciscan friends she took souvenirs of Paris: her clothes, 'they always create such a sensation', and three paintings by Matisse, including the portrait of Madame Matisse with a green stripe on her face. 'Since the startling news that there was such stuff in town has been communicated, I have been a very popular lady,' she wrote.

Harriet Levy, whose house was destroyed in the fire, took Alice and Annette to see the pictures. 'Mrs Stein received Alice and me graciously', wrote Annette,

and seemed pleased to introduce us to French art and to show the three paintings she had brought with her, the first by this French artist to be seen in America. Our initiation was a portrait painted on a splotchy background. On the right side of the head was a green daub, and on the opposite side a splash of crimson and mauve. But the crowning affront was a green streak running from the center of the forehead down the nose, lips and chin. It was grotesque and to me, conditioned by my training at Mark Hopkins Institute of Art in San Francisco, it seemed a demented caricature of a portrait. Another picture showed a fat distorted little nude who struck me as a gross unesthetic monster, a far cry from the nude paintings in our life class. The last horror was a small head painted with dots, with spotty bits of the canvas left uncovered by paint. Speechless and nonplussed, I believed that these paintings were the accepted French art of the day.

Alice, intrigued by the Matisse portrait and the stories of salon life, told Sarah of her desire to go to Paris. Two days later Sarah invited Alice and Harriet to travel back with her. But Alice had no money, still felt responsible for her brother Clarence and was unable to confide in her father. He referred to Sarah Stein, with what Alice called 'all a Pole's prejudice', as 'the German

*Henri Matisse*, Portrait with a green stripe, 1905.

memorial monument'. Nor did Harriet particularly want to travel with Sarah. She thought her opinionated and domineering. Alice suggested that Annette should go instead. So Annette travelled with Sarah, as a herald for Alice, who would make the journey when the time was right.

Two 'besandled and unusual-looking people' met Annette at the Gare St Lazare, 'a short squat woman and a tall slim bearded man'. She was taken to 27 rue de Fleurus for supper and then to her *pension* - a little room at the top of the house where Sarah lived. Leo collected her at nine the next morning to take her to the Louvre.

Annette was enamoured of Gertrude's 'dynamic magnetism', her 'inner distinction', the 'power in the beauty of her splendid head', her 'infectious chuckle', her 'low guffaw', the lot. Like Alice who came after her, Annette, at the sight of Gertrude, heard bells ringing 'with a deep sonorous note', and she described her impressions in her letters to Alice.

Gertrude was working on character analyses for her book *The Making of Americans*. Annette went round to the rue de Fleurus at four every afternoon for psychotherapy sessions of an unorthodox sort. She said she felt like a case-study. In these sessions she showed Gertrude all letters from family and friends. She said that Gertrude 'had a passion for letters'. So, for nearly a year before meeting Alice, Gertrude formed some opinion of her through her letters. She decided that Alice was a controlling character and 'an old maid mermaid' with a 'higher nature but a lower ideal' than Annette.

One day Annette tried to tell Gertrude about her turmoil at first meeting a homosexual:

> I was incapable of describing him or what had been said or to give any details of the meeting except my shock over the experience. I remember most vividly Gertrude that day, hugging herself, saying in glee, 'no memory, no consciousness'.

The remark affected Annette, 'this salient matter of consciousness', but she felt that Gertrude did not find where or how she was blocked. 'She had little appreciation of how crippled I was or incapable of responding to any love gesture.' Annette got unblocked twelve years later, after intensive analysis with a Dr Godwin Baynes in Zurich, and then 'all the distorted misshapen emotions came tumbling out helter-skelter in my miniature sculpture'.

Nor did she find Gertrude helpful about sex. 'My Victorian ignorance received little help or enlightenment.' Gertrude said that 'sex was an individual problem that each one had to solve for herself or himself'. She told Annette to reflect about each day and her meetings with people before going to sleep at night, and to attempt to understand her own responses.

After four months of daily sessions with Gertrude, Annette was in a state. Her mother and sister, holidaying in Europe, were shocked at the change in her and asked her to go home with them. Annette felt too dependent on Gertrude to leave. She wrote to her father for permission to stay and continued as Gertrude's subject until Alice arrived in September 1907.

San Francisco was still in a parlous state in 1907. The city was without an infrastructure, or adequate hospital provision and there were outbreaks of bubonic plague and other contagious diseases. More than ever Alice wanted to leave. Her brother Clarence was twenty-one and she was thirty. 'I wanted to go to Paris like all good Californians . . . I would see what would happen in Paris,' she said. But she had debts and no money. Grandfather Levinsky had left her a quarter of his estate when he died, but the money had not yet come through. Harriet Levy had $1,000 in the Wells Fargo Bank. She agreed to travel with Alice and to lend the money to her. Alice told her father she was off. 'He made no comment but gave a sigh.' She was leaving home never to return.

On board ship, in September 1907, Alice read Flaubert's letters and talked to a 'distinguished oldish man, a commodore'. Harriet thought she was being indiscreet. 'A most compromising letter' from him was waiting for Alice at her bank in the Place Vendôme when she got to Paris. 'There was no question of my answering it,' she said. She threw it into a pond in the Tuileries.

She and Harriet stayed first at the Hotel Magellan which was near the avenue du Bois de Boulogne. Nellie Jacott recommended them. 'You had to be recommended because it was small.' Alice loved the avenues of trees flanking the boulevards and thought Parisians had exceptionally intelligent faces, but she wondered why they all wore black.

On their first day Harriet said, 'Let's go and see the Steins'. She sent a *petit bleu* to the rue Madame saying they were on their way. So Alice found herself in Sarah Stein's large living room with the large furniture, large windows, Persian rugs, paintings everywhere and Gertrude:

> She was a golden presence burned by the Tuscan sun and with a
> golden glint in her warm brown hair. She was dressed in a warm
> brown corduroy suit. She wore a large round coral brooch and
> when she talked, very little, or laughed, a good deal, I thought
> her voice came from this brooch. It was unlike anyone else's
> voice - deep, full, velvety like a great contralto's, like two voices.
> She was large and heavy with delicate small hands and a
> beautifully modeled and unique head.

*Alice B. Toklas in 1906. Photograph by Arnold Genthe.*

Gertrude spoke little, though Buddha-like she smiled. 'Just a small smile.' Her eyes, thought Alice, reflected the richness of her inner life. Alice heard bells ringing - a sure sign that she was in the presence of genius. This only happened to her three times in her life. (The others in the trinity were Picasso and the philosopher Alfred North Whitehead.) She felt like a child on meeting Gertrude, whose experience she knew must have been deeper than her own:

I was so much younger in experience. I wasn't so much younger in years. I was only two years and a few months younger. But it was the enormous life she'd led that you could see ... An enormous sense of life. All the past experience gives a richness to every new vision - that's part of the genius.

Leo joined them for dinner. He too was a golden presence though, unlike Gertrude, he had a golden beard. He asked Harriet if she was a Monist and she did not know what it was, but she said she was not. Alice stared into space. As she was leaving, Gertrude took her aside and asked her to call at the rue de Fleurus the following afternoon so that they might walk together in the Luxembourg Gardens.

Alice was late. Harriet had wanted to lunch in the Bois de Boulogne. With the forethoughtfulness that Gertrude was to grow to love, Alice sent a *petit bleu* apologising in advance:

When I got to the rue de Fleurus and knocked on the very large studio door in the court, it was Gertrude Stein who opened it. She was very different from the day before. She had my petit bleu in her hand. She had not her smiling countenance of the day before. She was now a vengeful goddess and I was afraid. I did not know what had happened or what was going to happen ...

After she had paced for some time about the long Florentine table made longer by being flanked on either side by two smaller ones, she stood in front of me and said, Now you understand. It is over. It is not too late to go for a walk. You can look at the pictures while I change my clothes.

Alice looked with trepidation at the paintings on all the walls right up to the ceilings. She saw the two Gauguins, the Toulouse Lautrec, little paintings by Daumier and Delacroix, many Cézanne watercolours, enormous Picassos of the Harlequin period, two rows of Matisse, 'there was in short everything'. She looked at the big Tuscan furniture that in the ensuing years she was to get to know so well from dusting it. Gertrude returned in a better mood and laughed again from her brooch. They walked in the Luxembourg Gardens. Gertrude said, 'Alice look at the autumn herbaceous border,' and Alice looked, but did not reciprocate the familiarity by calling Gertrude 'Gertrude'. Gertrude asked her what books she read on the steamer and whether Flaubert was translated into English, because she did not like to read or speak any other language. They went to a patisserie off the boulevard St Michel where Gertrude said you could get the best cakes and ices on the Left Bank. She invited Alice to bring Harriet to dinner on Saturday, and to meet the painters and writers who would call round afterwards.

Back at the hotel, Alice told Harriet only of the walk, the cakes, the ices. She did not mention the 'vengeful goddess', provoked because she was half an hour late, nor the ringing bells, nor the promise of it all.

Leo opened the door to them on Saturday. He was wearing sandals and brown corduroy. Alice thought him amiable and incomparably graceful. 'Later, when he and Gertrude Stein disagreed about Picasso's pictures and her writing, he became unreasonable and unbearable,' she said. Hélène had cooked a simple but delicious meal. Every so often she came in and filled the large cast-iron stove with coal. Alice's legs did not reach the ground on the Renaissance dining chairs so she had to sit with them tucked under her.

Again Gertrude cast her spell. As well as her brown everyday kimono she had a 'gala' one decorated with a long heavy Chinese chain of lapis lazuli, with corals at the waist. Alice was

> impressed with her presence and her wonderful eyes and beautiful voice – an incredibly beautiful voice. I don't know any speaking voice that has its quality, its resonance and its fullness. It was like a very fine mezzo-soprano singing. Her voice had the beauty of a singer's voice when she spoke.

As for Harriet, she regarded the Steins as 'authority incarnate'. She said of them, 'In spite of my affection for them I hated them because I never had the courage to tell them to go to hell, as I so often wanted to do.'

Soon Picasso arrived 'very dark with black hair, a lock hanging over one of his marvellous all-seeing brilliant black eyes'. Alice heard bells for the second time that week. He was with Fernande, and they were late because she had been waiting for delivery of the dress she was to wear at the next day's preview of the Autumn Salon.

It was, Alice thought, one of the most important evenings of her life. After dinner they moved to the studio and Gertrude sat in a high leather Tuscan Renaissance armchair, with her feet on a pile of saddlebags. The room was full of Hungarians and Americans who had called to meet the painters, to listen to Leo and to look at the pictures. Germans were not popular because they tended to break things. Braque was there and Apollinaire, Marie Laurençin, and Miss Mars and Miss Squire. Ethel Mars had painted her lips orange and talked to Alice about how to apply make up.

Gertrude called Alice over and introduced her to Matisse. Alice thought he looked like a German professor: 'a medium sized man with a reddish beard and glasses. He had a very alert although slightly heavy presence and Miss Stein and he seemed to be full of hidden meanings.'

Alice left with an invitation card to the private view next day. She went to it with Harriet and they saw the Saturday crowd again. 'It was indeed the vie de Bohème just as one had seen it in the opera.' When Alice was sitting exhausted in front of a Braque and a Derain, she felt a hand on her shoulder and heard the laugh from the brooch. 'Right here in front of you is the whole story,' Gertrude said. All Alice could see were strange pictures of rather wooden figures. Gertrude was much amused at her consternation. 'Well, she said, still laughing' and then 'was quickly lost in an excited and voluble crowd'. But she soon came back and asked Alice if she wanted to have French lessons with Fernande Olivier, who was going to separate from Picasso and needed the money.

Alice agreed. So, for one of their first trips together, Gertrude and Alice took the horse-drawn omnibus across Paris to Picasso's studio in the Bateau Lavoir. There was a smell of dog and paint, and Alice thought it very untidy. Picasso called her 'the Miss Toklas with small feet like a Spanish woman and earrings like a gypsy and a father who is the king of Poland like the Poniatowskis'. Alice found his paintings dazzling:

> Against the wall was an enormous picture, a strange picture of
> light and dark colors, that is all I can say, of a group, an
> enormous group and next to it another in a sort of red brown of
> three women, square and posturing, all of it rather frightening.

She listened while Gertrude and Pablo talked. She thought the way they said each other's names, 'Gertrude' and 'Pablo', was proof of the bond between them. Then they visited Fernande, and Alice's long association with the 'wives of geniuses' began.

Every morning, Alice and Harriet had French lessons with Fernande. Harriet said Fernande only wanted their money. They had no common ground and conversation in any language was hard. They talked of the Steins and poodles. Fernande talked of French poodles, Alice talked of San Franciscan poodles and Harriet, who hated poodles, stayed quiet. Every day Gertrude asked Alice, 'Did Fernande wear her earrings?' She took this as a barometer of Picasso's financial state. If Fernande was not wearing them, they were in hock and he was in trouble.

Alice and Harriet became 'guests of importance' with the Steins when it was found they had lived through the earthquake and that Harriet's house had been destroyed. 'Any sense of inadequacy, of being in an intellectual world beyond our background left us,' said Harriet. They told the story many times. 'I fear we shall have to add to our earthquake experience if we hope to maintain our position,' Harriet said to Alice. 'We may even have to be buried with the house,' Alice replied.

After a few weeks in Paris they wanted to stay somewhere more like home than a hotel. Alice found an advertisement in *Le Figaro* from a Monsieur de Courcy, who offered to rent a floor of his house to two suitable people. He lived in a stone house, in the rue de la Faisanderie, near the Bois de Boulogne. He was a young man and proved an over-attentive landlord. He told them his mother was visiting friends in the Loire Valley, but would be back soon. He fed Alice and Harriet on shellfish salad, wild strawberry ice, and wine from the Loire, serenaded them with Chopin piano pieces, filled their rooms with flowers and took them to the *Folies Bergère*, of which, said Alice, 'what was not understood, was happily not understood'.

Gertrude put a stop to it. She came to lunch and considered Madame de Courcy's continued absence explicable only because her son had not told her of his lodgers. She suspected Monsieur de Courcy's intentions. She insisted that Alice and Harriet move that week to a hotel near the rue de Fleurus. Monsieur de Courcy was upset. 'But I thought you were pleased here,' he kept repeating. 'Quite content - indeed happy - with everything. My mother will be disappointed . . . What shall I say to her?' Harriet smiled in silence and Alice offered no explanation.

As they unpacked, at the Hôtel de l'Univers on the boulevard St Michel, Gertrude arrived with flowers for Harriet and chocolates for Alice. She commended them on their move and pointed out that they were now only twenty minutes walk through the Luxembourg Gardens to the rue de Fleurus. 'It was the beginning of my friendship with Gertrude Stein and I was to call her Gertrude,' said Alice.

Alice began to make herself useful at the rue de Fleurus. She went there every day. Gertrude talked to her about *The Making of Americans*. She confided her theory of bottom nature and dependent independent, and independent dependent characters. She gave Alice pages of her work in progress. Alice read:

The strongest thing in each one is the bottom nature in them. Other kinds of natures are in almost all men and in almost all women mixed up with the bottom nature in them. Some men have it in them to be attacking. Some men have it in them to be made more or less of the mixing inside them of another nature or of other kinds of nature with the bottom nature of them. There are two kinds of men and women, those who have dependent independent nature in them, those who have independent dependent nature in them. The ones of the first kind of them always somehow own the ones they need to love them, the second kind have it in them to have power in them over others only when these others have begun already a little to love them, others loving them give to such of them strength in domination.

Alice thought it very exciting. More exciting than anything else had ever been - more exciting even than Picasso's pictures.

By the time Alice arrived in Paris, Gertrude had already filled up many exercise books with work on her book, which was to be a thousand pages long, had no chapters and had sentences twenty lines long, and in which she was

> ... escaping from the inevitable narrative of anything of everything succeeding something of needing to be succeeding that is following anything of everything consisting that is the emotional and the actual value of anything counting in anything having beginning and middle and ending.

The book was, she said, the difference between American and English literature. English literature made the nineteenth century, and American literature made the twentieth, and Gertrude felt that she made twentieth-century American literature.

Alice started typing it all up. She did all the backlog then transcribed each night's output. Her routine was to go to the rue de Fleurus in the mornings while Gertrude was still in bed. (Gertrude worked from eleven at night, but liked to go to bed before the dawn was too clear or the birds too lively. One of her most poignant irritations was the early morning beating of rugs in the courtyard.)

Alice taught herself to type on a worn out Blickensdorfer typewriter:

> The typewriter had a rhythm, made a music of its own I don't mean the script I mean the typewriter. In those complicated sentences I rarely left anything out. And I got up a tremendous speed. Of course my love of Henry James was a good preparation for the long sentences.

She developed what she called 'a Gertrude Stein technique, like playing Bach'. She could only type Gertrude's work, nothing else. And she was one of the few people able to decipher Gertrude's handwriting - Gertrude could not always do that. It was, said Alice, a very happy time in her life, 'like living history . . . I hoped it would go on forever'.

Through this labour of love, Alice got to know all about Gertrude and her work. As in the years that followed she got to know all about the paintings at the rue de Fleurus through dusting them:

> I always say that you cannot tell what a picture really is or what an object really is until you dust it every day and you cannot tell what a book is until you type or proof read it. It then does something to you that only reading can never do.

Gertrude liked to discuss her analyses of character with Alice and to walk round Paris meditating, making sentences and observing incidents, which she then incorporated into the writing of the day. When she wrote 'there was no hesitation, she worked as quickly as her hand would move and there were no corrections in the manuscripts,' said Alice.

Alice's enthusiasm for long sentences, bottom nature and the continuous present, and her love and praise, came at an important time for Gertrude. May Bookstaver married a 'man's man', Charles Knoblauch, in August 1906. Some months later Mabel Haynes married an Austrian army captain called Heisig. Leo, who had been Gertrude's mentor, friend and support, had no interest in her work. He called her a barbarian in her use of language and said that she could not write plain English effectively.

Much of his sourness came from thwarted ambition. He gave up painting as he gave up everything else. Gertrude felt that he had to analyse and talk about painting before he could do it and that he talked himself out of everything. He was also going deaf and she felt this extended, metaphorically, to not listening to her. His lack of faith in her was 'to destroy him for me'. She began to reject him, as he held forth at the Saturday salons, while she sat listening. She stopped confiding her ideas in him. The final rift between them did not happen until 1913, six years after Alice arrived in Paris, but it was a slow attrition.

So it was timely that Alice came, heard bells ringing, had a deep regard for Gertrude and knew that she was a genius and the most exciting writer ever. Gertrude pined for American food, so Alice cooked her dishes of a Californian flavour - chicken fricassee, roast turkey with stuffing of mushrooms and chestnuts and oysters, cornbread, and apple and lemon pies. Everything Gertrude wanted, Alice tried to provide. Annette Rosenshine, who was pushed into the shade, thought that Alice had 'found the brilliant personality worthy of her talents' and that she could use her 'efficiency and cleverness' to further Gertrude's literary career: 'In the past, friendships with both Harriet Levy and me had shown her need to pull strings, but we, her San Francisco puppets, were too inconsequential.'

Gertrude and Alice went everywhere together and so were seen as a couple. One memorable outing was to 'Rousseau's Banquet'. This began with Leo saying he wanted to hear Rousseau playing his violin. Fernande Olivier then took up the idea and invited Rousseau to play at a dinner, given in his honour, at Picasso's studio. 'I'll ask the Steins and Braque and Apollinaire and Marie Laurençin,' she said. Word got about and so many people wanted to come, that dinner changed to a picnic supper. Alice bought a new hat for the occasion; a big black velvet thing with yellow feathers. Fernande ordered the food from Félix Potin, a delicatessen. She cooked a large quantity of *riz à la Valencienne* to go with it. The idea was for guests to meet for an aperitif at a café in Montmartre, near the rue Ravignan, and then to go on to the supper.

By the time Gertrude, Leo, Alice and Harriet arrived at the café, Marie Laurençin was drunk. 'She was falling in and out of the arms of Guillaume Apollinaire, who would put her back on her chair only to find her back in his arms,' said Alice. He slapped her, leaving a red mark on her face. Then Fernande came into the café in a distraught state and said that Potin's had failed to deliver the food. (It arrived the next day at noon.) Alice tried to help, but she could not easily find a phone, and when she did, the shop was closed. She and Fernande then went to buy what they could. Meanwhile guests moved from the café to the studio and went on drinking there. Most of them got extremely drunk.

Fréderic, who ran the café opposite the studio, arrived with his donkey, Lolo. Marie Laurençin sang old French songs, fell into the jam tarts, and insisted on kissing everybody. She was packed off home to mother. Apollinaire stood on the table and recited a eulogistic poem to Rousseau. Rousseau went to sleep and a wax lantern dripped on his head and then caught fire. He woke up and played endless dull music on his violin. When fighting broke out, Leo protected him and his violin, and Braque protected the sculptures.

Apollinaire wanted Alice to sing the national anthem of the Red Indians. She said she did not think they had one. Instead, Harriet sang her college song from the University of Berkeley:

> Oski wow wow
> Whisky wee wee
> Ole Muck I
> Ole Berk-keley i
> California
> Wow!

A man called Maurice Cremnitz gave an impression of delirium tremens by chewing a bar of soap, and Lolo ate a telegram, a box of matches and the yellow flowers off Alice's hat. 'The immense dish of rice,' said Alice, 'was indeed excellent.'

For Alice, it was all very different from Hanchen Levinsky's music soirées and the 'gently bred existence of my class'. She took to spending more and more time with Gertrude. Often she did not leave the rue de Fleurus until midnight, busy as she was with typing and listening and cooking. Harriet declared herself worried at the thought of Alice walking the streets of Paris alone so late. Harriet was also left alone too much, abandoned in a strange city, and she began to have problems with her feelings and her relationship with God.

She started suffering from some sort of hysterical paralysis which meant she was unable to walk. She found respite from her problems through God. Sarah Stein introduced her to Christian Science. One night Harriet said she was sitting alone with Sarah under a painting by Matisse 'of a woman with an extravagantly large bosom, antagonizing in its voluptuousness'. Harriet had never been able to look at it directly, but Sarah was reading a poem by Rabindranath Tagore aloud and

> lifted by the power of the Spirit I looked up at the Matisse.
> Something had happened to the painting. No longer was I
> looking upon heavy breasts, exaggerated, vulgar. Instead I was
> aware of a Giving, so generous, so universal . . . it moved me as I
> had never been moved . . . Here was love.

Soon after this experience, Harriet bought Matisse's *Girl with the Green Eyes*, still wet and unsigned.

Harriet confided her problems to Gertrude. 'Gertrude told Harriet there was nothing for her, Harriet, to do but to kill herself.' Harriet took this advice in silence, went back to her hotel alone and left a note by Alice's bed saying not to wake her in the morning. 'I fell asleep,' said Alice,

> reading one of the thirty volumes of George Sand's life I had
> found in a second-hand bookshop on the rue Vaugirard. It was
> early when Harriet woke me with a repeated call, Alice come at
> once. I threw on my dressing gown and hurried into Harriet's
> room. She was sitting up in bed, her small bright eyes brighter
> than ever. I have seen God she said in a hushed voice. He came
> to me in a drop of water from Heaven. I am so happy for you, I
> started to say, but she made a gesture to stop me. Go over to
> Gertrude she said and bring her over at once.

Gertrude was not much help. Sarah Stein took charge and told Gertrude she 'would not tolerate her participation in Harriet's salvation'. For a time, Harriet would see no one but Sarah and other Christian Scientists, leaving Gertrude and Alice entirely free to be together and to get to know each other better.

Annette Rosenshine was lonely too. Gertrude was no longer interested in her after Alice arrived, and the four o'clock therapy sessions stopped. Annette felt burdened by the fact that for a year she had shown all of Alice's letters to Gertrude. She felt that it violated their friendship. She told Alice about it one day when they were walking in the Luxembourg Gardens. Alice said nothing and just went on walking. But thereafter she referred to Annette as 'the Stinker'.

Alice kept a residual sense of responsibility for Harriet. They were, after all, ostensibly living together and it was Harriet who had made the trip to Paris possible. In 1908, when summer came, Michael Stein rented the Villa Bardi in Fiesole for himself, Sarah, their son Allan, and Gertrude and Leo. Gertrude suggested that Alice and Harriet rent the Casa Ricci, which was nearby, where she and Leo had stayed the year before. Alice readily agreed. It was to be a momentous holiday.

*Venice,* 1908.

# 7

---

# OUSTING THE OTHERS

*'We can't carry boxes of fruit and prunes around.
That's what I say'*

The train journey to Florence was hot, Alice's tolerance of heat was low. (Heat, high buildings, bombs and stepping stones were among the things that made her tearful and fractious.) She took off her corset in the lavatory and threw it out of the window. It was cherry-coloured and Harriet saw it fly by. From Florence they had a cool drive to Fiesole where Gertrude met them.

Gertrude wanted to explore the Tuscan countryside with Alice, the steep hills, piazzas and Roman ruins. It was a romantic setting. Alice's villa was high on the hills overlooking the valley of the Arno with the domes and spires of Florence in the distance. Each morning Alice did Gertrude's typing, then they went to Florence to borrow library books and to shop. Alice bought handmade boots and shoes, a Tuscan table, chairs and a *credenza*, a small table used for the Eucharist bread and wine, an intimation of the religious conversion she would later undergo.

They lunched in Florence with Etta and Claribel Cone. 'Dr Claribel was handsome and distinguished, Miss Etta not at all so,' said Alice, jealous of Etta's interest in Gertrude. Though Etta had typed *Three Lives*, she was now redundant. 'Has my successor done her duty by my place what she usurped? I am sometimes envious,' she said to Gertrude.

They visited Bernard Berenson at his Villa, I Tatti, in Settignano and went to tea at the Villa Gamberaia with Miss Florence Blood and her friend, the Princess Ghyka, who had been to bed with Napoleon III and Natalie Barney. Alice's coral necklace broke and she admired their grottoes and pools.

They went to the Tuscan hill towns. In Perugia they stayed in a hotel that had been a palace, the bedrooms painted with hunting scenes. At sunset the valley was filled with glow-worms, fireflies and noisy swifts and swallows. They dined on 'perfect scampi and *fritto misto*'. In Assisi they climbed to the cathedral. Alice wore a cotton batik dress, Gertrude a corduroy skirt, silk shirt and straw hat crocheted by a woman in Fiesole. They walked in torrid heat and Alice took off her silk underwear and stockings under a bush. 'It was all I could do,' she said. After many hours they reached the cathedral and Alice understandably went in to pray.

Most of all they went on long 'unforgettable walks'. Gertrude liked to walk for miles in the midday sun. When tired, she lay stretched on the ground and stared at the sun. She said it cleared her head. One blistering day, Alice packed sandwiches and they walked to the mountain top where, she said, Saint Francis and St Dominic met. Gertrude and Alice slipped on the dry earth of the steep path. Gertrude took off her sandals and advised Alice to do the same. The higher they climbed, the finer the view of the valley. At the top they had their picnic in the clouds.

On one such walk Gertrude proposed. It was her wish 'to win my bride'. The conversation began with a discussion of the comparative heat of the various places in which they had lived. Then Gertrude said, 'I have been very happy today.' She asked Alice whether her San Franciscan friends had loved her. She knew something of such matters for she had read all Alice's letters to Annette. 'Didn't Nelly and Lilly love you?' Gertrude asked. They had not loved Alice in the way Gertrude intended so to do. Gertrude was to be the husband and Alice the wife. Alice was to dote and depend. 'A wife hangs on her husband that is what Shakespeare says a loving wife hangs on her husband that is what she does.' But most of all, and at the root of the tryst, was desire. 'When all is said one is wedded to bed', wrote Gertrude.

What with the heat, the emotion and the happiness, Alice could not stop crying. Harriet counted thirty sodden handkerchiefs a day. 'Day after day she wept because of the new love that had come into her life,' said Harriet, who was not having much fun and began to have spiritual experiences involving the moon and a nightingale, and again became afflicted with an hysterical inability to walk.

Gertrude invited Alice to live with her and Leo at the rue de Fleurus, but Alice stalled. It was difficult to leave Harriet, marooned in a foreign city, with only the questionable support of her Christian Science acquaintances. On their return to Paris, Alice found a flat for herself and Harriet on the rue des Saintes-Pères, close to the rue de Fleurus. She put in the furniture she had bought in Florence, made curtains and cushion covers, gave instructions to the Swiss maid, Marie Enz, then left Harriet there alone and spent most of her time with Gertrude.

She started on her career as Gertrude's editor, amanuensis, secretary, housekeeper, lover, wife and friend. No publisher wanted *Three Lives*. They thought it too unconventional, too literary, too strange. May Bookstaver, now Mrs Knoblauch, in 1908 found a private American firm, the Grafton Press, who would publish 1,500 copies at a cost to Gertrude of $660. The director, Mr F. H. Hitchcock, sent Gertrude the galleys in January 1909. 'My proof-readers report that there are some pretty bad slips in grammar, probably caused in the typewriting.' He offered to make the corrections for a small additional fee. He thought perhaps she had an imperfect knowledge of English, or no experience of writing. Alice had to check that every repetition and grammatical irregularity was there as pencilled by Gertrude.

After it was published, Mr Hitchcock sent another letter: 'I want to say frankly that I think you have written a very peculiar book and it will be a hard thing to make people take it seriously.' He was worried that Gertrude's stylistic oddities would be construed as his firm's incompetence. The *Boston Morning Herald* thought it extraordinary, the *Kansas City Star* called her 'a literary artist of such originality', Sarah Stein liked it a lot and was deeply moved and H. G. Wells said that at first he was repelled by her strange style, but then read with 'deepening admiration and pleasure', and would watch for her name curiously and eagerly. Leo said it was not art.

Alice helped with the distribution, sent seventy-eight free copies to reviewers and friends, and pasted all reviews in a book. But despite her efforts the book did not do well. A year after publication, seventy-three copies had been sold.

Gertrude and Alice started calling each other Lovey and Pussy. Alice was Pussy. They did not mind who heard, because they cared more about each other than what anyone else might think or say.

One Sunday evening in 1908, when Alice was serving supper, Gertrude came into the kitchen waving a tiny notebook, saying it must be read immediately. She liked her food tepid, Alice liked it hot. Alice sat down to read. Called *Ada*, the story was all about Alice and her idyllic relationship with 'some one' who loved her. 'I began it and I thought she was making fun of me,' said Alice 'and I protested . . . Finally I read it all and was terribly pleased with it. And then we ate our supper.'

It was the first of Gertrude's 'portraits' of people she knew. In *Making of Americans* she wrote about everyone who had ever lived. In her portraits she wrote about everyone she knew. Alice collaborated on *Ada* and it became a joint declaration of their love. It began with an account of what a good daughter Alice had been and how she looked after her mother, then, when her mother died,

> kept house for her father and took care of her brother. There
> were many relations who lived with them. The daughter did not
> like them to live with them and she did not like them to die
> with them.

She went away and her father waited for her to return. She wrote him 'tender letters' but she never went back – because she met 'some one' who loved her: 'She came to be happier than anybody else who was living then. It is easy to believe this thing.' Alice endorsed this with a declaration of love at the end of the story, in her own handwriting, but in Gertrude's style:

> Trembling was all living, living was all loving, some one was then the other one. Certainly this one was loving this Ada then. And certainly Ada all her living then was happier in living than any one else who ever could, who was, who ever will be living.

Happiness had its thorns, one of which was Harriet. She was vague about her plans, as Gertrude explained in another of her portraits:

> She said she did not have any plans for summer. No one was interested in this thing in whether she had any plans for the summer. That is not the complete history of this thing, some were interested in this thing in her not having any plans for the summer. She was interested in this thing in her not having any plans for the summer. Some to whom she told about this thing were interested in this thing. Her family were interested in this thing in her having not yet made any plans for the summer. Others were interested in this thing, her dress-maker was interested in this thing and her milliner . . .
>
> Some who were not interested in this thing in her not having made any plans for the summer would have been interested in this thing in her not having made any plans for the summer if she had made plans for the winter . . .
>
> What would be her plan for the summer. She would not have any plan for the summer. She would not really come to have a plan for the summer and the summer would be a summer and then there would be the winter. She would not have any plan for the winter and some would ask her what was her plan for the winter. There would not be then any more summer. There would be then a winter . . .
>
> She could not tell any one in the beginning of winter that she had not a plan for the winter because she would be knowing then that it was winter and she would be knowing then that what she was doing then was her plan for that winter, every one could know that, any one could know that, she could know that that what she was doing in the winter was the plan she was carrying out for that winter. There was then coming to be the

end of summer and she was then not answering anything when
any one asked her what were her plans for the winter.

It continued in the same vein for several pages. The gist of it was that Harriet
had no plans for the summer or winter. She seemed to have gone into a
state of melancholy withdrawal. She was alone in Paris in a rented flat, tended
to see God in drops of water, had very little money and her flatmate had
fallen in love with a woman.

She wrote to a friend in San Francisco, Caroline Helbing, inviting her
to visit Paris. Caroline was about to marry the man to whom she had been
engaged for twenty-five years, but agreed to take a holiday first. She arrived
in Paris in the winter of 1909, and this temporarily eased the burden for
Alice and Gertrude.

When Caroline went home, Alice took her to the boat-train and on the
way said:

> Caroline dear, you must see that when Harriet goes back to
> America she does not return to Paris because it is already
> arranged that I should go to stay with Gertrude and Leo at the
> rue de Fleurus. That is what I suspected, said Caroline, you can
> count on me. Whereupon Caroline kissed me and I put her on
> the train.

In July 1910, Sarah Stein had to go to San Francisco because her father
was dying from a brain tumour. She boarded ship with Michael, Allan and
Harriet. Harriet then wrote to Alice from San Francisco telling her to close
up the Paris flat and carefully to pack Harriet's paintings, particularly Matisse's
*Girl with Blue Eyes* and a landscape by Harry Phelan Gibb, and to send them
to her along with furniture she had bought in Florence, because she would
not be returning.

Annette Rosenshine had returned home the year before. Her relationship
with Alice was tense. Alice would brook no competition for Gertrude's time
and attention. Sarah Stein told Gertrude:

> seeing her with Alice is a strain - just because Alice jars so on
> her and I find myself siding with Annette in my insides, although
> I'm very noble when I discuss it afterwards, that's my job isn't it?

Annette spent her last night in Paris with Sarah, who wrote:

> She clung to me literally with both her claws from 7.30 until
> midnight and that sensation hung on all night. Last night I was
> haunted by her shriek of 'I'm going Sally Oh . . .' as the train
> pulled out.

When Gertrude said goodbye, Annette found 'little meaning in her expression or words'. Annette was ill on the boat and back in San Francisco her mother said that she kept sighing. She wrote to Gertrude practically every day, 'the brightest spot in my day by day existence was the lifeline of letters from Gertrude'.

She got a job with difficult children, went deep into therapy, changed her name to Rhodes, wrote to Jung, wrestled with her feelings of guilt, introversion, repression and the significance of her dreams, then took up art as a means of self-expression. She made figures that represented aspects of her personality.

Alice moved in with Gertrude, free of her past connections. Her mother was dead. She never saw her father again, though she wrote him affectionate letters and wired him when she needed money. She had no particular feeling for her brother. Harriet and Annette were back in San Francisco. Her relationship with Gertrude was exclusive, and the people she now met were Gertrude's friends. As time went on, she chased away those who threatened to become too close to Gertrude, or who disturbed their routines.

At first, Leo was agreeable to Alice's arrival. He gave up his study so that she could have a room of her own, and was discreet about leaving the house so that she and Gertrude could be alone together. 'It was very considerate of him,' said Gertrude. He travelled a lot and became 'more and more impressed by the supreme importance of nutrition and sexuality in the determination of human personality'. This conviction, and perhaps the atmosphere of Gertrude's new love, prompted him to begin an affair of his own - with a street singer and artists' model, Nina Auzias, known as Nina of Montparnasse for the favours she conferred.

He wrote to Mabel Weeks in 1910 explaining that he was perhaps not passionately in love with Nina, but very deeply absorbed:

> She looks like a feminine version of the James the Less in
> Corregio's Dome picture in Parma and in her moments of
> radiance she's extraordinarily like the Angel in his Madonna with
> St Jerome.

He found her eyes 'absolutely bottomless', unlike Gertrude's findings on human nature, though some of his friends thought she looked menacing and overwhelming.

Nina Auzias was the daughter of a provincial professor of mathematics. She rebelled at home, went to Paris when she was eighteen, 'formed a liaison with a socialist workingman', and sang in the streets to provide for them both. She lost her voice from the cold and so took to posing for artists in the nude, which led to many an affair. She first saw Leo in the Luxembourg

Gardens in 1905. She thought he looked like an Egyptian statue of a handsome giant, and felt certain that he was the man of her dreams.

Four years later he saw her at a friend's studio, kneeling naked on a soapbox with her hands raised in a pose of supplication and admiration. Soon after, she saw Leo playing billiards and stuck her tongue out at him. He asked her, perhaps disingenuously, to pose naked for him too. She refused, saying she was too badly built, a consideration that had not deterred her in the past. He persuaded her, then set her nerves on edge by whistling as he sketched. Then he said 'Yes, you are right, you are badly built and not at all inspiring'. Suddenly, Nina

> rushed toward him, seized his head and kissed him. Without a word he arose and spat on the floor. 'That was too much,' I said. 'No I do not wish to pose any more. I am too ugly. I am going.'

Leo described her behaviour as 'a most desperate effort at seduction'. Some months later he asked her to pose again. She reminded him of his opinion. 'Yes, that is right,' said Leo,

> But you can come to visit me as a psychological model. I am sincere. You have had many experiences and have much to tell me. That interests me a great deal, and I shall pay much more than for an ordinary model. Come tomorrow.

He offered her four times the going rate for modelling, so the sessions continued:

> Very dignified and calm I sat on the sofa. Not far from me he sat also. And looking only at the wall opposite I began to relate to him my fantastic adventures, like a modern Scheherazade to her modernistic Sultan.

Leo found her adventures irresistible and was soon caught in 'a perfect whirlpool of tragicomic romance'. In bed he told her, when asked, that he loved her, but he had difficulty in saying it spontaneously. She told him she loved him all the time.

She was twenty-six when Leo met her in 1909 and she was involved in affairs with three other men. One, an English artist, had painted 'innumerable bad portraits of her for seven years'. Another, 'M.R.', kept threatening to kill Leo and himself if she left him. A third, more vague, felt murderous at the prospect of her leaving M.R. for anyone but himself. Leo counselled her on the progress of her affairs and took a portion of her love for himself. In July 1910 he wrote to her:

I deeply hope that this summer it will be possible to be together
for at least a month. I do not think I shall be capable of a
passionate love like that of R. or B. etc., not because I am too
much soul and not enough flesh, but rather because these
elements are not sufficiently mixed.

By 1910, he felt that Nina was 'one of the great realities of his life', but
he was having terrible problems with insomnia and his bowels. He took
to eating zucchini with grated walnuts, starved himself for twelve days, then
tried Fletcherism, the dietary code of a nutritionist called Horace Fletcher,
'the Moses of Mastication', who advocated chewing each mouthful forty-
two times.

Nina reassured him that he was better than all her other men and even
offered to rid herself of his rivals. But Leo wanted them there. He did not
want her to depend upon him, nor to be around him all the time. He needed
to hear that he was the best and most intelligent of them all. It excited
him to hear of her adventures with other men and he was impressed by
the inspiration he believed she gave to them. He boasted to Gertrude of
a composer's affair with Nina:

> . . . he writes to her every day. He can't live except in the light
> of her eyes. If she will only take him he will have a real
> inspiration and write the music of the future.

Leo liked to believe that the woman with whom he was involved had the
power to make a man great. And he rationalised his own lack of commitment
in a self-effacing way:

> In truth if I were more egotistical, I should like to have you all
> to myself, but knowing how little I can offer you I always have a
> fear of making you miss a greater self by putting myself between
> you and your fate.

He turned to Nina after Gertrude's betrothal to Alice. Gertrude chose a
wife who was monogamous, directional, domestic, adoring and extremely
possessive. Leo chose a woman who, like his ambition, was all over the place.

Gertrude turned away from Leo for her own survival because he was
contemptuous of her work. He did not have a good word to say about it,
for any success or self-conviction of hers emphasised his own failure and
self-doubt. He said her writing was all to do with her and nothing to do
with literature. 'He said it was not it it was I. If I was not there . . . what
I did would not be what it was.'

The more he criticised, the more Gertrude turned away. And the more
she turned away, the more critical he became. He said that he could not

understand her work and that she could not think consecutively for ten seconds: 'She doesn't know what words mean. She hasn't much intuition but thickly she has sensations and of course her mania, herself. Her idea of herself as a genius.'

Being a genius became a point of contention. Gertrude's assessment was, 'It was I who was the genius, there was no reason for it but I was, and he was not.' Leo did not agree: 'Gertrude and I are just the contrary. She's basically stupid and I'm basically intelligent'. Gertrude said his failure to appreciate her worth 'was the beginning of the ending and we always had been together and now we were never at all together. Little by little we never met again.'

Leo rowed with Picasso, too. One evening he took Picasso into the dining room at the rue de Fleurus and told him what he thought of his work. Picasso came out furious and went in to Gertrude and Alice saying, 'He does not leave me alone. It was he who said my drawings were more important than Raphael's. Why can he not leave me alone then with what I'm doing now?' Leo slammed the door between the two rooms, then came in to continue the argument. Gertrude 'dropped books on the floor to interrupt him'.

Gertrude allied herself with Picasso. 'I was alone at this time in understanding him,' she said. 'Perhaps because I was expressing the same thing in literature.' She felt they both sought 'to express things seen not as one knows them but as they are when one sees them without remembering having looked at them'. She said that what they were producing was beyond realism, or 'things remembered', or 'reconstruction from memory'. They were dismantling the components of reality and reconstructing them in their own highly individual ways. She felt that this subjective expression put them into the vanguard of the twentieth century. They were its chroniclers, working at a time when 'belief in the reality of science commenced to diminish'.

Alice affirmed. She heard bells for them both. Leo hated it all; hated cubism and Gertrude's word portraits. He was hurt that Gertrude turned her back on him, stopped being his disciple, thought her own worth greater than his and found a partner she preferred. And the more she stonewalled Leo, proclaimed her worth as a writer and looked to Alice for everything, the more he lost his sense of self-esteem and lashed out at her. He felt he had no *métier*, that he could not write, had no talent for conversation and that he was alone in his dislike of cubism.

Gertrude expressed her disaffection with Leo in her work. He 'continued to believe in what he was saying when he was arguing and I began not to find it interesting', she wrote. His criticism of her work 'destroyed him' for her. She wrote of their fracture from each other in a word portrait called *Two: Gertrude Stein and Her Brother*:

She was thinking in being one who was a different one in being one than he was in being one. Sound was coming out of her and she was knowing this thing. Sound had been coming out of him and she had been knowing this thing. She was thinking in being a different one than he was in having sound come out of her than came out of him. She was thinking in being a different one. She was thinking about being a different one. She was thinking about that thing. She had sound coming out of her. She was knowing that thing. She had had sound coming out of her, she was knowing that thing. He had had sound coming out of him, she was knowing that thing. He had sound coming out of him, she was knowing this thing. Each one of the two was different from the other of them. Each one of them was knowing that thing. She was different from him in being one being living. She was knowing that thing. She was different from him in having sound come out of her. She was thinking this thing. She was thinking in this thing. She had sound coming out of her. She was thinking in this thing. She had sound coming out of her. She was different from him. She had sound coming out of her. She was different in being one being one. She was knowing that thing.

She was different in being one having sound coming out of her she was different in being that one from any other one. She was one having had sound coming out of her, she was different in being that one from any one.

She had sound coming out of her. This was a thing she was being. Sound was coming out of her, sound had come out of her, perhaps sound would come out of her.

She was different from any other one in being one having sound come out of her. She was one having sound come out of her. She was one having had sound come out of her. She had been then different from any other one. She might, this thing is not certain, she might go on being different from any other one. She might not be different then from any other one. Certainly she was different from one other one. She was different from the other one, the other one of the two of them.

He was different from her. He was completely a different one. He had sound coming out of him. He had had sound coming out of him. He would have sound coming out of him. In a way he was different from any other one in having sound coming out of him. Certainly he was different from her, he was different from the other one of the two of them. He had sound coming

out of him. He had had sound coming out of him. Some sound
would come out of him. He was in a way different from any
other one in being one having sound come out of him.

Sound coming out of her, sound coming out of him is
something that is completely that thing is completely sound
coming out of her, is completely sound coming out of him.

Sound coming out of him is completely that thing is completely
the sound coming out of him. Sound coming out of her is
completely that thing, is completely the sound coming out of her.

Sound coming out of him is something that coming very often
is that thing is the sound coming out of him. Sound coming out
of her and coming very often is that thing is the sound coming
out of her.

Sound coming out of him is that thing is sound coming out of
him. Sound coming out of him is that thing the thing . . .

It continued for 147 pages. Publishers did not like it any better than did
Leo. They bundled her *Portraits* up and sent them back to her. Mr Fifield
of Clifford's Inn, London, wrote:

19 April 1912
Dear Madam
I am only one, only one, only one. Only one being, one at the
same time. Not two, not three, only one. Only one life to live,
only sixty minutes in one hour. Only one pair of eyes. Only one
brain. Only one being. Being only one, having only one pair of
eyes, having only one time, having only one life, I cannot read
your MS three or four times. Not even one time. Only one look,
only one look is enough. Hardly one copy would sell here.
Hardly one. Hardly one.

Many thanks. I am returning the MS by registered post. Only
one MS by one post.
Sincerely yours
A. C. Fifield

Mabel Dodge blamed Alice for the break between Gertrude and Leo:

Alice Toklas entered the Stein ménage and became a handmaiden.
She was always serving someone, and especially Gertrude and
Gertrude's friends. She was perfect for doing errands and was
willing to run all over Paris to get one a special perfume or any
little thing one wanted . . . But lo and behold she pushed Leo
out quite soon. No one knew how exactly and he went off to

Florence and from that time I date his extreme neuroticism . . .
Before that he had a human contact with life through his sister.

In Florence, Leo would meander over to the Villa Curonia in Arcetri, where
Mabel Dodge lived. He used to talk very close into her ear. Being deaf himself,
he thought everyone else was too. When they were doing a jigsaw together
in her grand salon (which she pronounced 'gran salone') he said, 'I think
this angle is susceptible to a conjunction,' and slipped a piece into place.
'All his speech was like that,' said Mabel Dodge. 'Boring, I thought then.
But he was grieving over Gertrude and Alice.' Leo talked to Mabel about
the atmosphere at the rue de Fleurus after Alice moved in:

> He had always had an especial disgust at seeing how the weaker
> can enslave the stronger as was happening in their case. Alice did
> everything to save Gertrude a movement - all the housekeeping,
> the typing, seeing people who called and getting rid of the
> undesirables, answering letters - really providing all the motor
> force of the ménage and Gertrude was growing helpless and
> foolish from it and less inclined to do anything herself . . . he
> had seen trees strangled by vines in the same way.

Leo stopped going to the Saturday evening salons. 'I would rather harbour
three devils in my insides than talk about art,' he wrote to Mabel Weeks.
So Gertrude presided, and Alice sat with the wives. The atmosphere at the
rue de Fleurus became frosty. Gertrude and Leo stopped speaking and left
irritable notes. One from Leo read:

> I told you one time since that I found it very disagreeable to
> come downstairs or into the house in the morning and find the
> light burning in the front hall. You said then that it was
> accidental. Now if you leave it on on purpose because you don't
> like to go upstairs in the dark or what not I'll try and get used
> to it but if it's only carelessness I wish you'd jog your memory a
> little.

There was bickering about the gas bill, the laundry bill, postage, a painting
Leo took from Gertrude's bedroom, who should have the money from the
sale of their Japanese prints. By 1913 Gertrude and Alice were looking for
another apartment in Paris. They thought of moving to one that overlooked
the Palais Royale gardens. Then Leo resolved matters by moving to the Villa
di Doccia in Settignano near Florence. 'It will take days', he wrote to Nina,
'to have the floors fixed and the closets constructed'. He took the Renoirs
and the Matisses, and Gertrude kept the Cézannes (apart from a painting
of apples Leo particularly wanted) and the Picassos.

Gertrude and Alice decided never to see him again.

Do you remember how we decided that indeed if he came we would have it said that there would be no admittance. Do you remember that we decided that we had entertained him as frequently as we would and that now when he came we would have him told that we would not receive him. Do you remember that.

Leo made conciliatory gestures, but was rebuffed. For Gertrude, the rift was absolute and she never spoke to him again. She distrusted his emotional make-up and his effect on her. She was the artist, he was the critic and she did not want criticism, she wanted praise - which Alice gave her in abundance.

Without Gertrude, Leo turned to Nina. By 1912 he was describing his relationship with her as a 'whirlwind of passion' which had as its foundation 'absolute confidence, perfect candor, complete toleration and unlimited goodwill, affection and mutual esteem'. Mabel Dodge said Leo and Nina made one of those odd combinations of people that baffle the onlooker, but whose essential reality is indisputable. She thought Leo was driven to incessant thinking because his other responses were so few.

Gertrude's erstwhile friends felt the breeze of Alice's arrival too. Mabel Weeks, when writing to Gertrude about Leo, added a coda, 'Don't read this to Alice. Unless I feel that sometimes I can write just to you it's no fun to write.'

Mabel Dodge disliked Alice and thought that she separated Gertrude from her friends. Gertrude took Alice to visit her at the Villa Curonia in 1911. Mabel patronised the arts, kept peacocks in the garden, called her dog Climax, her monkey Madame Bovary and her white cat Princess. In the drive, which was lined with cypresses and roses, stood an antique statue of Atlas with a globe on his shoulders. There was a ninety-foot living room in the Villa with Venetian candelabra, china dogs and statues. There were stone stairways, wide arches, a terracotta figure of Jesus, a life-size Gothic madonna, twelve-foot high mirrors, Flemish tapestries, an altar with a Chinese terracotta Kwannon of the Han dynasty, Florentine oil lamps and red curtains.

Mabel had four consecutive husbands, an uncertain number of male and female lovers and liked to fill the villa with assorted guests. 'On summer nights before going to bed,' she wrote,

Domenico [a servant] would bring enormous platters of sliced watermelon and bunches of grapes to us here - and the groups of shadowy women eating the ripe fruit in the dim light were as sumptuous as ever Sheba was, surrounded by her maids.

*Mabel Dodge at the Villa Curonia in 1912.*

*Leo and Nina.*

André Gide came to supper one evening when Gertrude and Alice were there. 'It was a rather dull evening', Gertrude said. Alice remembered him talking in a low voice to Mabel, who was stretched out on one of her long sofas, while another guest, Mina Loy, danced with an imaginary partner.

At night, between midnight and dawn, Gertrude wrote *The Portrait of Mabel Dodge at the Villa Curonia*. She worked in the room next to Mabel's bedroom. Alice was given a small room next to Gertrude's so that she could get up early to do the typing. Mabel said that each day Alice and Gertrude were both equally delighted at what Gertrude had written the night before, and that Gertrude had no recollection of it by the time she got up at noon.

Mabel's husband at that time, an architect, Edwin Dodge, was in America. Mabel was having a flirtation with the twenty-two-year-old tutor of her children, who liked playing football and had 'long limbs and swaying shoulders'. Mabel wore long white silk dresses and white turbans, her bedroom was white and the twenty-two-year-old tutor veered her towards the

> wide, white hung bed - until we were lying, arms about each
> other - white moonlight - white linen - and the blond white boy
> I found sweet like fresh hay and honey and milk.

Mabel said:

> I can't, I can't, I can't . . . and so we remained for heaven knows
> how long - while Gertrude wrote on the other side of the wall,
> sitting in candlelight like a great sybil, dim against the red and
> gold damask that hung loosely on the walls.

A good deal of heavy breathing found its way into Gertrude's portrait of Mabel Dodge:

> So much breathing has not the same place when there is that
> much beginning. So much breathing has not the same place when
> the ending is lessening. So much breathing . . .

Mabel liked the portrait. She had 300 copies privately printed, bound in flowered paper and distributed. She thought it a 'masterpiece of success' and, even if she did not altogether understand it, 'some days I don't understand things in myself, past or about to come'. Leo called the portrait 'damned nonsense'. He said he knew Mabel Dodge well, and the portrait 'conveys absolutely nothing to me'. 'Mabel Dodge hodge podge,' was his opinion.

Mabel was an energetic and efficient publicist. She was the main publicist for the 1913 Armory Show in New York, which took modern European art to America. Writing in the issue of *Arts and Decoration* devoted to the Armory exhibition, she described Gertrude's language as exquisitely rhythmical and cadenced and, like Picasso's painting, finely patterned and 'finding the hidden and inner nature of nature'.

Mabel was attracted to Gertrude's fat and appetite and steam, and in her own flamboyant memoirs wrote:

> She loved beef and I used to like to see her sit down in front of five pounds of rare meat three inches thick and with strong wrists wielding knife and fork, finish it with gusto, while Alice ate a little slice daintily, like a cat . . .
>
> Gertrude Stein was prodigious. Pounds and pounds and pounds piled up on her skeleton - not the billowing kind, but massive, heavy fat . . .
>
> She would arrive just sweating, her face parboiled. And when she sat down, fanning herself with her broad-brimmed hat with its wilted, dark-brown ribbon, she exhaled a vivid steam all around her. When she got up she frankly used to pull her clothes off from where they stuck to her great legs. Yet with all this she was not at all repulsive. On the contrary, she was positively, richly attractive in her grand *ampleur*.

As for Alice, Mabel found her sinister, sycophantic and drooping: 'So self-effacing that no one considered her very much beyond thinking her a silent, picturesque object in the background.' Mabel described her as

> slight and dark, with beautiful gray eyes hung with black lashes, a drooping Jewish nose, and her eyelids drooped and the corners of her red mouth and the lobes of her ears drooped under the black, folded Hebraic hair, weighted down, as they were, with long heavy Oriental earrings.

Mabel thought her batik dresses made her look like something out of the Old Testament. She gave her jobs to do - meeting visitors from the station or talking to guests, while Mabel dressed. She said Alice wore 'barbaric chains and jewels' and was forever manicuring her nails. 'Every morning for an hour, Alice polished her nails - they had become a fetish with her.' One morning at breakfast Mabel said to her, 'Well I can't understand you. What makes you contented? What keeps you going?' Alice replied, 'Why I suppose it's my feeling for Gertrude.'

Trouble came one lunchtime at the Villa in summer 1912. Mabel thought that during the writing of the portrait Gertrude 'seemed to grow warmer to me'. Mabel responded in 'a sort of flirtatious way', even though her 'fire was drawn' to the smells, tastes and limbs of the blond white boy:

Gertrude, sitting opposite me in Edwin's chair, sent me such a strong look over the table that it seemed to cut across the air to me in a band of electrified steel - a smile traveling across on it - powerful - Heaven! I remember it *now* so keenly!

Alice left the table and went out to the terrace. Gertrude 'gave a surprised, noticing glance after her and as she didn't return, got up and followed after'. Gertrude came back alone. 'She doesn't want to come to lunch,' she told Mabel, 'she feels the heat today'.

'From that time on Alice began to separate Gertrude and me - poco poco.' Mabel's friendship with Gertrude ended. The end was, she felt sure, 'Alice's final and successful effort in turning Gertrude from me - her influencing and her wish and I missed my jolly fat friend very much.'

For Alice the 'band of electrified steel' was between her and Gertrude alone. And no one else should come too near it.

*Gertrude and Alice in the 1920s.*

# 8

## MARRIAGE

*'Cow cow, coo coo coo'*

Such bands of steel are forged by sex and in the stack of manuscripts that eluded publication, for the most part until after her death, Gertrude wrote a great deal about the delights of it with Alice. She called her gay, kitten, pussy, baby, queen, cherubim, cake, lobster, wifie, Daisy and her little jew. Gertrude was king, husband, hubbie, Mount fattie and fattuski. She penned her love for Alice. 'She is very necessary to me. My sweetie. She is all to me . . .'

> I marvel at my baby. I marvel at her beauty I marvel at her perfection I marvel at her purity I marvel at her tenderness. I marvel at her charm I marvel at her vanity . . . I marvel at her industry I marvel at her humor I marvel at her intelligence I marvel at her rapidity I marvel at her brilliance I marvel at her sweetness I marvel at her delicacy, I marvel at her generosity, I marvel at her cow.

Cows, some Steinian scholars surmise, are orgasms. Gertrude, in her bedroom pieces, made repeated reference to them and to caesars which have something to do with cows, though it is not quite clear what. 'Cows are very nice. They are between legs,' wrote Gertrude. Cows made both Gertrude and Alice very pleased:

> A cow has come he is pleased and she is content as a cow came and went . . . And now a little scene with a queen contented by the cow which has come and been sent and been seen. A dear dearest queen.

As for caesars, it seems they are what cows need. 'Have Caesars a duty. Yes their duty is to a cow. Will they do their duty by the cow. Yes now and with pleasure.' Gertrude described one of her stories, *A Book Concluding As A Wife Has A Cow. A Love Story*, as her Tristan and Isolde:

Have it as having having it as happening, happening to have it as happening, having to have it as happening. Happening and have it as happening and having to have it happen as happening, and my wife has a cow as now, my wife having a cow as now, my wife having a cow as now, my wife having a cow as now and having a cow as now and having a cow and having a cow now, my wife has a cow and now. My wife has a cow.

She went some way toward explaining cows in *A Sonatina Followed By Another*:

All of us worship a cow. How. By introducing and producing and extension.
How.
You know about pipes. A shepherd has pipes. So he has. And so have I.
I do mention this and that, it is true of a pussy and a cat, that this is that and that is this and you are sleepy with a kiss. Who miss, us.
Why misses us, who dismisses us.
We kiss us.
Very well.
She is very well.
And as to cow which is mentioned anyhow. A cow is mentioned anyhow.
Thank you Romans Caesars and all.
I say it to you and I say it to you I say it to you how I love my little jew. I say it to you and I say it to you. I say it to you and I say it to you. I say it to you.
How can I have the air of here and there and I say it to you I say it to you I love my own little jew. How can I have the air and I do care I care for her hair and there for the rest of her too my little jew. I lover her too my little jew. And she will have endured the cold that is cured, it is cured it is cured and a cow how can a cow follow now a cow can follow now because I have a cow. I had a cow you have a cow, you have a cow, you have a cow now.
She is that kind of a wife. She can see.
And a credit to me.
And a credit to me she is sleepily a credit to me and what do I credit her with I credit her with a kiss.

1. Always sweet.
2. Always right.
3. Always welcome.
4. Always wife.
5. Always blessed.
6. Always a successful druggist of the second class and we
know what that means. Who credits her with all this a husband
with a kiss and what is he to be always more lovingly his missus'
help and hero. And when is he heroic, well we know when.

Win on a foul pretty as an owl pretty as an owl win on a fowl.
And the fowl is me and she is pretty as an owl. Battling Siki and
Capridinks capridinks is pretty and winks, winks of sleep and
winks of love. Capridinks. Capridinks is my love and my Coney.

Leo got out of the rue de Fleurus in 1913. He said Alice's advent was a
'godsend' because it allowed the separation between him and Gertrude to
happen without 'an explosion'. 'I hope that we will all live happily ever after
and continue to suck our respective oranges,' he wrote to her when he left.
He told anyone who would listen that Gertrude's writing was 'silly twaddle',
'sub-intelligent gabble' and 'utter bosh'. 'Like all children and madmen she
adequately communicates only to herself'. Her writing and her confidence
infuriated him. She was self-assured in her weird prose style and she rejected
him through it and with it. He wrote peevish letters to Mabel Weeks:

Gertrude knows that everything changes and that the more it
changes the more it's the same thing. Also that people repeat to
insist. None of this is analyzed or developed, but simply asserted
in paradoxical simplicity and baby language. It's the oldest stuff
in the book and long before there were books ... When Jesus
said Verily Verily, he was insisting, but if he had said Verily Verily,
Verily, verily, verily, verily, verily, verily, verily, verily, some one in
the audience would have yelled, 'Say Mr Jesus you said that
already' ... If all the fools were drowned in Noah's flood, the
seed was saved.

Mabel Dodge thought that he went to pieces after he left the rue de
Fleurus:

He wasn't very neurotic before that. He was very shut into
himself and he had his own queer ways of wearing sandals, eating
mostly nuts and looking down his long ram-ish nose.

A kind of depression and anger settled on him after he separated from Gertrude. He went from boastfulness to self-despair. Nothing worked out for him. The relationship with Nina was there, but he made little conscious commitment to it. He wrote to her and broached the subject of marriage, but in a very lukewarm way:

> I love you for always more than any other woman. But I do not know how, the love which at a certain moment was more than budding, really flowering, has vanished. And now I do not know when it will reawaken or how. In any case, time passes. I do not see a rosy colored future.

For Gertrude and Alice love budded and flowered and grew more like a rose each day. 'It happened very simply that they were married . . . They had likeness. Likeness to what. Likeness to loving.' They wrote notes to each other inscribed 'DD' and 'YD' (Darling Darling and Your Darling), vowed commitment, discussed everything 'including individual feeling' and put a great deal of energy into creating for themselves an extremely social, pleasurable and stress-free style of living. Their happiness and routines depended on no one but themselves and they were everything to each other. 'Our pleasure is to do every day the work of that day,' wrote Gertrude:

> to cut our hair and not want blue eyes and to be reasonable and obedient. To obey and not split hairs. This is our duty and our pleasure . . . Every day we get up and say we are awake today. By this we mean that we are up early and we are up late. We eat our breakfast and smoke a cigar.

'I have so much to make me happy,' she wrote. 'I know all that I am to happiness, it is to be happy and I am happy. I am so completely happy that I mention it.' And mention it she did. She mentioned it and mentioned it and mentioned it.

When Gertrude and Alice had the rue de Fleurus to themselves, they spent time and money on home improvements. They took out the cast-iron stove in the studio and had a fireplace put in. They took out the gas lamps and had the place wired for electricity. They had a covered hallway built between the studio and living area, and everywhere was repapered and decorated. They looked for comfortable armchairs to replace the furniture Leo had taken with him to Florence. They sold three Picassos to Kahnweiler and bought paintings by Juan Gris to replace the Renoirs Leo had taken. Gris was twenty-seven at the time and living with his wife Josette in the Bateau

Lavoir. He had come late to cubism and Gertrude thought he brought an order and clarity to it. She bought *Glass and Bottle*, *Book and Glasses* and a cubist collage painting called *Roses*.

Alice's work of the day was to serve Gertrude, who liked to read, write, wander around, drive cars (she learned to drive in 1916) and talk. Anything else made her nervous. Alice was secretary, cook, publisher, housekeeper and ministering angel. She did the knitting, sewing, house-keeping, dusting, typing, ordered books from Mudie's lending library in London, supplied etymologies of words, references for poets, pronunciations of Spanish, corrected Gertrude's French, kept the house filled with acacia, honeysuckle roses and tulips, answered the telephone, did the filing, carried Gertrude's bag and served all meals promptly. When they went on holiday, Alice did the packing. On the Saturday salon evenings while Gertrude talked to the creative men, Alice sat with the wives, or showed them round the kitchen. And of course she supervised the cooking. Food was extremely important to Gertrude. 'In the menu there should be a climax and a culmination,' wrote Alice. 'Come to it gently. One will suffice.'

Throughout her life Alice collected recipes. Into her Polish dumplings went sour cream, cottage cheese, butter, eggs and flour. Her hard-boiled eggs she served with whipped cream, truffles and Madeira wine. She cooked a young hare in a quart of dry champagne, cognac, fat salt pork, truffles, cream, butter and more. She made her chicken liver omelettes with six eggs and cognac, stuffed the duck with beef fat and chestnuts, stewed the apples in rum, flamed the bananas in Kirsch, concocted a chocolate whip of eggs, bitter chocolate, icing sugar, cream and Cointreau and for colic, indigesion, vomiting, stitch, liver complaint, difficulty in urinating, giddiness, rheumatism, shortness of breath or worms, she recommended a mixture she called Vespetro, made from two pounds of sugar, two quarts of brandy, three sliced lemons, angelica, orris and coriander. She made elaborate preparations for the Saturday salons, buying cakes and making 'a heavenly punch with a sweet innocuous taste but which packed a terrific wallop'. She served it with little spiced sugar biscuits. 'She is very necessary to me . . . My sweetie. She is all to me,' wrote Gertrude, who was freed from all domestic chores and could concentrate on her work. 'It's hard work being a genius. You have to sit around so much doing nothing,' she said. Fortunately for Alice, being a genius did not take up all Gertrude's time. There was plenty left for her, and for travelling, visiting friends and shopping.

They took lots of holidays and travelled in Europe for months at a time. Alice particularly liked Spain. They went on a long trip there in 1912-13. Alice abandoned her batik dresses and beads and adopted her 'Spanish disguise' of a long black dress, long black gloves and a black feather hat with flowers of the sort that Lolo the donkey ate, and which children wanted to touch.

Gertrude was mistaken for a bishop. On her little finger she wore a rhinestone ring which local people tried to kiss. Outside the cathedral at Burgos, a little girl with green eyes followed her saying 'a penny kind sir'. Alice exploited their compelling appearance to get maximum comfort and service. 'La Baronne', she would say if their rooms had a poor view, or dinner did not pass muster, 'is not satisfied'.

Alice loved Avila for its cathedral, cloistered walls, cobbled streets, excellent dinners and pastry shops. She told Gertrude, 'I am enraptured with Avila and I propose staying.' But Gertrude said she could not work there. Alice was drawn to Christianity and religious devotion. When she was old, and Gertrude had died, she converted to Catholicism and spent much of her time in an Italian convent.

In Madrid, they looked at paintings most mornings in the Prado. They stayed in a hotel close by, on the calle San Geronimo. Alice saw her first bullfight. She told the box office attendant: 'I must have the very best seats in the first row in the shade under the President's box.' Gertrude warned her when not to look, because horses were being gored. But Alice's favourite Spanish spectacle was La Argentina, a flamenco dancer, born in Buenos Aires, whose real name was Antonia Marcé. She danced in traditional costume with a tortoiseshell comb in her hair. Alice and Gertrude went back again and again to see her. She inspired Gertrude to write a poem called *Susie Asado*. Alice thought her to be in the same class as Isadora Duncan and Nijinsky. 'The audience was silent, spellbound, and went off its head when the dance was over,' said Alice, who thought it more exciting than the Russian ballet.

They got back late to their hotel and had to step over the concierge asleep on the floor, rolled in a blanket. They bought lots of things from the antique shops - apothecary pots and arabesque ornaments - and had special luggage made to carry it all back to Paris. They went to Toledo and El Escorial and saw religious processions and El Greco's paintings. At Cuenca, they had wild game for supper and Gertrude slept with the windows closed, afraid of the deep drop down into the valley. Alice tossed in the airless room. Nor could she sleep in Cordova because of the heat. Gertrude fetched a basin of cold water and a bath sponge, and Alice squeezed cold water over herself throughout the night. The sun blazed all the way. In Seville, said Alice, 'it was very hot and I ate innumerable ices during the day, which upset Gertrude's stomach'. Perhaps their 'likeness to loving' had gone too far. Gertrude then had an attack of colitis and could not eat anything, even though they were staying at a hotel recommended by Matisse for the excellence of its food.

'We fell madly in love with Granada,' said Alice. She particularly liked the gypsies, who 'danced and walked beautifully with their wide skirts and swinging step'. But everything about Spain was right for her. She preferred it to France. It was her spiritual home. 'I can sit anywhere out of doors in Spain and be thrilled, thrilled.' She liked the light, the way Spaniards moved and their beautiful gutteral voices. Gertrude communicated a more singular view of the country in her writing. She wrote of Spain:

> A little pan, that is to please it, a little which is a point to show that co-incident to a lively boat there is nearly places. That is nobody touching. All the plays garden. Little screen. Not collected and spacious not at all so old. And more places have the behold it. The best example is mustard. A little thing. A little no old shut.

She wrote in hotel rooms. She went through what she called her '*Tender Buttons* and early Spanish and Geography and Play period'. People and events of the day inspired her. In Madrid there was a café singer called Preciosilla. Gertrude wrote a portrait of her:

> Preciosilla. Please be please be get, please get wet, wet naturally, naturally in weather . . . in vacant surely lots, a single mingle, bait and wet . . . Toasted Susie is my ice-cream.

Gertrude was ambitious to have her work published. Her manuscripts were piling up in the cupboard. After writing the history of everyone in *The Making of Americans* and the history of anyone in her portraits, in *Tender Buttons* she wanted to write the history of anything. She said she 'needed to completely face the difficulty of how to include what is seen with hearing and listening'. She said it was her 'first conscious struggle with the problem of correlating sight, sound and sense and eliminating rhythm'. She said she was trying to live in looking and not mix it up with remembering, and to reduce to its minimum listening and talking, and to include colour and movement:

ORANGE
A type oh oh new new not knealer knealer of old show beef-steak, neither neither.
RHUBARB
Rhubarb is susan not susan not seat in bunch toys not wild and laughable not in little places not in neglect and vegetable not in fold coal age not please.

Gertrude said that what excited her was that the words that made what she looked at be itself, were words that, to her, exactly related themselves to the thing at which she was looking, 'but as often as not had nothing to do with what any words would do that described that thing'.

Such excitement made comprehension difficult and there were those confused enough to think that Tender Buttons were clitorises. Others thought they were marinated mushrooms. Others, more prosaically, imagined the book got its title simply because of Gertrude's liking for buttons. Gertrude's handwriting became rather wild when she was writing it. But, whereas she privately printed *Three Lives* and *The Portrait of Mabel Dodge*, *Tender Buttons* found a publisher.

The man responsible for this literary launch was Carl Van Vechten. Mabel Dodge had given him a copy of her portrait by Gertrude in 1912. He read it with enthusiasm and then went to supper at the rue de Fleurus, in June 1913, with a letter of introduction from Mabel. Hélène cooked a strange meal of a series of hors d'oeuvres followed by a sweet omelette. Van Vechten became an indispensable friend. 'It was on all sides love at first sight', said Alice, 'and the beginning of a long rare friendship, indescribable loyalty on his side, complete dependence on Gertrude Stein's.'

After he had visited the rue de Fleurus, Carl Van Vechten wrote to his actress friend, Fania Marinoff:

Last night I had dinner at Gertrude Stein's. She is a wonderful personality. I wish you could meet her. You will sometime . . .
She lives in a place hung with Picassos and she showed me some more sketches of his including men with erect Tom-Tom's much bigger than mine.

Carl Van Vechten was big and burly, with buck teeth and porcelain blue eyes. He wore dandyish clothes and his wife Ann, from whom he was separated, had previously told Gertrude about 'the tragedy of her married life' with him. After they divorced, he married Fania Marinoff, though he had affairs with men too. The Van Vechten married life was a succession of storms and reconciliations. Their apartment in New York was like a bazaar, with a bust of Paul Robeson by Epstein, a self-portrait by de Chirico and a jumble of folk art and Mexican toys.

Carl Van Vechten championed Gertrude and did everything he could to see that her work was printed, published, publicised and performed. He helped her because he believed in her importance. He was a man of huge enthusiasms, an eclectic dilettante, with a liking for the avant-garde. In 1913 he was assistant music critic for the *New York Times*. He was a photographer, he wrote more than twenty books, including novels, and he promoted all forms of African art. His preferences were, he said, for 'the odd, the charming, the glamorous'.

Gertrude and Van Vechten wrote to each other regularly from 1913 onwards. Alice wrote too, though less often. For fifteen years he misspelled Alice's name, and called her Miss Taklos. (Many other friends writing to Gertrude spelled Alice's name wrongly. They called her Toklus or Tocklass or Taclos.) Gertrude did not correct his mistake, though she herself wrote that to call someone by the wrong name was to deny their identity.

Van Vechten found a publisher for *Tender Buttons* - an American poet friend of his called Donald Evans, who had started up his own press, Claire Marie, which promised 'New Books for Exotic Tastes'. Evans advertised:

> Claire Marie believes there are in America seven hundred
> civilized people only. Claire Marie publishes books for civilized
> people only. Claire Marie's aim, it follows from the premises, is
> not even secondarily commercial.

Mabel Dodge, who was in the States, tried to dissuade Gertrude from publishing with Claire Marie Press. She said that it was absolutely third rate, decadent and in bad odour. She wrote a cautionary letter to Gertrude in March 1914:

> I think it would be a pity to publish with him if it will
> emphasize the idea in the opinion of the public that there is
> something degenerate and effete and decadent about the whole
> of the cubist movement which they all connect you with.

But Mabel Dodge was herself in bad odour with Gertrude and Alice, who were fed up with accounts of her sexual adventures and marital problems, and Gertrude stayed with Claire Marie, though she never received any money from them.

In June, 1,000 copies of *Tender Buttons* were printed and bound in canary yellow covers. In his promotion copy Evans said:

> The last shackle is struck from context and collocation, each unit
> of the sentence stands independent and has no commerce with
> its fellows. The effect produced on the first reading is something
> like terror.

Such publicity did little to woo readers. The *Chicago Tribune* reviewer did not know 'whether "Tender" of the title means a row boat, a fuel car attached to a locomotive or is an expression of human emotion.' Another critic described it as 'a sort of Wonderland or Luna Park for anyone who is not too busy'. Max Eastman, less respectfully, said it was like the ravings of a lunatic. The *Detroit News* said that after reading excerpts from it, a person feels like going out and pulling the Dime Bank building over onto himself. The *Commercial Advertiser* wrote:

> The new Stein manner is founded on what the Germans call 'Wort salad', a style particularly cultivated by crazy people . . . The way to make a wort salad is to sit in a dark room, preferably between the silent and mystic hours of midnight and dawn, and let the moving fingers write whatever comes.

The *New York Post* reviewer wondered if Gertrude had been eating hashish. None of the reviewers claimed to understand *Tender Buttons*, but they all thought it unlike anything else, and Gertrude was described as a literary cubist, though her following was small. People found it less taxing and time-consuming to look at cubist paintings, than to read *Tender Buttons*. Discussions on multiple perspective in cubist painting, and multiple points of view in Gertrude's work, tended only to interest a few.

Carl Van Vechten did all he could to promote Gertrude. In the August edition of *Trend* he wrote that 'words surged through her brain and flowed out of her pen', that the book was irresistible, sensuous, fresh and with majestic rhythm, and that Gertrude was 'massive in physique, a Rabelaisian woman with a splendid thoughtful face, mind dominating her matter'.

In June 1914 the publisher John Lane visited Paris and Archduke Ferdinand, heir to the Habsburg throne, was assassinated at Sarajevo. John Lane said that his wife, Camille, had read and liked Gertrude's early book *Three Lives* and that, if Gertrude visited him in London in July, a contract would await her. Alice thought Camille Lane looked like her French piano teacher from San Francisco, and that this boded well. Alice had already tried to persuade most of the London publishers to take *Three Lives*. They all said they could make nothing of it.

Gertrude assured Mabel Dodge that she would do her best to look like a genius in London. She wore a short corduroy skirt, white silk shirt, sandals and a tiny hat. Muriel Draper, a friend of Mabel's living in London, said Alice shadowed Gertrude 'draped in some semi-oriental gauze of sorts, with clinking bracelets, tinkling chains and ear-rings as big and oval as her gaunt eyes'.

Gertrude and Alice intended only to stay in London for a few weeks. Everybody was talking about the war. Alice overheard the editor of *The Times* saying, 'I shall not be able to eat figs in Provence this year.' At first they took little notice of the prospect of a European war. They shopped with enthusiasm and visited friends. In Paris they had been unable to find a suitable three-piece suite to replace the chairs Leo had taken to Florence, so they had themselves measured for chairs and a couch – to accommodate Gertrude's bottom and Alice's short legs. Then they took a lot of time choosing chintz for the suite that would go with all their pictures.

They went to Cambridge for ten days and stayed with Hope Mirrlees' mother. Hope Mirrlees was a friend from Paris. Gertrude liked the food, the beautiful weather and the house, which was quiet and conducive to work. Alice found English breakfasts painful:

> That gathering of conversation before you get your coffee, at the
> end of the meal that I don't eat so I have to sit there and look
> amiable and try to say something and wait for the coffee which
> was half an hour after you were at table.

At a supper party given in their honour by Mrs Mirrlees, Alice met the philosopher, Alfred North Whitehead, and for the third and last time in her life heard the bells connoting genius ring. She said he had a most benign sweet smile and the simplicity that comes only in geniuses.

Gertrude went to John Lane's office at the Bodley Head on the morning of 31 July, and came away with an agreement from him that he would publish *Three Lives*. Alice waited for her and window shopped. Late that afternoon they took a train from Paddington to Lockeridge in Wiltshire, to stay with the Whiteheads. What was intended as a weekend visit, lasted for eleven weeks, because while they were there, Britain entered the war against Germany.

With what Alice called 'quiet serenity', Alfred North Whitehead each day read aloud from the papers all the details about the war. Gertrude cried, and could not believe it. Alice said, 'It's true, really, really, really. This isn't one paper it's all the newspapers.' Gertrude did not like unpleasant things, and had a habit of not believing or remembering them. Whitehead read out to them about the destruction of Louvain. 'Where is Louvain?' Gertrude asked Alice. 'Don't you know?' said Alice. 'No, nor do I care,' said Gertrude. 'But where is it?'

They could not get back to Paris because of travel restrictions. 'Do you remember it was the fifth of September we heard of asphyxiating gases?' Gertrude wrote. 'Do you remember that on the same day we heard that permission had been withheld. Do you remember that we couldn't know how many h's in withheld.' They had money sent to them from America – from Alice's father and Gertrude's Baltimore cousins. John Lane said he could not now publish anything but war books, but he hoped things would be different soon.

When the German army came within striking distance of Paris, Gertrude refused to get out of bed. She stayed there with her eyes closed, but she was not asleep. She said she was worried about Mildred Aldrich. Mildred

Aldrich was an American journalist living in Paris, who said that she did not really understand Gertrude's work, but that she was sure Gertrude knew what she was doing. When Gertrude and Alice first met her, she lived on the top floor of an apartment block on the boulevard Raspail. She often accidentally dropped her key down the stairwell when she called goodnight. She had a great many canaries. One friend had asked her to look after her canary. A second friend thought it might be lonely and gave her another to keep it company. Soon she had a great many. When she gave them all away she confided to Alice that she had always hated canaries.

Three months before the war started, Mildred Aldrich, who was sixty-one, had said that she wanted quiet, calm and perfect peace. She found a peasant's house with open rafters and a hazel hedge in Huiry, a hamlet thirty miles outside Paris. Her small garden looked out over the valley of the Marne: over grain and sugar-beet fields, orchards and asparagus beds. From her house she saw the Battle of the Marne in September. She saw the French and English fighting the Germans, and the Germans' defeat. She saw the artillery fire, palls of smoke, bombs, fires and dead soldiers. She wrote a book about it called *A Hilltop on the Marne*, which was published in 1915 and went into seventeen printings.

Bertrand Russell used to call round to the Whiteheads and talk about pacificism and Gertrude argued fiercely with him. She maintained that the Germans could not win the war because they were a backward people. She said that they had method but no organisation. Alice went up to Gertrude's bedroom to give her news of the German defeat in the Battle of the Marne. She said, Paris is saved, the Germans are in retreat. Gertrude did not believe her and said, Don't tell me these things. Then they both wept with relief.

After more weeks of waiting, they managed to get the necessary papers to allow them to go home. Alice packed in such haste she broke a Wedgwood plate by putting it under a heavy malachite bowl. They arrived in Paris on 17 October 1914. Paris was 'beautiful and unviolated', said Gertrude, but many of their friends had gone. Derain and Braque had been conscripted. Picasso said, 'On August 2, 1914 I took Braque and Derain to the Gare d'Avignon. I never saw them again.' Matisse, whose eyesight was not good, was given a job guarding railway bridges. Apollinaire, who had a Polish mother and an Italian father, had never taken French nationality, but he volunteered as an artillery officer. Marie Laurençin had married a German and was living in Spain. Kahnweiler's gallery was closed and all his paintings confiscated as the property of an enemy alien. There were blackouts, fuel and food shortages and Zeppelin alarms.

Alice trembled in fear, so Gertrude covered her with a blanket. Alice said she discovered that knees knocked together just as described in poetry and prose. The chintz-covered three-piece suite arrived from London in 1915.

*Gertrude, Alice and Auntie, with nurses and soldiers at the Simon
Violet Hospital, during the 1914-18 war.*

# 9

## THE FIRST WAR

*'trust a cold bit of pickle
usefully in an emergency'*

Paris was too dangerous, deserted and expensive for Gertrude and Alice in wartime. In the spring of 1915 they decided to go to Majorca, thinking it to be peaceful, cheap, Spanish and sunny. Gertrude was short of money so she sold her remaining Matisse, *Woman with a Hat*, for $4,000 to Sarah and Michael Stein, who had moved to the French Riviera because of the war. They had loaned nineteen of their paintings by Matisse to an exhibition in Berlin, in the summer of 1914, and when war was declared they could not get them back.

Gertrude and Alice travelled by train to Barcelona, then by boat to the island. A German submarine was rumoured to be following in their wake. Alice kept spotting Germans everywhere. She and Gertrude stayed first at the Hotel Mediterraneo which overlooked the harbour and the cathedral. Then the postman told them of a villa to rent in Terreno, just outside Palma. It belonged to a retired army major. It was high on a hill above the sea, with a terrace filled with carnations and roses. In the garden were almond, fig, tangerine and pomegranate trees and vegetables.

They found that they knew people on the island: an American painter called William Cook and his Breton wife Jeanne, a Swedish count, the French consul and his wife. When William Cook went back to Paris in 1916 he worked as a taxi driver because he was hard up and taught Gertrude to drive in his Renault taxi.

Gertrude and Alice settled in their villa and bought a dog, a Mallorcan hound, reddish brown with black stripes. They called him Polybe, which was the *nom de plume* of Salomon Reinach, a writer for *Le Figaro*. Polybe the dog had an insatiable appetite for eating filth. Gertrude and Alice muzzled him, but were criticised for doing so by the Russian servant of the English consul. Unmuzzled, Polybe chased sheep and goats. Alice then tethered him, but he cried all the time and a neighbour threw a note on to the terrace saying he would kill him if the noise went on. Polybe's one nice trait was sitting in a chair, smelling large bunches of flowers that Alice bought in the market and arranged in vases. In the end they gave him away. Gertrude mentioned him in plays she wrote at this time like *Turkey Bones And Eating And We Liked It: A Play*, which had twelve pages and seventeen scenes. She wrote of him:

> Minorca and Dogs
> I like a dog which is easily understood I have never had the habit
> of going out except Sunday. Now I go out every day.

She mentioned other things too in the play: 'I do not like cotton drawers. I prefer wool or linen. I admit that linen is damp. Wool is warm. I believe I prefer wool.' Scene VI of the play was 'A water faucet'.

Neither Gertrude nor Alice would have anything to do with the Germans on the island. Alice, in particular, was vehement in her prejudice. 'We made a vow never to speak to a German,' Gertrude wrote in *All Sunday*, one of her Mallorcan poems. The German governess of one of their neighbours used hang out the German flag every time there was a German victory. Gertrude and Alice retaliated by hoisting the American flag over their house whenever there was news of an Allied victory, 'but alas just then there were not many allied victories,' said Gertrude.

They were totally in each other's company with few visits from anyone else. They settled into harmonious domestic life. Gertrude changed her routine and took to working in the days. She got up at nine, Alice at seven-thirty. Most days Alice went shopping for food in Palma market. She bought melons, lobsters and chickens for their dinners. There were no peas, but plenty of beetroots which Gertrude loved. Their Breton cook, Jeanne Poule, tried to teach Alice to kill pigeons by smothering them. She said they tasted better when killed that way and that it was more humane than cutting off their heads. She gave Alice a lesson in the market and a disapproving crowd gathered. Jeanne Poule said they were hypocritical when they paid big money to see bulls killed at bullfights and then ate the meat from the dead animals. She taught Alice a recipe for cooking the smothered pigeons – braising them with salt pork and butter, and serving them on a bed of croutons and puréed mushrooms, with Madeira sauce poured over them.

Gertrude and Alice went for long walks over the island. Alice packed picnics of eggs, salad, vegetables, brown bread and contraband tobacco. She was hysterical about lizards and called them crocodiles and screamed, which irritated Gertrude. And she was very much discomfited by the heat and the wind, and the privations of Mallorcan life. In the summer months she slept under a mosquito net, by an electric fan. Gertrude fixed the fan when it broke. There was no electricity on Sundays. The butter was always rancid, so they stopped using it. Gertrude thought the Majorcans were 'a very foolish lot of decayed pirates with an awful language'. Winter was dreary, windy and rainy, the wood fires smoked over the walls and the house had to be painted.

In the afternoons, Gertrude read aloud to Alice all Queen Victoria's letters. Alice, who had learned to knit from Madame Matisse, knitted socks and sweaters out of Scottish wool for French soldiers while she listened. She also found she could knit and read at the same time. Gertrude, who had very catholic taste in reading, developed a passion for the autobiographies of missionaries and for the military diaries of English officers. Lord Roberts' *Forty One Years In India* was one of her favourite books. Alice ordered them from Mudie's in London. 'It was my pleasant duty to make out the list of books and pack those that were being returned,' she said.

On rare occasions, they made excursions off the island. They went to Barcelona to buy their winter clothes and woollen stockings, and to get their teeth fixed. There was an American dentist there, apparently the only one in Spain. He looked after the King of Spain's teeth too. They went to Valencia, with William Cook as their guest, for a week's fiesta of peasant dancing and bullfights. They saw five of the best fights with toreadors Gallo, Gallito and Belmonte. Gertrude said it was the only thing that made her forget the war. The King and Queen of Spain were there, but the Queen turned away for the gory bits.

Most of the time, though, Gertrude and Alice were totally absorbed in their work and each other, 'she with a sheet of linen and he with a sheet of paper'. The roles polarised into husband and wife. And their use of the words 'husband' and 'wife' and 'he' and 'she', determined their obligation to each other: Gertrude was to dictate and protect, Alice was to serve and to please. Gertrude wrote about their personal world. She said that she was writing plays but perhaps they were poems. It is not always easy to interpret the genre of her work. What with the war, and so many rejections from publishers, she sometimes became dispirited. Carl Van Vechten tried to reassure her,

Your name pops up in current journalism with great frequency. You are as famous in America as any historical character - and if you came over I think you might have as great a reception as say Jenny Lind [a popular Swedish soprano].

Gertrude replied

Alas about every three months I get sad. I make so much absorbing literature with such attractive titles and even if I could be as popular as Jenny Lind where oh where is the man to publish me in series. Perhaps some day you will meet him. He can do me as cheaply and as simply as he likes but I would so like to be done. Alas.

Lack of a publisher did not deter Gertrude. She wrote for herself, the 'lined page' and Alice, who typed every word of it and relived in the mornings the cows, Caesars and wifely delights of the previous night. Gertrude's eulogies on the delights of sex became less veiled. She wrote of kisses and stickiness, preferred positions and bed. 'Lifting Belly', which Virgil Thomson described as 'concerning the domestic affections', is a fifty-page lyric on the glory of it all:

I am fondest of all of lifting belly . . .
Lifting belly is in bed
And the bed has been made comfortable . . .
Lifting belly
So high
And aiming.
Exactly
And making
A cow
Come out . . .
I say lifting belly and then I say lifting belly and Caesars. I say
lifting belly gently and Caesars gently. I say lifting belly again and
Caesars again. I say lifting belly and I say Caesars and I say lifting
belly Caesars and cow come out. I say lifting belly and Caesars
and cow come out . . .
Lifting belly high.
That is what I adore always more and more.
Come out cow.

Gertrude was also fond of the sort of cows that graze in fields. She said they gave her a nice feeling of being quiet, peaceful and softly restful.

But Alice was the focus of her world. The outside world might be at war, but her private world was bliss:

Tiny dish of delicious which
Is my wife and all.
And a perfect ball.

Or

kiss me kiss me . . . I'll let you kiss me sticky

In their roles of writer and amanuensis, Gertrude and Alice continued their remarks, conversations, arguments and flirtations of the days and nights. Life and literature were one.

Some of Gertrude's lyrics had a sado-masochistic edge. Compliance, dominance and supplication crept into the tone:

> You will give me orders will you not. You will tell me what you prefer. You will ask for what you want . . . I see what you wish, you need to have instant obedience and you shall have it. I will never question. Your lightest wish shall be my law . . . If you want to be respectable address me as sir I am very fond of yes sir.

Gertrude's writing broke all rules. Structures were strange and word play free. A piece called 'One Sentence' ran to thirty pages of mostly one-line statements. Chances of publication were slight. Van Vechten kept trying to place her work with New York publishers. He did not get very far. 'I am doing more important things than any of my contemporaries and waiting for publication gets on my nerves,' Gertrude wrote to him. She was forty-two, there was a war and her literary prospects seemed unclear. Her rejection letters from publishers read: 'I really cannot publish these curious studies', or, 'I have only read a portion of it because I found it perfectly useless to read further as I did not understand any of it'.

Nor was Alice always entirely satisfied with her spouse's performance. Irritable and inconsequential asides crept into the typed copy. 'You can't put that in a book', or 'that doesn't mean anything', or 'Miss Toklas wishes Roberts to kindly send her by registered mail - under separate cover - 1 Ivory soap and a good face soap that Roberts can recommend'. And Alice was anxious because Gertrude's writing earned them no money. When her allowance ran out she sent a telegram to her father, 'wire me money - I need more money'. Then he wrote to her saying, 'That's no way of living because you are drawing on your future. You will have to come to some conclusion.' Gertrude promised her: 'Some day we will be rich. You'll see . . . and then we will spend money and buy everything a dog a Ford letter paper, furs, a hat, kinds of purses.'

For the most part, though, life was cosy.

> S is for sweetie sweetie and sweetie
> Y is for you and u is for me and we are as happy as happy can be.

She hogged the fire and confessed her selfishness in her writing:

You mean that I make it too cold. Well to be sure I am selfish I
sit before the fire. I really ought to give you the best place only I
don't like to change. You dear you are so sweet to me.

The factual, commonplace, esoteric and mad all merged in Gertrude's word
games:

I'd like to go back. Cook knows everybody. I am going to put
grease on my face do you mind. A continuance roundness makes
a shimmer . . . Shawls have hair. Bicycles are skylarks and a silk
night has stars . . . What are you doing my precious. Taking
grease off my face my love.

After a time, both of them yearned for home. They were worried about
their friends and cut off from the life they liked. Alice became fractious
because of the weather – the heat in summer, the wind and the rain in
winter, the absence of comforts. The Paris group had dispersed, the future
seemed unpredictable and insecure. Picasso's lover, Eva, was dying from
tuberculosis. (He had been with her since 1912.) He wrote to Gertrude that
life was hell, that he could not work and that he spent half his days in the
Metro going to and from the nursing home. The war took its toll. Braque
had been wounded, Juan Gris was stuck in Collioure, impoverished and
ill, Apollinaire was a brigadier with an artillery regiment, Leo was being
psychoanalysed in the States, there was great uncertainty as to how the world
would turn out.

When, in 1916, the French won the Battle of Verdun and stopped the German
advance into France, Gertrude and Alice went back to Paris. They travelled
by steamer and train, and reached the rue de Fleurus in June. They decided
they wanted to help with the war effort, like their friend Mildred Aldrich.

One day, when they were walking down the rue des Pyramides, an American
woman in uniform got out of a Ford van near to them. 'There,' said Alice
to Gertrude, 'that is what we are going to do. At least you will drive the
car and I will do the rest.' The woman worked for the American Fund for
French Wounded, an organisation that distributed supplies to hospitals
throughout France. She took Gertrude and Alice to meet her director, Mrs
Isabel Lathrop.

Isabel Lathrop was wearing a matching pink hat and dress and a string
of pearls when she met Gertrude and Alice. 'In spite of her frivolous
appearance she had a great instinct for work,' said Alice. She told them
that it would be most useful if they could provide a truck and deliver hospital
supplies. She asked Alice, in the meantime, to draw up an inventory of
everything sent out to the hospitals.

For her part, Gertrude took driving lessons in William Cook's taxi and wrote to her cousin in New York asking for a Ford van. While waiting for it to arrive, she wrote war poems, two of which were then published in *Life*, which had previously printed spoofs on *Tender Buttons*. Gertrude told the editor that her real work was funnier, and that he should publish it. He printed a poem by her about Woodrow Wilson and one about war work. Gertrude published the poems in 1928 in a volume called *Useful Knowledge*.

The winter of 1916 was cold and there was a coal shortage. Gertrude and Alice could not heat the studio. Gertrude, with her flair for getting people to help her, chatted to a local policeman about their problems and he turned up that evening in civilian clothes with two sacks of coal. After that, said Gertrude,

> he became our all in all. He did everything for us, he cleaned our home, he cleaned our chimneys, he got us in and he got us out and on dark nights when Zeppelins came it was comfortable to know that he was somewhere outside.

In February 1917 the Ford arrived. It was delivered to a special workshop, in order to be converted into a supply truck. On the day Gertrude and Alice collected it, driving into Paris, it stalled on the tram rails, between two trams, and had to be pushed clear. The next day they drove as far as the Champs Elysées and then it stopped dead. Gertrude cranked. Passers-by cranked. Then an elderly chauffeur said, 'no gasoline'. Someone stopped a passing convoy of military trucks. Soldiers tried pouring petrol into the Ford from an over-large tank. In the end Alice bought a tin of petrol from a broom shop.

It was the beginning of Gertrude's driving days. She never learned to stay in lane, or to reverse satisfactorily, and she and Alice had 'violent discussions' about this. They called the car Auntie, after Gertrude's aunt Pauline, who was married to her father's brother Solomon and 'who always behaved admirably in emergencies and behaved fairly well most times if she was properly flattered'. Auntie looked more like an assemblage of parts, than one solid piece. She had wooden wheels with bicycle-size tyres. The windscreen was split in the middle to let in air. Gertrude had a 'scary habit of talking and forgetting about driving'. And she took no notice of Alice's careful instructions. If the map said Avignon was on the right, and Gertrude preferred the left, she went left.

Alice wanted her to practise taking the engine to pieces and putting it together again, but Gertrude refused. In time, Gertrude became known to car mechanics throughout France. Auntie required a great deal of cranking. Gertrude would say as she cranked, 'I'm going to scrap it. I'm going to scrap it.' She was always dragooning passing men into helping her crank, or change the tyres, or clean the spark plugs. Mrs Lathrop complained that nobody did those things for her. Gertrude said that was because Mrs Lathrop looked so efficient. As for herself, she said, she was not efficient, she was good-humoured, she was democratic and she knew clearly what she wanted done:

> If you are like that anybody will do anything for you. The important thing is that you must have deep down, as the deepest thing in you, a sense of equality. Then anybody will do anything for you.

It was an attitude that worked well for her, from her childhood on. For she was also, on her own admission, fond of doing nothing.

Mrs Lathrop sent them to Perpignan, way down in the south of France, near the Spanish border, to open a distribution depot for hospital supplies. They set off in March 1917, armed with a Michelin Guide to hotels and restaurants and innumerable maps. Gertrude drove in sandals that buckled over the ankles, and woollen stockings. Going down a snowy hill they had some sort of altercation with a gaggle of ducks. 'Gertrude's skill in driving did not include the unexpected,' said Alice. Then they got stuck in the snow. Then Alice was sure they were on the wrong road. 'Wrong or right,' said Gertrude 'this is the road and we are on it'.

Alice planned the route according to the gastronomic promise of hotels and restaurants in her guide. She collected recipes *en route*. Auntie would only go at thirty miles an hour, so they were often late for lunch and dinner and had to have special things cooked for them at odd times. The first night they stopped at Seaulieu and stayed at the Hôtel de la Côte d'Or. They ate bread soup, ham croquettes and peaches flamed in peach brandy and sugar. Alice said it was a plain but delicious meal. She thought the proprietor of the hotel was German because of his clothes. Apparently he had been the Kaiser's chef at Potsdam.

At Lyon, they lunched at the restaurant of La Mère Fillioux. They had trout from the lakes of the Haute Savoie cooked in butter, hearts of artichokes with truffled *foie gras*, capon steamed in white wine and veal broth with *quenelles* and then *tarte Louise*. It was not for them a war of hunger and hardship.

They stayed in a small, quiet, friendly hotel in Perpignan. A letter from Mildred Aldrich was waiting for them: 'Well I am proud of you. Think of you two rushing through the passes in a snowstorm. Now I feel as if there were nothing you could not do.' They collected the hospital supplies, which had already arrived at the station, and turned the erstwhile banqueting hall of the hotel into a storeroom, distribution depot and office.

*With Auntie and war supplies,* 1917.

The food at the hotel was Catalan. One of their favourite desserts was called Millason. It was a mixture of cornflour, sugar, eggs, butter and orange flower water, fried in oil and served sprinkled with sugar. It reminded them of Southern fried cornbread and comforted them. They also liked the little lobsters served with a sauce of white wine, basil, fennel, saffron, cayenne, garlic and tomato purée, the roasted wild boar in a sauce of grated lemon and orange peel and redcurrant jelly, the spring duckling served with asparagus, butter, lemon juice and cream.

They enjoyed distributing their supplies of medicines, blankets and food parcels to the hospitals in the region. Alice said it was like a continuous Christmas. She did all the stocktaking and paperwork. She sent weekly reports of their activities to the Paris office of the American Fund for French Wounded and many of her reports were published in the Fund's *Weekly Bulletin*. All the bureaucratic jobs went to Alice. Gertrude said offices were obnoxious and she refused to have anything to do with officials. But as she was the driver, all the papers about the car were in her name.

They needed extra petrol for their work, so Alice went to see the major in charge of this at Perpignan. Gertrude waited in the car. The major called Alice Mademoiselle Stein, but it did not seem to matter, for that was in a sense who she was. But then he said, 'Mademoiselle Stein, my wife is very anxious to make your acquaintance and she has asked me to ask you to dine with us.' Alice had to explain that she was not Mademoiselle Stein, that Mademoiselle Stein was sitting in the car and had no patience and would not go into offices and wait around and explain things to people. But they both went to supper and had very good soup. The major's wife came from Bordeaux and the soup of Bordeaux, said Alice, 'remains to me the standard of comparison with all the other soups in the world'.

To boost money for the American Fund, Alice had a photograph taken of Gertrude, herself and Auntie, outside the birthplace of General Joffre, the Commander-in-Chief of the French army. This was at Riversaltes near Perpignan. She had 1,000 postcards of it printed to sell in the States.

She and Gertrude always gave lifts to soldiers on their travels. They called the soldiers their military godsons. Their own obligations, as military godmothers, were to write letters as often as they received them and to send food parcels every ten days. Alice thought the soldiers liked the letters better than the food parcels. On one occasion she mixed her letters up. She asked a soldier whose mother was dead, and who had told her all about his wife, to remember her to his mother, and she asked the one with the dead mother to remember her to the wife he did not have. 'Their return letters were quite mournful', she said.

When inspired, Gertrude wrote poems. Sometimes she wrote in the car, or in the hotel, or in a field. A conversational poem called 'Work Again' related somewhat loosely to their war effort:

> The wind blows
> And the automobile goes.
> Can you guess boards.
> Wood.
> Can you guess hoops.
> Barrels.
> Can you guess girls.
> Servants.
> Can you guess messages.
> In deed.
> Then there are meats to buy.
> We like asparagus so.
> This is an interview.
> Soldiers like a fuss.
> Give them their way.
> Yes indeed we will.
> We are not mighty
> Nor merry.
> We are happy.
> Very.
> In the morning
> We believe in the morning
> Do we.

When America entered the war, in April 1917, Gertrude and Alice cut up ribbons printed with stars and stripes and gave them to the wounded soldiers.

In the autumn they were recalled to Paris by Mrs Lathrop. Alice gave Gertrude half a roast chicken to stave off hunger pangs on the journey back. Gertrude ate it with one hand and drove with the other. On the way home everything went wrong with Auntie. The sun was very hot and even Gertrude, who loved the heat, said she felt like a pancake – 'the heat above and the heat below and cranking a car besides'.

At Nevers they met some American soldiers. Gertrude was thrilled and talked to them all. She wanted to know what state and city they came from, what they were called, how old they were and what they liked. Two of them helped her fix the car. She called them California and Iowa, because that was where they came from. This gave her the idea for a history of the United States, 'consisting of chapters wherein Iowa differs from Kansas, and wherein Kansas differs from Nebraska etcetera'. She wrote a little of it and it was printed in the book she called *Useful Knowledge*.

They spent only a few days back in Paris - long enough to get Auntie properly serviced. Alice invited some American relief workers and nurses, who were on leave in Paris, to lunch. She gave them meat balls, called Kneppes, made of calves' liver. There were power cuts and severe rationing of meat, butter and eggs. Mrs Lathrop told them that, for their next assignment, they were to open a supply depot at Nîmes, serving the three departments of the Gard, the Bouches-du-Rhônes and the Vaucluse.

Alice took to wearing an officer's jacket, with lots of pockets, and a pith helmet. Gertrude wore a greatcoat and a Cossack hat. Braque met them at Avignon:

> They looked extremely strange . . . their funny get-up so excited the curiosity of the passers-by that a large crowd gathered around us and the comments were quite humorous. The police arrived and insisted on examining our papers. They were in order alright, but for myself, I felt very uncomfortable.

At Nîmes, Gertrude and Alice stayed in the best hotel, but it was in a sorry state. The proprietor had been killed in the war, the chef was in the army, and the usual suppertime fare was a tired-looking whiting with its tail in its mouth.

Auntie became an ambulance and was used to ferry wounded soldiers from the trains to the hospitals. Gertrude and Alice worked with the Red Cross nuns. There was a scarcity of cigarettes, and wounded soldiers smoked the stuffing from the hospital mattresses. Alice managed to get them contraband tobacco from Marseilles. She and Gertrude spent a good deal of their own money on supplementing supplies for soldiers.

An American regiment was stationed at Nîmes and they made friends with several of the young soldiers there. This was their link with America. One of the soldiers, W. G. Rogers, corresponded with Gertrude until her death. They called him the Kiddie. He was with the Ambulance Unit in Nîmes, had no money and was interested in Roman ruins. Gertrude and Alice invited him to tea in their hotel dining room. They plied him with cakes, and Gertrude questioned him like a policeman grilling a prisoner - where was he born, who were his parents, what did his father do, where did he go to college, who were his professors, how did he happen to be in the army, was this his first visit to France, what would he do when the war ended. He thought that Gertrude was like Stonehenge, and said that her laughter rumbled like thunder.

After his interrogation Alice told him that, as the Roman remains he wanted to see were difficult to get to by train, he was welcome to tour the region with them during his ten-day leave. He would have to obey certain rules. If the car went wrong, he must fix it. He must not get in the way. He must sit on the floor, on a pillow next to Alice, with his feet on the running board so that Gertrude would have as much room as if he were not there. They must always be back at the hotel by nightfall, because Gertrude did not like driving in the dark.

They took the Kiddie sightseeing all over Provence and they paid for everything. He sat on a pillow, half out of the open door, with his knees drawn up to his chin, crowding Alice but not Gertrude. 'Miss Toklas,' said the Kiddie, 'devoted practically all her adult life to the prevention of any crowding of Gertrude Stein.' The more he got to know them, the more he wondered 'whose light was being hidden under whose bushel'. For over the years a paradox developed in Gertrude and Alice's relationship and what, ostensibly, were Alice's acts of service to Gertrude became her means of control.

At Christmas in 1917 there was a dinner and dance at the hotel for convalescing British soldiers stationed at Nîmes. Gertrude and Alice took turns dancing with the men. 'It was as gay as we could make it, but the British Army was not cheerful,' said Alice. War news became more cheerful as the allies advanced. Gertrude wrote some short works. One of them, *Have They Attacked Mary He Giggled*: *A Political Caricature*, was published in *Vanity Fair*. After the war Gertrude gave a copy of it to Sylvia Beach's bookshop and lending library, Shakespeare and Company, in Paris. Sylvia Beach called it, 'that thing with a terrifying title'.

All through the war years Gertrude and Alice were cut off from the people they knew. Claribel Cone was stuck in the Regina Palace hotel in Munich and no one heard anything of her until the end of the war. Leo was in New York, 'psychoanalyzing and being psychoanalyzed, philosophizing and perambulating'. Carl Van Vechten, now permanently in New York with Fania, told Gertrude that he met Leo from time to time, 'scowling in galleries at manifestations of modern artists, and *talking* but never to me. He seems to be quite certain that he doesn't like me. Why, I don't know.'

Both Apollinaire and Braque had been wounded in the head. Apollinaire had married 'a real young lady' and was living in a smart apartment on the boulevard St Germain. Sarah and Michael Stein stayed in the south of France, but when there was shelling close to the rue de Fleurus in the Luxembourg Gardens, Michael arranged for the packaging up of two of Gertrude's paintings by Cézanne and one by Manet, insured them for $40,000, sent them to her at Nîmes, and told her to leave them in the Credit Lyonnais.

Picasso, after Eva's death, had several love affairs, then married a Russian ballet dancer, Olga Koklova. To celebrate his marriage he sent Gertrude a little abstract painting. Years later he copied it for Alice on to a tapestry canvas and she embroidered it, 'and that was the beginning of my tapestrying'. She covered two small Louis XV chairs with these canvases. Picasso told her what colour silks to use.

When the armistice was signed by the Germans, on 11 November 1918, Alice wept with relief. 'Control yourself', said Gertrude. 'You have no right to show a tearful countenance to the French whose sons will no longer be killed.' The next day Mrs Lathrop sent them a telegram asking if they spoke German. If so they should close the depot, return to Paris and then go to Alsace to open a depot for civilian relief. 'Gertrude,' said Alice 'spoke a fluent incorrect German . . . I tried to remember the correct German I had been taught.'

They stopped in Paris long enough to buy fur-lined aviators' jackets and thick sweaters, then set off for Alsace. On the way a horse pulling an army canteen kicked Auntie. A mudguard came off and the tool chest and steering column broke:

> We went on, the car wandering all over the muddy road, up hill and down hill, and Gertrude Stein sticking to the wheel . . . We had never realised before what mudguards were for but by the time we arrived in Nancy we knew.

Alice was 'disgracefully covered in mud' and all they had for supper were two hard-boiled ducks' eggs. They made up for it the next day with a quiche of ham, salt pork, eggs and cream. But then the car's fan belt broke and Gertrude tried unsuccessfully to fix it with a hairpin.

In Alsace, they set up their distribution headquarters in the school in Mulhouse and went to all the surrounding devastated villages. Their job was to distribute two blankets, underwear, children's woollen stockings and babies' booties, to every refugee family. They usually asked the local priest to help them. People were coming back to their ruined homes. Alsace had been a battlefield. 'It was not terrifying it was strange,' said Gertrude. 'We were used to ruined houses and even ruined towns, but this was different. It was a landscape and it belonged to no country.'

Alice found lots of provisions in the shops: real coffee, large hams, milk and pastries. Gertrude told her not to buy sausages though. 'It might be Claribel,' she said. Gertrude wrote a play-poem, *Accents In Alsace. A Reasonable Tragedy*. There were two Act Twos followed by an Act 425. She mentioned that Alsatian wine was dear and that they had eaten dry potatoes, but the main theme was love for Alice:

Let me kiss thee willingly.
Not a mountain not a goat not a door.
not a whisper not a curl not a gore
In me meeney miney mo.
You are my love and I tell you so.

When it was the season of 'orange blossoms and storks', they closed their depot and headed back to Paris 'by way of Metz, Verdun and Mildred Aldrich'. Mildred had used all the money earned from her book *A Hilltop on the Marne* to help wounded soldiers. Alice said, 'she had given it to the hilltop from which she had earned it'.

Gertrude and Alice were awarded Reconnaisance Française medals for their war work. They painted out the red cross and the lettering 'American Fund for French Wounded' from the side of Auntie. Paris was different. 'The city like us was sadder than when we left it,' said Alice. Gertrude and Picasso quarrelled - 'they neither of them ever quite knew about what' - and stopped talking to each other for a year. Apollinaire died, two days before the armistice, from the head wound he received in 1916, and from flu that he caught in Spain. Matisse had moved to Nice with his family. Juan Gris was ill. Daniel Kahnweiler's collection of cubist paintings, taken over by the government during the war, got sold for very little money. No one was interested in cubism any more. Leo returned from the States thinner, weaker, deaf and self-rejecting:

> my first attempts at psychoanalysis did not work satisfactorily, every little advance was countered by as great a relapse. If it hadn't been for that I might have had a successful time over there.

He could not work, except in spurts - an article about Cézanne, a talk on art - 'and that amounts to nothing', he said of his efforts.

He and Nina were apart during the war. She could not get the necessary papers for admission to the States. He wrote and asked her to marry him on 19 September 1915. He said it could be legal or otherwise if she preferred. He said that he loved her honestly, greatly and deeply and that she was something real. He also sent her money. His income was $1,000 a month. He gave her $600 and she would ask him for more. This left him with not enough for himself after he had paid the rent at Settignano, insurance on his pictures and his high psychoanalysis bills. He asked her to try to find work and she took his request very badly.

He told her that most of the time he wished he was dead, or at least not alive 'for it is neither pleasurable nor productive'. In December 1917 he wrote to her about the other women in his life – a young married one of twenty-three who said she wanted to kiss him and crush him. A tall slim one, 'she is the most androgynous woman who has ever known love', and

> about fifteen women and an equal number of men who interest me for the moment, but that would take too long, especially since in spite of all this galaxy I always return to you, my beloved, as the only one that I love, I love, I love.

They finally married in 1921 when he was fifty.

In December 1919 he wrote to Gertrude seeking to heal the breach between them. He told her that his antagonism had dissipated and that he felt amiable toward her. He said he had found that all his digestive troubles were neurotic symptoms, and that he had spent nearly all his time in America trying to cure his neurosis:

> But they're damned hard things to cure . . . and I was in almost utter despair. Then I got on a tack that has led to better states. This has finally led to an easing up & simplifying of most of my contacts with things and people and brought about a condition where it was possible to write to you . . .
>
> The 'family romance' as it is called is almost always central in the case of a neurosis just as you used to get indigestion when we had a dispute. So I could tell pretty well how I was getting on by the degree of possibility I felt of writing as I am doing now.

But Gertrude had no desire to go back to disputes, indigestion and the 'family romance'. She did not answer his letter. There could anyway be no return to the pre-war life. She and Alice were both overdrawn at the bank. They had spent a lot of their own money on war work. They had bought X-ray equipment, bandages, blankets, Woodbine cigarettes and 5,000 thermometers. Before the war, said Alice, 'we spent money without knowing what we were doing at all'. Now they had to economise. They had no cook or maid, and every morning they went to the market to get their provisions. Alice said they 'would live like gypsies and go everywhere in left-over finery, with a pot-au-feu for the many friends we would be seeing'. But most of the friends were gone. 'Everybody was dissatisfied and everyone was restless. It was a restless and disturbed world.'

However disturbed the world, the relationship between Alice and Gertrude followed a tranquil path. On the day of the *defile*, the victory procession under the Arc de Triomphe, they got up at sunrise and walked to join Jessie Whitehead in her hotel room which had a perfect view of the celebrations.

'It was a wonderful day,' wrote Gertrude.

> Everybody was on the streets, men, women, children, soldiers,
> priests, nuns, we saw two nuns being helped into a tree from
> which they would be able to see . . .
> They all marched past through the Arc de Triomphe . . .
> Everybody except the germans were passing through. All the
> nations marched differently, some slowly, some quickly, the french
> carrying their flags the best of all . . .
> However it all finally came to an end. We wandered up and we
> wandered down the Champs Elysees and the war was over and
> the piles of captured cannon that had made two pyramids were
> being taken away and peace was upon us.

*At Home*, 1922. *Photograph by Man Ray.*

# IO

## FAMOUS MEN. AND WOMEN

*'You can be a museum or you can
be modern but you can't be both'*

In Paris after the war, Auntie did not qualify as a civilian vehicle, and was not allowed in the Bois de Boulogne. She looked like a second-hand hearse and broke down frequently. She finally gave up in 1920, outside the Luxembourg Palace, obstructing the entrance when the Prime Minister, Raymond Poincaré, was due to arrive. The police towed her out of the way.

Gertrude and Alice went to the Ford factory and ordered a new two-seater. Riding in the car for the first time, Alice remarked that she was nude. The car that is. 'There was nothing on her dashboard, neither clock nor ashbox nor cigarette lighter. Godiva, was Gertrude Stein's answer.' Gertrude became fond of writing in Godiva while Alice did the errands and the shopping. She derived inspiration from the sounds of the street. The movement of other cars set the rhythm of a sentence for her, like a tuning fork or metronome. She wrote to that rhythm and tune. She wrote *Mildred's Thoughts*, *The Birthplace of Bonnes*, *American Biography* and *One Hundred Prominent Men* while sitting in Godiva. She thought *Mildred's Thoughts* the most successful of these car pieces.

She also found her own rhythms of splashing in the bath helped her to say what she wanted to say and when, later, she and Alice got a dog, she said the noise of him lapping water made her recognise the difference between sentences and paragraphs: that paragraphs are emotional and that sentences are not. She communicated this in the 'Sentences and Paragraphs' section of her book *How To Write*:

> Now what is a sentence. A sentence hopes that you are very well and happy. It is very selfish. They like to be taken away. A sentence can be taken care of. The minute you disperse a crowd you have a sentence. They were witnesses to it even if you did not stop. There there is no paragraph. If it had a different father it would have.

Cows and the clunking of their bells also inspired her. The American writer, Bravig Imbs, said he saw her sitting on a camp stool in a field and instructing Alice to bat a cow with a stick to one side of the field. Gertrude then wrote in her exercise book. Then she folded up her camp stool, moved to a different part of the field, and signalled to Alice to bat the cow in a different direction.

Bravig Imbs met them in 1926. Around this time Gertrude became friendly with about a dozen young men who were painters and writers. She eventually quarrelled with all of them. Imbs arrived with a letter of introduction from the painter Pavel Tchelitchew. He was quizzed by Alice before being allowed to talk to Gertrude. He said of Alice: 'She acted both as sieve and buckler; she defended Gertrude from the bores and most of the new people were strained through her before Gertrude had any prolonged conversation with them.' He said that degrees of intimacy were carefully graded and keenly felt, 'so that when the first important degree was reached, that of being invited to lunch, one was all but overcome by the honor'. The supreme degree of intimacy was a quarrel. Gertrude told him he had true brilliancy after she read his short stories, but that he should not use crutch phrases. 'In my own writing, as you know,' Gertrude told him:

> I have destroyed sentences and rhythms and literary overtones
> and all the rest of that nonsense, to get to the very core of this
> problem of the communication of intuition. If the
> communication is perfect the words have life, and that is all
> there is to good writing, putting down on the paper words which
> dance and weep and make love and fight and kiss and perform
> miracles.

He said that Gertrude had the most engaging and infectious laugh he had ever heard. 'It began abruptly at a high pitch and cascaded down and down into rolls and rolls of unctuous merriment. It was straight from the heart.'

Soon after acquiring Godiva, and getting stuck in a traffic jam on the boulevard St Germain, near the church of St Germain des Prés, Alice saw Gertrude bowing to a man who had taken off his hat and bowed to her. 'I said to her, Who was that? and Gertrude answered, Leo . . . I said, Not possibly. And she said, Yes, it was Leo.' That was the only communication the two of them had after 1913. Gertrude then went home and wrote a story, *How She Bowed To Her Brother*.

Leo married Nina on 5 March 1921 in Italy. Then he began 'nursing in the womb of his mind' a book called *Others, Do They Exist?*. It was to be about 'the morphology of irrational belief'. He felt that marriage did not come at the right time for him and that his progressive deafness was a blight. He felt 'almost a passion to be a father', but thought that a deaf father would

*Gertrude and Alice in Godiva.*

be like the father of a living doll. Most days he woke up wishing that he was dead and he said that sex was continually related to conflict for him.

Gertrude and Alice went off in Godiva for frequent picnics. They picked violets at Versailles, daffodils at Fontainebleau and hyacinths and forget-me-nots in the forest of St Germain. For these outings Alice prepared two basic picnic lunches. One was of chicken cooked in white wine and paprika, with hard-boiled eggs stuffed with mushrooms, and a dessert of cream puff shells filled with strawberries and sugar. The other was toasted sandwiches of roast beef chopped with sour cream, mustard, parsley and shallots, lettuce leaves filled with sweetbreads and truffles cooked in sherry, and a dessert of caramelised apples fried in puff pastry and dusted with icing sugar.

Gertrude got too fat and had to go on a diet. Alice joined her on it for no other reason than what Gertrude did, she tended to do too. As Alice was very thin and never ate much anyway, she soon completely lost her appetite. This, as with many of Alice's ways, made Gertrude laugh. When Alice was being obsessive, Gertrude liked to provoke and tease her. Alice told their dinner guests that Gertrude was having one of her stupid days. Gertrude also gave up alcohol, smoking and putting salt on her food. And the doctor told her to change her work habits and not write late into the night. Alice could not stop smoking. She chain-smoked Pall Mall until she was eighty-six, then switched to tipped cigarettes.

Alice was the brusque and uncompromising manager of Gertrude's life. She guarded, promoted and protected Gertrude. Visitors commented on Gertrude's sense of repose. Alice had none. She got up at six in the morning and did the cleaning because she did not trust the *femme de ménage* with the porcelain and fragile things. She said she could contemplate violence toward a servant who broke anything and her relationships were bad with a succession of cooks and servants. None of them could do their work well enough.

Annette Rosenshine, revisiting Paris in the twenties, noted how efficient Alice's power over Gertrude had become. She went to tea wearing a new Paris hat and her best earrings, hoping to show her sculpture to Gertrude. Alice looked at the pieces in silence then, when Gertrude came over, turned the lights off. Alice answered the questions Annette put to Gertrude. When they went for a drive in Godiva, Alice decided what streets Annette should see. 'It was first-rate team work,' Annette said. 'I was ostracised as far as Gertrude was concerned.' Though the logistics were left to Alice, Gertrude was not the victim. It suited her to be managed, shielded and freed.

In the pre-war years when Leo lived with Gertrude at the rue de Fleurus, the Saturday salons focused on painters and paintings. Between the wars they focused on new, mainly American writers. Gertrude's prestige was enormous. She had been the person to have faith in Picasso and cubism. High respect developed for her opinions, though few people claimed to read her writing. 'She could make or mar an exhibition with little more than a movement of her thumb,' said Bravig Imbs. If she approved of an exhibition, she carried off the best painting at a bargain price. If she disapproved, a coterie of American buyers followed her view. But after she and Leo separated, and in the years between the wars, Gertrude wavered in her convictions about painting. She began by buying Cézanne, then Matisse, Picasso and Juan Gris. Then Francis Picabia. Then she wavered over the work of several neo-romantics: Pavel Tchelitchew, Christian Bérard and Genia Berman, but she rejected each in turn. Finally she gave equivocal support to Francis Rose (though she bought 130 of his paintings) and Riba-Rovira. Art historians noted the lessening in merit of the painters she patronized. She said that after its cubist high point, painting lapsed into a secondary form of expression.

With writers, as with painters, she was emphatic about who was good and who was not, and her approval, encouragement and help meant much. Her callers were like a court, with intrigues for the sovereign's favour. Virgil Thomson said the lines 'Will you come into my parlour, said the spider to the fly' came into his mind.

Sylvia Beach opened her bookshop and library, Shakespeare and Company, in Paris in 1919, the year Gertrude and Alice came back from Alsace. It was a picturesque and homey place in a little street on the rue de l'Odeon. There were black and white Serbian rugs on the wood floor, antique furniture and racks for the England and American literary reviews: *Dial, Nation, Chapbook, New Republic, New Masses, Poetry, Egoist, New English Review* – the little uncommercial magazines that, said Gertrude, died to make verse free. On the walls were Blake drawings and pictures of Edgar Allen Poe, Walt Whitman and Oscar Wilde. At the back of the shop was a storage room and a little kitchen.

Sylvia Beach said she learned to run the shop from her friend and lover Adrienne Monnier, whose bookshop, *La Maison des Amis des Livres*, was on the other side of the road. Both shops held readings and literary meetings, and Sylvia Beach said there should have been a tunnel under the road to join the shops. She and Adrienne Monnier were together for thirty-eight years. They met when Sylvia was thirty and Adrienne, twenty-six. Sylvia was angular, brisk and witty, and Janet Flanner said she dressed like a schoolgirl, in skirts and velvet jackets, with a big bow at her throat. Adrienne Monnier was contemplative, philosophical, religious, a gourmet cook, earthy and rather plump. They spoke together in French, both had sisters and no brothers, and were helped by their parents to start their businesses. They were given the financial and moral support that ordinarily at that time would have gone to sons.

Gertrude was the first American writer to visit Shakespeare and Company:

> Not long after I had opened my bookshop two women came walking down the rue Dupuytren. One of them, with a very fine face, was stout, wore a long robe, and, on her head, a most becoming top of a basket. She was accompanied by a slim, dark whimsical woman: she reminded me of a gypsy ...
>
> Gertrude's remarks and those of Alice which rounded them out, were inseparable. They saw things from the same angle, as people do when they are perfectly congenial. Their two characters, however, seemed to me quite independent of each other. Alice had a great deal more finesse than Gertrude. And she was grown up. Gertrude was a child, something of an infant prodigy.

Sylvia told Gertrude how few American customers she had, so Gertrude offered her services as a publicist. She wrote a poem, *Rich and Poor in English*. Alice typed it and posted it to their friends to encourage them to subscribe to the bookshop:

> A curry comb
> or
> A matter of dogs
> It is this I please
> Please
> Seals go a long way
> Or better.

Alice said that it induced many people to join the bookshop.

Sylvia thought that Gertrude's subscription was only a friendly gesture. 'She took little interest of course in any but her own books.' Sylvia went for rides with them in Godiva. 'Off we roared to Mildred Aldrich's hilltop on the Marne.' She was very impressed when they equipped Godiva with headlights that worked from the inside and with an electric cigarette lighter for Alice.

She visited them at the rue de Fleurus, but never met any French people there. Gertrude, she observed, had a way of looking at the French without seeing them, like a tourist 'glancing with amusement at the inhabitants as she passed'. On one occasion, Sylvia took Adrienne Monnier to the rue de Fleurus. Gertrude told Adrienne that the French had 'no alps' in literature or in music. 'You have no Shakespeare and no Beethoven . . . your genius is in those things that generals say: on ne passera pas . . . yes fanfare is what the French do best: the bombastic.' Adrienne thought her rude and had no desire to visit again.

Sylvia Beach felt like a guide from a tourist agency because so many young American writers visited Shakespeare and Company and asked her to introduce them to Gertrude Stein. Gertrude stayed friendly with her until she published James Joyce's *Ulysses* in 1922. Then she transferred her subscription to the official American Library on the Right Bank. Joyce was her rival in literary innovation. She said that he smelled of museums and that was why he was accepted and she was not. 'You see it is the people who generally smell of the museums who are accepted and it is the new who are not accepted.' Joyce never made any mention of her. They met once, at a party given by Jo Davidson, who did a sculpture of Gertrude. Sylvia introduced them to each other. Gertrude said to Joyce, 'After all these years'. Joyce said, 'Yes and our names always linked together.' Gertrude said, 'We live in the same *arrondissement*', and he said nothing so she went back to talk to a Californian.

Ezra Pound was another of Gertrude's literary rivals who, she said, smelled of museums. Alice thought him disagreeable and pretentious. They first met him at Grace Lounsbery's house. (She was a friend from Gertrude's Johns Hopkins days.) Pound and Scofield Thayer, the editor of *Dial* magazine, then went to dinner with Gertrude and Alice. Pound talked about Japanese prints and T. S. Eliot. Gertrude called him a village explainer, 'excellent if you were a village, but if you were not, not'. He got over-animated and fell out of his chair, the one Alice subsequently tapestried with Picasso's designs. He broke the back leg of it which annoyed Gertrude: 'All he has to do is to come in and sit down for half an hour. When he leaves, the chair's broken, the lamp's broken. Ez is fine, but I can't afford to have him in the house.' When he expressed the desire to visit them again, she told him, 'I am so sorry but Miss Toklas has a bad tooth and beside we are busy picking wild flowers.'

A decade later, when everyone who knew anyone wrote memoirs, many of those slighted by Gertrude and Alice became acidic in print. Ezra Pound called Gertrude an 'old tub of guts', and in a published parody had her say, 'Yes the Jews have produced only three originative geniuses: Christ, Spinoza and myself.' From Gertrude and Alice's point of view, though they liked to see people come, they equally well liked to see them go. And if they banished many, then there were always more. They were endlessly hospitable but, as Gertrude saw it, 'either people lived with you or they did not, and if not, not'.

Sherwood Anderson arrived at the rue de Fleurus in 1921, with a letter of introduction from Sylvia Beach. He had left his first wife, family and respectable job to be a writer. He had written novels called *Poor White* and *Winesburg Ohio*. Sylvia wrote to Gertrude, 'He is so anxious to know you for he says you have influenced him ever so much and that you stand as such a great master of words.' As he was very flattering to Gertrude, the meeting was a great success. In his diary he described her as 'a strong woman with legs like stone pillars sitting in a room with Picassos'. His second wife, Tennessee, a music teacher, did not fare very well. Every time she tried to join in the conversation, Alice took her across the room to show her something interesting. Sylvia Beach could not see the necessity for the cruelty to wives practised at the rue de Fleurus:

> This was not the way Adrienne and I treated wives. Not only did we always make a point of inviting Mrs Writer with her husband, but we found them quite interesting. Many a time a wife will be more enlightening on the subject of writers than all the professors in the classrooms.

Gertrude was disheartened about all her unpublished manuscripts and meagre literary prospects, so she was very pleased to receive Sherwood Anderson's flattery. He had read *Tender Buttons* in 1914. He said his mind did a 'jerking flop' and that for days afterwards he jotted down new combinations of words: 'Perhaps it was then I really fell in love with words, wanted to give each word I used every chance to show itself at its best.'

When she met him, Gertrude was again paying for the publication of a book of her short pieces. She called it *Geography and Plays*. Four Seas Press in Boston was publishing it. Gertrude called the editor, Edmund Brown, 'Honest to God Brown'. Sherwood Anderson agreed to write the preface. The book included the portrait of Alice called 'Ada', 'Sacred Emily', which had in it the immortal line, 'Rose is a rose is a rose is a rose', and other less immortal lines like, 'Electrics are tight electrics are white electrics are a button.' The book also included a piece called 'IIIIIIIII', with the observation in it, 'The seam in most tight legs are looser and not secure politely'.

'Dear Miss Stein,' wrote Honest To God Brown on 5 January 1922,

> I am sure that Sherwood Anderson's explanatory preface to your book will be very helpful, not only as an aid to the general reader but also to us in marketing.
>
> I am glad to enclose contracts providing that we will make an edition of 2,500 copies at a cost of only $2,500 and that we will pay you a royalty of 15% and in addition that we will pay you $1 a copy on every copy sold of the first edition, which will bring you back the return of your investment.

I assure you that even if we never succeed in making any great amount of money on this book, we appreciate the value of having your name on our list, and you may be sure that we shall not lose the opportunity offered by such an unusual book to get special publicity and comment.
Yours sincerely
Edmund R. Brown

In his introduction Sherwood Anderson wrote that Gertrude's was the most important pioneer work being done in the field of letters. He said that she was doing totally new things with words:

> Here is one artist who has been able to accept ridicule, who has even foregone the privilege of writing the great American novel ... to go live among the little housekeeping words, the swaggering bullying street-corner words, the honest working money saving words, and all the other forgotten and neglected citizens of the sacred and half-forgotten city.

'We began to meet new people all the time,' said Alice. Gertrude always liked to see Ernest Hemingway. She thought he was wonderful, with 'passionately interested rather than interesting eyes' and she had a 'weakness' for him. This irritated Alice. 'Don't you come home with Hemingway on your arm,' she would say.

Hemingway thought that Gertrude looked like an earth mother, talked like an angel, and had beautiful eyes and a strong German-Jewish face that could have been from Friulano. She reminded him of a northern Italian peasant woman with her clothes, her mobile face and 'her lovely, thick, alive immigrant hair which she wore put up in the same way she had probably worn it in college'. He said that Alice's hair was cut like Joan of Arc, that she had a very hooked nose, did needlepoint, saw to the food and drink, talked to their wives and often interrupted Gertrude's conversation to put her right.

Hemingway was twenty-three when he arrived at the rue de Fleurus in 1922 with a letter of introduction from Sherwood Anderson. Gertrude was forty-eight. He was working as a journalist and Gertrude told him to give it up. She read his poems and stories and told him, 'There is a great deal of description in this, and not particularly good description. Begin over again and concentrate.' He wrote to Gertrude, 'It was a vital day for me when I stumbled upon you.' He particularly liked Alice's fragrant colourless alcohols that tasted of raspberries and blackcurrants, but packed a fiery punch. Alice and Gertrude were godmothers to his baby boy and Alice embroidered a chair and knitted a bright jacket for the baby.

Hemingway said Gertrude told him of the difference between homosexuality in men and women. According to him, she said:

> the act male homosexuals commit is ugly and repugnant and afterwards they are disgusted with themselves. They drink and take drugs to palliate this, but they are disgusted with the act and they are always changing partners and cannot be really happy ... In women it is the opposite. They do nothing that they are disgusted by and nothing that is repulsive and afterwards they are happy and they can lead happy lives together.

Hemingway became commissioning editor of Ford Madox Ford's magazine, *transatlantic review*, in 1924 and persuaded Ford to serialise some of Gertrude's book *The Making of Americans* in it. Gertrude had been hoping for publication for thirteen years. Carl Van Vechten and May Knoblauch [Bookstaver] had tried very hard to get it published in America. The publishers Knopf and Liveright prevaricated, so Gertrude was 'quite overcome' with excitement at the prospect of serialisation. Hemingway wrote to her:

> Ford alleges he is delighted with the stuff and he is going to call on you. He is going to publish the 1st installment in the April No. going to press the 1st part of March. He wondered if you would accept 30 francs a page and I said I thought I could get you to. (*Be haughty but not too haughty.*) I made it clear it was a remarkable scoop ... obtained only through my obtaining genius. He is under the impression that you get big prices when you consent to publish ... Treat him high wide and handsome ...
> They are going to have Joyce in the same number.

Ford had thought it was a short story, not a book of 565,000 words. He and Hemingway fell out, the magazine foundered for want of money and Gertrude did not get paid.

It was a pattern for Gertrude, prompted by Alice, ultimately to quarrel with and banish most of the young men, the painters and writers, she encouraged and advised. Hemingway gave his account of how his relationship with her ended in his memoir, *A Moveable Feast*. He called on Gertrude one morning at the rue de Fleurus, and the maid gave him a glass of *eau de vie* and said Gertrude would be down in a moment. Then he heard Alice speaking to Gertrude as he had never heard one person speak to another, 'never anywhere, ever':

> Then Miss Stein's voice came pleading and begging saying, 'Don't pussy. Don't. Don't, please don't. I'll do anything pussy but please don't do it. Please don't. Please don't pussy.'

Hemingway did not want to hear any more so he left. He said that Gertrude stopped looking like a beautiful peasant woman from Friulano, got to look like a Roman Emperor and started buying worthless pictures and quarrelling with everybody. He implied that it was Alice who could be cruel to Gertrude. Certainly Alice was fiercely possessive and jealous and wanted absolute fidelity. When, in 1932, she learned of Gertrude's early affair with May Bookstaver – which Gertrude had never admitted to her – she was destructively jealous. And that was over an affair that had finished thirty years previously. As for Gertrude and Hemingway, Virgil Thomson thought they were perhaps in love with each other. 'That's why Alice had to get rid of him,' he wrote. However unlikely the idea, there was enough between them to provoke Alice. And Hemingway wrote a letter to W. G. Rogers (the Kiddie) in July 1948, saying of Gertrude: 'I always wanted to fuck her and she knew it and it was a good healthy feeling and made more sense than some of the talk.'

Hemingway took Scott Fitzgerald to meet Gertrude and Alice in 1925, just after the publication of *The Great Gatsby*. Gertrude compared Fitzgerald to Thackeray. She said of *This Side of Paradise*, 'it really created for the public the new generation'. Fitzgerald told her that she was a very handsome, acutely sensitive, gallant, kind lady. He wrote to her in June 1925:

> I am a very second rate person compared to first rate people . . . and it honestly makes me shiver to know that such a writer as you attributes such a significance to my factitious, meritricous (metricious?) [sic] 'This Side of Paradise'.

He often called to see her and they talked about his drinking. Gertrude was fond of a number of people who were always more or less drunk. 'There is nothing to do about it they are always more or less drunk.' Her rule was to treat them as if they were sober. 'It is funny,' she said:

> the two things most men are proudest of is the thing that any man can do and doing does in the same way, that is being drunk and being the father of their son . . . If anybody thinks about that they will see how interesting it is that it is that.

She told Fitzgerald he would write an even greater novel. When *Tender is the Night* was published, eight years later, he sent her a copy inscribed, 'Is this the book you asked for?'

T. S. Eliot went to tea in 1924. He sat clasping his umbrella by the handle. He asked Gertrude why she so frequently used the split infinitive. He said he would print something of hers in the *Criterion*, the magazine he edited in London, but it would have to be her very latest work. Gertrude started writing a piece called 'the fifteenth of November', that being the date, so there could be no doubt as to its freshness. 'It was all about wool is wool and silk is silk or wool is woollen and silk is silken.' Alice sent it to T. S. Eliot and he printed it two years later. The critic Henry Seidel Canby said of it:

> If this is literature or anything other than stupidity worse than madness, then has all criticism since the beginning of letters been mere idle theorizing.

Alice had a long correspondence about the fate of the piece with T. S. Eliot's secretary. They each addressed each other as 'sir', not knowing that neither was a man.

In January 1926, Gertrude's friend, the Duchess of Clermont Tonnerre, called at the rue de Fleurus. (She wrote books about nineteenth-century French life and travel books. As a young girl she met Proust and served as the model for the Duchesse de Guermantes in his novel *A la Recherche du Temps Perdu*.) She took off her hat and her hair was cut short. She said to Gertrude, 'What do you think of it?' Gertrude said, 'It suits your head.' 'That is what you will have to come to,' said the Duchess of Clermont Tonnerre. That night Gertrude said to Alice, 'Cut it off.' 'Cut it off she said and I did.'

Alice took two days cutting Gertrude's hair. She did not know how to go about it so it got shorter and shorter. And the shorter it got, the better Gertrude liked it. Previously she had worn it long and wound into an 'ancient fashion'. She read, as Alice barbered, and had a revelation:

> I found that any kind of a book if you read with glasses and somebody is cutting your hair and so you cannot keep the glasses on and you use your glasses as a magnifying glass and so read word by word reading word by word makes the writing that is not anything be something.
> Very regrettable but very true.
> So that shows to you that a whole thing is not interesting because as a whole well as a whole there has to be remembering and forgetting, but one at a time, oh one at a time is something oh yes definitely something.

By the time Alice finished cutting, Gertrude did not have much hair left. Sherwood Anderson was the first caller to see the new style. He thought she looked like a monk. Pavel Tchelitchew had been planning to paint her portrait, but the shape of her head now seemed changed. He had wanted to paint her because he thought she looked like his aunt, but no longer.

While the barbering went on, Alice did not answer the door to callers. Virgil Thomson was one of the young men turned away. He had met Gertrude and Alice a few days previously at their Christmas Eve party. This was always

*The Duchess of Clermont Tonnerre and Gertrude with short hairstyles.*

a big affair with carols, a tree and a cake cooked by Alice with ribbons and candles on it. Virgil Thomson had read Gertrude's poems when he was a student at Harvard. He left at the door a music manuscript he had written, a setting for voice and piano of Gertrude's *Susie Asado*. Gertrude replied immediately:

> I like its looks immensely and want to frame it and Miss Toklas who knows more than looks says the things in it please her a lot and when can I know a little other than its looks but I am completely satisfied with its looks, the sad part was that we were at home but we were denying ourselves to everyone having been xhausted by the week's activities but you would have been the xception you and the Susie, you or the Susie, do come in soon we will certainly be in Thursday afternoon any other time it is luck but may luck always be with you and a happy New Year to you always
> Gertrude Stein

In the next few months, Virgil Thomson set several of her pieces to music. Because her meanings were so abstract, or absent, or multiplied, he felt no temptation toward tonal illustration of birds babbling by the brook or of scudding clouds. His settings were for sound and syntax only, his accompaniments functional:

> I had no sooner put to music one short Stein text than I knew I had opened a door. I had never had any doubts about Stein's poetry; from then on I had none about my ability to handle it to music.

He asked Gertrude to write an opera libretto. She wanted it to be about late eighteenth-century or early nineteenth-century saints. She wrote to him in March 1927: 'Four saints in three acts. And others. Make it pastoral. In hills and gardens. All four and then additions. We must invent them.'

She persuaded some of her wealthy American friends to give him money to live on while he wrote the music. Her libretto contained her famous lines about 'Pigeons on the grass alas', and was a great success when staged in New York at the Forty-Fourth Street Theatre in 1934.

In 1926, Virgil Thomson introduced Gertrude and Alice to Bernard Faÿ, who was Professor of American history at the University of Clermont-Ferrand. He had praised Gertrude in all manner of published articles. He said she was 'le plus puissant écrivain américain d'aujourdhui', and that she was conducting a great revolution in literary art all by herself. In his memoir he wrote of Gertrude and Alice,

Between the two women, one seemingly stronger and the other more frail, one affirming her genius and the other venerating it, one speaking and the other listening, only a blind man could ignore that the most vigorous one was Alice, and that Gertrude, for her behavior as much as for her work and publications, leaned on her, used her and followed her advice . . .

Alice kept house. On her fell the tedium of servants, provisions, upkeep and finances. Alice knew how to entertain, listen to, stimulate Gertrude and to calm her. She knew how to guide her and divert her. In a word she gave her good advice. Even in her friendships, she played a discreet but influential role, because she drew in or rejected those who came near Gertrude, according to her own judgement.

'I am always beaten in discussion,' Alice told Faÿ. But she scored her victories in other ways.

One day, Gertrude and Alice invited Edith Sitwell and Pavel Tchelitchew to lunch. Twenty years later, Alice wrote of their visit to Annette Rosenshine:

Shortly after lunch they left together . . . They had a very violent affair . . . They have written to each other every day for years and years and each promised to give the others letters sealed of course to Yale University Library not to be opened until 2000. I say Edith will go over for the breaking of the seals.

Alice thought Edith Sitwell's nose the most distinguished nose she had ever seen on any human being. She thought she looked like 'nobody under the sun, very tall, rather the height of a grenadier'. As well as her nose, Alice liked her double-breasted coat with buttons. Edith Sitwell regarded Gertrude as a great writer and a pioneer, quite different from 'the vulgar little clothes moths that sit drinking and pretending to be geniuses in the cafés'. She thought *Geography and Plays* a beautiful book, and she tried to persuade Leonard and Virginia Woolf to publish *The Making of Americans* in England.

She urged Gertrude to lecture at Oxford and Cambridge colleges in England. Harold Acton sent a formal invitation in March 1926. Gertrude was very agitated at the thought of it, but then managed to write a lecture, in a garage in Montrouge, while Godiva was being repaired. She sat on the running board of another Ford and wrote:

Everything is the same except composition and as the composition is different and always going to be different everything is not the same. So then I as a contemporary creating the composition in the beginning was groping toward a

continuous present, a using everything a beginning again and
again and then everything being alike then everything very simply
everything was naturally simply different and so I as a
contemporary was creating everything being alike was creating
everything naturally being naturally simply different everything
being alike.

The lecture was called *Composition As Explanation*. It took her three hours
to write and she arrived home cold. She delivered it in June 1926 and it
lasted an hour. Alice was proud. Harold Acton said she surpassed all
expectations, 'a squat Aztec figure in obsidian, growing more monumental
as soon as she sat down. With her tall bodyguard of Sitwells and the gipsy
acolyte, she made a memorable entry.' Gertrude also read from her portrait
of Edith Sitwell:

Miss Edith Sitwell have and heard.
Introduces have and had.
Miss Edith Sitwell have and had.
Introduces have and had introduces have and had and heard.
Miss Edith Sitwell have and had and heard.
Left and right.
Part two of Part one.
If she had a ball at all, if she had a ball at all too.
Fill my eyes no no.

Alice said they had a beautiful time and that the audience was quiet, attentive,
large and intense. Many had to stand. Gertrude's voice was friendly and
made everybody feel at home until they pondered the subject matter. Harold
Acton found it difficult not to fall into a trance:

She forged ahead without any attempt at compromise: take it or
leave it . . . While she read Edith Sitwell's portrait I glanced at
the model. No, I could not see the likeness, nor, apparently,
could Edith, for she was trying not to look as embarrassed as she
felt. Sachie looked as if he were swallowing a plum and Osbert
shifted in his insufficient chair with a vague nervousness in his
eyes . . . The illusion that we were living in a continuous present
was certainly there, a little too continous for my taste.

After the lecture, the men asked questions but the women said nothing.
Gertrude wondered whether 'they were supposed not to or just did not'.
One man told Alice that listening to Gertrude had been his greatest experience
since reading Kant's *Critique of Pure Reason*. Gertrude was unperturbed by
any of the questions. 'She was like a solid rock among the brambles,' said
Harold Acton.

Gertrude's reputation was greater than her readership. She was in her fifties, with only a few things privately printed and some short stories and articles published. When the author William Carlos Williams went to tea at the rue de Fleurus in 1924, she one by one took all her unpublished manuscripts out of a cupboard, told him their titles and asked him what he would do if they were his. 'If writing were my *métier* and they were mine,' he replied, 'having so many I should probably select what I thought were the best and throw the rest in the fire'. 'No doubt,' said Gertrude, 'but then writing is not of course your *métier*.' Williams left soon after that and did not visit the rue de Fleurus again. 'I told the maid I was not in if he came again. There was too much bombast in him,' said Gertrude. She and Alice intended that every word of every page she had written should find its way into print.

Although Gertrude's acolytes were young American men, and wives were consigned to Alice and the kitchen, there were, in Paris between the wars, women writers, artists and publishers of great rebelliousness and innovation. But Gertrude was not a woman's woman when it came to affairs of the mind and she could be chauvinistic as Djuna Barnes recalled:

> Do you know what she said of me? Said I had beautiful legs!
> Now what does that have to do with anything? Said I had
> beautiful legs! Now I mean what did she say that for? I mean, if
> you're going to say something about a person ... I couldn't stand
> her. She had to be the centre of everything. A monstrous ego.

Djuna Barnes drank a lot, took drugs and lived tempestuously for a decade with the artist Thelma Wood. She wrote an anonymous book, *Ladies Almanack*, for the expatriate lesbians of Paris. It was thought too obscene for America and the customs officials banned it. Djuna and her friends sold copies on the streets of Paris. Thelma Wood threatened daily to leave Djuna, who would go looking for her in all the louche Paris bars. After the relationship ended, Djuna wrote about it in 1936 in her book *Nightwood*.

Natalie Barney and Gertrude were good friends. Natalie Barney was from Cincinnati and had inherited a fortune. She wrote poems and memoirs, which she paid to have printed. She started her famous salon after the war in 1919, the year Sylvia Beach started Shakespeare and Company, and continued it for a decade. She had a house on the rue Jacob, with a large pavilion in a shady garden which had lots of trees but no flowers. A narrow passageway led from the pavilion to a Temple of Friendship, which had a huge domed ceiling of stained glass and an alcove with four harps and hung with tapestry where recitations took place. Natalie Barney's Friday teas were held in the temple. There were cucumber sandwiches, 'like damp handkerchiefs', made by the housekeeper Berthe, strawberry and raspberry tarts and chocolate cake.

At these teas one met lesbians, said Sylvia Beach:

> Paris ones and those only passing through town . . . ladies with high collars and monocles, though Miss Barney herself was so feminine. Unfortunately I missed the chance to make the acquaintance at her salon of the authoress of *The Well of Loneliness* in which she concluded that if inverted couples could be united at the altar, all their problems would be solved.

Natalie Barney was blonde, wore white clothes, rode a horse in the Bois de Boulogne every morning and always had lots of lovers. Alice said she got them from the toilets of the Louvre department store. Natalie wanted as her epitaph, 'She was the friend of men and the lover of women, which for people full of ardor and drive is better than the other way around.' She and the painter Romaine Brooks met when they were forty and were lovers, on and off, until they died in their nineties. Romaine Brooks was always faithful to Natalie, whom she painted wearing a cravat and with her hand on her hip holding a whip.

Natalie was not faithful. For ten years she had an affair with Dolly Wilde, Oscar Wilde's niece. Dolly longed for a home and instead found excitement, jealousy and insecurity. Romaine would arrive when Dolly was with Natalie, 'the herald of unimaginable suffering', and Dolly would be banished. Dolly took opium and cocaine and twice tried to kill herself. She died of cancer in 1941. Alice remembered her 'mythical pristine freshness that, alas, became a bit tarnished'. Gertrude said of her life, 'Well, she certainly hadn't a fair run for her money.'

Mata Hari came to some of the teas. She wanted to ride in on an elephant, but Natalie said 'No, you'll get in the way of Berthe. There are cookies and tea and we can't have an elephant stamping around in my garden.'

Natalie Barney and Romaine Brooks first met Gertrude and Alice at the Russian ballet in 1926 and invited them to the Temple. Gertrude sat at the centre of the group and Natalie Barney thought that in her stout tweeds and with her cropped hair she looked like a game warden scrutinizing the exotic birds. Gertrude declined several invitations to read her work but then in January 1927, Natalie Barney held four consecutive salon evenings to introduce the work of American and French writers to each other. Gertrude's evening was called 'Homage to Gertrude', after the painting Picasso had done for her, which she hung above her bed, of naked ladies bringing her fruit on plates. Mina Loy read some of Gertrude's work, there were songs Virgil Thomson had written to her texts and Natalie Barney translated passages of *The Making of Americans* into French.

Natalie Barney was a writer of *pensées*: 'I like to find a thought as in a nut or seashell, but while I make for a point Gertrude seems to proceed by avoiding it.' She liked Gertrude's 'staunch presence, pleasant touch of hand, well-rounded voice always ready to chuckle'. In later years they used walk round Paris together in the evenings. There was a kind of equality between them. Both had faithful partners, private incomes, assured egos, idiosyncratic imaginations. There was no need for the kind of assertion that troubled many of Gertrude's other relationships.

Many of the literary magazines of the time were edited by women: *Poetry* by Harriet Monroe, the *Egoist* by Harriet Shaw Weaver, the *Little Review* by Jane Heap and Margaret Anderson. Margaret Anderson started the *Little Review* in New York, then took it to Paris in 1922 and published Gertrude and Mina Loy, Djuna Barnes and H.D. Then she fell in love with a singer, Georgette LeBlanc, and lost interest in the magazine. She published the last edition in 1929. She said, 'Even the artist doesn't know what he is talking about. And I can no longer go on publishing a magazine in which no one really knows what he is talking about.'

In 1925 she asked Gertrude and Alice to 'watch over' her two nephews, Fritz and Tom Peters, who were at the Gurdjieff Institute at Fontainebleau. Their mother was too ill to look after them. Fritz Peters wrote:

> We were very startled when we were told that Gertrude Stein was going to take care of us. We went the first time in trepidation. But she was wonderful to us, always gave us what we wanted, not what she wanted to give us.
>
> I didn't like sightseeing much as a child, but I liked what she arranged for us. 'Go up to the top of Notre Dame and here's a red handkerchief to wave so I can see you've got there.'
>
> At the Louvre she told us one or two things we should look at, but didn't go round with us. 'You must like what you like not what I like. Art is something you must live with.'
>
> Once she asked me what I thought of the pictures at the rue de Fleurus. I began slowly explaining I didn't like Picasso's portrait of her. She cut in quickly: 'Remember you don't have to like them.' And she pointed a finger at me repeating emphatically: 'Remember.' Another time she found me looking at one of her books and asked me what I thought of it. 'It doesn't make sense.' 'You've more courage and intelligence than most people', she said. 'No it doesn't make sense. That's the point.'
>
> I was a little scared of Alice. She came and went so

mysteriously. And although she often came in bearing some
wonderful cake or other concoction I gave Gertrude the credit
for it. I knew Alice was doing it for her.

Gertrude owed the eventual publication in book form of her *magnum
opus*, *The Making of Americans*, to a woman - Bryher. Bryher's father, Sir
John Ellerman, was the richest man in England. He was a shipping magnate,
the founder of Ellerman Lines, and owned most of the shares in *The Times*,
the *Illustrated London News*, the *Sphere*, *Tatler* and *Sketch*. When he died in
1933 he left £30 million. Bryher's real name was Winifred Ellerman, and
she called herself Bryher after one of the Scilly Isles. She was in love with
the imagist poet Hilda Doolittle and adopted her daughter, Perdita. H.D.
wrote that Bryher loved her 'so madly it is terrible. No man has ever cared
for me like that.'

Bryher needed to marry a man to appease her parents. She met Robert
McAlmon in New York. He wanted to go to Paris, but had no money. 'I
put my problem before him', said Bryher, 'and suggested that if we married,
my family would leave me alone. I would give him part of my allowance,
he would join me for occasional visits to my parents, but otherwise we would
live strictly separate lives.' She said of McAlmon, 'We neither of us felt the
slightest attraction towards each other but remained perfectly friendly.'

With Bryher's money, and editorial help, McAlmon set up the Contact
Publishing Company in Paris, which published, between 1922 and 1930, his
own work, Bryher, H.D., Gertrude, Ezra Pound, Ernest Hemingway, Nathanael
West, William Carlos Williams and Djuna Barnes. Contact's publishing legend
ran:

> Contact Editions are not concerned with what the 'public' wants.
> There are commercial publishers who *know* the public and its
> tastes. If books seem to us to have something of individuality,
> intelligence, talent, a live sense of literature, and a quality which
> has the odour and timbre of authenticity, we publish them. We
> admit that eccentricities exist.

Bryher also gave money to Harriet Weaver's *Egoist* and to Sylvia Beach's
bookshop. Her financial help made a lot of experimental publishing possible.

Bryher described her first meeting with Gertrude. She was walking with
McAlmon in Paris. Gertrude stopped her car and 'lumbered down':

> Two penetrating eyes in a square impassive face seemed to be
> absorbing every detail of my appearance. 'Why McAlmon' a
> puzzled voice remarked, 'you did not tell me that you had
> married an ethical Jewess. It's rather a rare type.'

Bryher's ancestors were English Protestants and German Lutherans but, said Bryher, 'You did not argue with Gertrude Stein. You acquiesced'.

Bryher and McAlmon went to tea at the rue de Fleurus and were impressed by the paintings and Gertrude's talk. 'She offered us the world, took it away again in the following sentence, only to demonstrate in a third that it was something that we could not want because it never existed.' Despite the fact that she wore a tie, was in love with a woman and called herself he, Bryher was consigned to Alice and the wives. They sat in the kitchen and talked of cooking and gardening. 'I am afraid that while I had a profound admiration for Gertrude,' said Bryher, 'it was Miss Toklas whom I loved. She was so kind to me.'

Gertrude was delighted at the prospect of seeing *The Making of Americans* published. Publishers had rejected it for more than a decade. Contact was to bring out 500 copies in one volume, with five deluxe copies printed on vellum. Printing was to be carried out by the firm of Maurice Darantière at Dijon. Gertrude was to be responsible for selling fifty copies.

Carl Van Vechten was very pleased. He had tried unsuccessfully to find an American publisher. He thought the book 'probably as big as, perhaps bigger than James Joyce, Marcel Proust or Dorothy Richardson' and a bit like the Book of Genesis. 'There is something Biblical about you Gertrude,' he wrote to her on 16 April 1923. 'Certainly there is something Biblical about you.'

The relationship between Gertrude and McAlmon soon soured. Gertrude would not give him a free hand. Without consulting him, she asked Jane Heap to find an American publisher for the book. Jane Heap approached Benjamin Huebsch, not knowing that he had turned it down thirteen years before. 'I cannot follow Miss Stein's theories with enough zest to be a foster father to her children,' he said by way of saying no. Then a firm called Charles and Albert Boni showed interest in buying up McAlmon's edition. Gertrude wrote to McAlmon on 16 September 1925:

> There is a syndicate which very seriously wants to put all my books on the market, Three Lives, the long book and several later and newer ones. It is for me an important opportunity. Their proposal is to buy the Making of Americans from you that is the 500 copies minus the 40 copies already ordered, for a thousand dollars which really means 1620 dollars a 1000 dollars for 460 books and 40 ordered at 87 dollars and the five bound in vellum at $60. They would pay for the unbound sheets and covers upon delivery that is as soon as they are delivered in France.
>
> Will you wire me your answer within 24 hours. You will realise how much this opportunity means to me.

McAlmon wired his reply on 17 September: 'Book bound offer too low and vague'. The same day he wrote a detailed letter saying he thought it unbusinesslike for the syndicate not to deal direct with him, the offer of $1,000 was too low because the book cost $3,000 to print, and that he did not see why this new scheme would give better publicity or distribution.

The correspondence became acrimonious. Gertrude wrote that it had been his idea to sell the edition, that he was not interested in any of it, that she had done all the publicity and that she wanted her book 'to go big and I want to get my royalties'. McAlmon replied citing all the work and expense he had put into the venture:

> I don't feel like making a gift to any publisher . . . The sudden
> violence of interest combined with an offer that is too low from
> an unknown company, or one that may not yet be organized
> doesn't look propitious for their later disposal of the book.

Nevertheless, Gertrude phoned the printer Darantière and asked him to send the sheets to the shipper. Darantière checked with McAlmon who told him he was not to take any orders except from Contact. And on 8 October, McAlmon wrote a chastising letter to Gertrude:

> Had you wished to give arbitrary orders on the book you could
> have years back had it printed yourself . . . the book is now
> complete, stitched, and will be bound. You will get your ten
> copies which will be sufficient for your friendly gifts, and at least
> more than commercial publishers give authors. Whatever others
> you want you can have at the usual author's rate of 50% on the
> sale price of eight dollars. We will send out review copies to
> some special reviewers if you choose to send us a list of names
> and addresses. Further panic and insistence and 'helping' us will
> not delight me.

Gertrude tartly told him that he forgot from one letter to the next what he had or had not agreed. Alice's view was that he was irresponsibly drunk throughout the whole affair.

By December 1926 only 103 copies had been sold and paid for. Reviews were thin and poor. Marianne Moore in the *Dial* likened it to *Pilgrim's Progress*, but Edmund Wilson in *New Republic* said he could not read it through:

> I do not know whether it is possible to do so . . . With sentences
> so regularly rhythmical, so needlessly prolix, so many times
> repeated and ending so often with present participles, the reader
> is all too soon in a state, not to follow the slow becoming of life,
> but simply to fall asleep.

The *Irish Statesman* said that it must be among the seven longest books in the world, the *Saturday Review of Literature* said, 'Miss Stein has exhibited the most complete befuddlement of the human mind', expressed concern for the mental well-being of the compositors and said they deserved sixteen bucks a day for the rest of their natural lives.

Six months after publication, McAlmon wrote another acrid letter to Gertrude:

> Contrary to your verbal statements that you would help rid us of your volume, you have done nothing. The Dial review I got for you. The Irish Statesman review came from a book sent them at my instructions. Books were sent to people you asked to have them sent to. Ten books were GIVEN you. You *asked* me to take on the book. You knew it was a philanthropic enterprise as the Ms. had been some twenty years on your hands. There is no evidence of any order having come in through your offices except from your immediate family . . .
>
> If you wish the books retained you may bid for them. Otherwise, by Sept - one year after publication - I shall simply get rid myself of them *en masse* by the pulping proposition.

Gertrude did not buy the copies from McAlmon, nor did he go to the expense of having them pulped. The book's reputation grew despite its difficult beginning. It was printed again in 1934 after Gertrude was a success with her *Autobiography of Alice B. Toklas*. But she and McAlmon were never friends again.

*Gertrude with Pépé and Basket in the garden at Bilignin.*

# 11

## COUNTRY LIFE

*'Think of the Bible and Homer think
of Shakespeare and think of me'*

Getting out of Paris, away from the razzmatazz and cultural ambitions of friends and enemies, was important to Gertrude and Alice. Godiva made this possible. In the summer of 1922 they went to try to find in the country the peacefulness they had so loved during the war. They travelled with their friend, Janet Scudder, from Indiana and her friend, Camille Sigard, a singer. They had a new Ford too. Janet Scudder was a sculptor. She made models for garden fountains of little boys blowing conch shells. Gertrude said she had the pioneer's passion for buying useless real estate. In every town they passed through she wanted to buy some uninspired dwelling and Gertrude tried to dissuade her. She was redeemed by her gift for locating good food and wine, though Alice said it was Godiva who led them to their best meals. They had a very good bouillabaisse in Marseilles of sea fish, lobster, crabs, clams, garlic, cloves, saffron and olive oil, with hors-d'oeuvres of baby artichokes, endives, radishes and asparagus tips.

Gertrude and Alice only intended to be away for a month or two, but they stayed all winter. Their friends bought a plain-looking house in Aix-en-Provence, and Gertrude and Alice settled in St Remy. The mistral blew and the hotel and food were mediocre. The only decent thing to eat in the town, said Alice, was the *glacé* fruit, but one could not live on that alone. The speciality was *melon glacé* filled with *glacé* cherries, apricots, plums and pears. They sent one to Hemingway, who said it was as big as a Thanksgiving pumpkin.

Apart from occasional visits to Janet Scudder, they saw no one but the local people all winter. They went to Avignon to shop, but for the most part wandered round St Remy and up into the Alpilles. They watched the huge flocks of sheep going up into the mountains, led by donkeys with water bottles. They called themselves Les Amis du Rhône. Gertrude said the river exercised its spell. They loved it, and the land through which it passed. She said the quietness of the long winter broke the restlessness of the war and early post-war years. She meditated 'upon the use of grammar, poetical forms and what might be termed landscape plays'. She wrote *Valentine to Sherwood Anderson,* a poem *Capital Capitals,* which Virgil Thomson later set to music, and a play *Lend a Hand or Four Religions.* She put more of her thoughts on grammar into her *Elucidation,* in which she tried to give examples of how her mind functioned when she wrote. It was printed in *transition* in 1927. She said, for example, that the words 'Madrigal' and 'Mardigras' were related in her mind, that they both began with the letter 'm', and so both reminded her of 'Em which is a name for Emma'.

Gertrude was prolific and happy that winter, but Alice did not have much to do and the weather made her miserable. One day, as the mistral blew, they were walking through a ploughed field: 'I could not walk on it. Suddenly I found myself crying. Gertrude said What is the matter? The weather I said, can we go back to Paris? She said, Tomorrow'.

The next summer, in 1924, they planned to motor down to visit Picasso in Antibes. They stopped for what they thought would be a night or two in Belley, at Monsieur Pernollet's hotel. It was in Alice's gourmet guide and she planned their route by its recommendations. They liked the area so much – the Rhône valley, the mountains, the wide countryside, the flowers in the gardens and the food, that Alice sent a wire to Picasso, 'Are staying on here at least for present'. Then Gertrude wrote to say they would not be coming to visit him, but would be staying in Belley all summer.

It was Monsieur Pernollet who coined the phrase *'une generation perdue'.* Gertrude repeated it to Hemingway, who used it as the epigraph for his novel *The Sun Also Rises.* Monsieur Pernollet believed that men became civilised between the ages of eighteen and twenty-six. Those who fought in the First World War were denied this opportunity and so were a lost generation. Monsieur Pernollet came from a family of chefs, but Alice said his cooking was not all it was trumped up to be, and that he preferred reading Lamartine in a corner of the kitchen. She and Gertrude used to go to Priay, a village an hour's drive away with 341 inhabitants, where Monsieur and Madame Bourgeois were the best cooks in the whole region. Alice said their kitchen was throughly organised and equipped and nearly noiseless and that Monsieur Bourgeois was a very good judge of wine.

La Baronne Pierlot, who lived in Béon across the valley from Bilignin and had a memory as good as Alice's, let Gertrude write during the day in a seventeenth-century house in the grounds of her estate. Gertrude became very interested in the commonplace there. 'I am trying to be as commonplace as I can be,' she said to Alice. She said she wanted to describe landscape as if anything she saw was a natural phenomenon:

> A natural phenomena is contained in all in six places. In the first
> place, as old and as often, and partly in return. In the second
> place imagine that it is not suitable for them or with the rest. As
> an advantage it is an advantage. The third place makes it nearly
> fairly near and if it has the same if the reliance upon it is the
> same it is nearly as well as decided. The fourth place we do not
> go south any more. In the fifth place we go to Belley an
> attractive place where we hope to be as well situated as ever. The
> sixth place makes it necessary that later there is as favorably a
> decision. Natural phenomena have this use. Let us consider coal
> and wood and candles. Let us consider paper and stones and oil.
> Let us consider chances and distance and origin. Let us consider
> it all at once.

She wrote *Natural Phenomena*, more meditations on grammar and sentences, and a short novel with 307 chapters.

Belley is a small town on a hillside in beautiful countryside, with high mountains, hills, rivers, streams, waterfalls and flowers. Alice said the children were pretty and that people had an air of well-being. The next summer, in 1925, she and Gertrude went back to the same place and corrected the proofs of *The Making of Americans*. 'What a summer it was,' said Alice. As the book goes on the sentences get longer and longer. Sometimes they are pages long and the compositors were French. Gertrude and Alice left the hotel every morning with camp chairs, a packed lunch and the proofs. 'All day we struggled with the errors of French compositors,' said Alice.

They chose lovely spots to do their work, 'but there were always to accompany us those endless pages of printers' errors'. One of their favourite places was a hill from where, in the distance, they could see Mont Blanc. They called the mountain Madame Mont Blanc. Another favourite spot was a crossroads by a small stream, where people met and talked, which Gertrude thought was like the Middle Ages.

They liked the whole area so much that they returned each summer and searched for a house to rent. In Bilignin in 1928 they saw the house of their dreams overlooking the valley. Gertrude told Alice, 'I will drive you up there and you can go and tell them that we will take their house.' Alice said, 'But it may not be for rent.' Gertrude said, 'The curtains are floating out the windows.' 'Well,' said Alice, 'I think that proves someone is living there.'

The house was owned by a local farmer and rented to a French army officer. Gertrude and Alice talked to 'two influential friends in Paris' in the hope of getting the officer promoted and posted overseas. With or without

*Their house at Bilignin.*

their influence, that was what happened and, after months of waiting, they 'were ecstatically tenants of a house which we had never seen nearer than two miles away'. Shortly after the soldier's transfer to Morocco, war broke out and they heard he had been taken prisoner. 'Alice Toklas' conscience troubled her,' said Gertrude. 'Mine did not trouble me but hers troubled her and then later came the news that he was not a prisoner and nothing happened to him.'

They moved in when Gertrude was fifty-five and Alice was fifty-three in Spring 1929. It was to be their summer home for thirteen years. They stayed there for six or seven months each year and went back to Paris for the winter. Before moving in, they bought a new Ford, had electric radiators that smelled installed at the rue de Fleurus and acquired Basket, a white poodle. Alice had wanted a white poodle for years, ever since reading Henry James's novel *The Princess Casamassima*. They bought him at the Paris dog show, at the Porte-de-Versailles, from a woman who had spent a great deal of money at the vet because Basket's mother had had a difficult pregnancy. They called him Basket because Alice said he should carry a basket of flowers in his mouth. He was two months old. People said how sweet he was, that he looked like a sheep, that they had not seen one like him before, that he must have cost a lot of money and did he have to be bathed every day, to which Gertrude replied, 'O no, twice a season.' But there was one dissentient, a man in Paris who threatened to shoot him and said: 'Piss you dog piss against the side of the house piss against the lamp-post a poor street cleaner has to clean the lamp-post that you have pissed against . . . piss dog piss.'

Gertrude and Alice's new summer home was a grand seventeenth-century manor house, the size of a small château. It stood on the only street in Bilignin, a small farming hamlet with a few humble houses and barns set high on a hill. There were often cows by the front door of the house. The walls were thick and the house was quiet. The gardens were on the far side and the furthest edge parapeted down to the lush valley below. From the opposite side of the valley, on a clear day, they could see Mont Blanc.

In front, the house had a high wall with iron gates. There was a courtyard, outbuildings, a fountain, a terrace with twenty-six formal flowerbeds, shaped by boxwood hedges, a plane tree, a garden house with a peaked roof and two vegetable gardens. There was no inside plumbing. They got their water from a pump in the garden.

The gardens were Alice's joy. She worked in them from April to October, and planned them in the winters in Paris. When they arrived there was one large apple tree. Gertrude called it The Nucleus, and around it Alice planted an apple orchard. The French officer had not cared about gardening and

*Basket. Photograph by Man Ray.*

had only planted potatoes. Alice hired seven men from the village to clear the rubbish and weeds. They unearthed a snake's nest and raspberry and strawberry bushes. Alice made a plan for the vegetable plots and paths, bought sacks of seeds of all the vegetables Gertrude cared for, cuttings from the Saturday morning market in Belley, fertiliser, topsoil and 300 feet of hose for watering. (One summer there was a drought and ox carts brought water in barrels from the stream in the valley.)

When Alice closed her eyes at night Gertrude asked her what she could see. 'Weeds,' Alice replied. In the mornings she got up at six, or before, and spent an hour gathering a punnet of wild strawberries for Gertrude's breakfast, 'before the sun kissed them'. And she was ecstatic about her vegetables:

> The first gathering of the garden in May of salads, radishes and herbs made me feel like a mother about her baby. How could anything so beautiful be mine ... And this emotion of wonder filled me for each vegetable as it was gathered every year. There is nothing that is comparable to it, as satisfactory or as thrilling, as gathering the vegetables one has grown.

Their friend, the Baroness Pierlot, had cultivated fifty-seven varieties of vegetables - 'like the Heinz pickles', said Alice, who felt competitive about it. But the more Alice grew the more she cooked, so by the end of the day she was not fit for much else. Gertrude tried to restrain her. 'Fewer vegetables would leave us still with enough variety,' she said.

Alice braised the lettuces, casseroled the artichokes, baked the beetroots, threw away the rhubarb and made some intoxicant out of the blackcurrants. She made strawberry jam and raspberry jelly. In October she harvested, packed and crated the winter vegetables for their return to Paris: turnips, squash, eggplants, tomatoes. Gertrude said the *expressage* would ruin them and it was enough to feed an institution. Alice conceded, 'There was no question that looking at that harvest as an economic question it was disastrous, but from the point of view of the satisfaction which work and aesthetic confer, it was sublime.'

'Most of our men guests', she wrote, 'had their breakfasts served on the terrace. The breakfast trays were my pride.' At the Chambéry market she found some Savoy coloured glass on which she liked serving berries, fruits, salads and vegetables.

Sometimes Gertrude cut the boxwood hedges and sawed wood. But it was Alice who excised the hornets' nests and killed the wasps. Gertrude was bothered by them, nor did she care for centipedes, spiders or bats. They did not worry her out of doors, but in the house she always called for Alice's help. Alice got rid of them with newspapers, a broom and pincers.

In the evenings Alice worked on her embroidery. Gertrude sat in a rocking chair with Basket on her lap. Francis Picabia gave them another dog, a Chihuahua. They called him Byron because of his sexual interest in his mother and sister. Basket was jealous of him and ran out into the night to 'try to escape the jealousy that was gnawing at him'. Gertrude and Alice brought him back and consoled him. When Byron died, he was succeeded by Pépé. He sat on Gertrude's lap too, while she meditated and concentrated on being a genius.

'It takes a lot of time to be a genius, you have to sit around so much doing nothing,' said Gertrude. Bilignin was the ideal spot for both occupations. Her routines there were leisurely: she got up late, had breakfast, read, wrote letters, played with the dog. Eventually she bathed, dressed, had lunch. Books were sent from the American Library in Paris. She particularly liked crime stories and read one a day. Dashiell Hammett was her favourite author. In the heat of the afternoons she walked with Basket - often twelve or sixteen kilometers. She had two favourite routes, up through the vineyards, or down to the river to follow the valley. She carried a cane and strode along swishing at the weeds in the hedgerows. Bravig Imbs said local people touched their caps with respect when Gertrude passed. She talked to everybody she met on her walks - or wherever she was: neighbours, farmers, passers-by, shop people, hotel staff, garage mechanics, policemen. She talked to farmers about crops and livestock, to mothers about the care of their children, to garagemen about gears and gasoline. She liked people and wanted to know everything about them. 'They were grist for her poetry, a relief from the solitudes of a mind essentially introspective,' said Virgil Thomson.

At some point in every day she wrote - usually for about half an hour. 'If you write a half hour a day it makes a lot of writing year by year. To be sure all day and every day you are waiting around to write that half hour a day.' She wrote in the same sort of way - fragmentary perception expressed in her idiosyncratic style, without sustained narrative or coherent paragraphs. Her essential interest was the theoretical foundation of her own style. The circumstantial details of her life crept in: the problems of the lease on the Bilignin house, tearfulness over Etta Cone when Claribel died of pneumonia in 1929, Alice's failure to have a cow, remorse about some argument - 'I have never been so sorry about anything as I was about Friday.'

She had no particular memory for facts or detail. She could not paint or draw, and seldom listened to music, though she liked playing what she called sonatinas on the white keys of the piano. Her memory was for the cadences of speech, impressions of events, the essence of character, the quirks of people's behaviour, the structural oddities of language. She liked the grand philosophical conundrums of time and space and being. Alice was terse, sharp, factual, down-to-earth and with a vivid memory for who did what and when and where. Virgil Thomson said that Gertrude, when recounting a story, would get repetitive and vague as to detail. Alice would say, looking up from her embroidery or knitting:

> 'I'm sorry Lovey; it wasn't like that at all.' 'All right Pussy,' Gertrude would say, 'you tell it.' Every story that ever came into the house eventually got told in Alice's way and this was its definitive version.

Gertrude's writing tantalised. Even at its most peculiar, it seemed to have some elusive implication of meaning. It was as if she was all the time asking the question, what do we mean by what we say and why do we say things in the way we do? The tone was unmistakeably hers. No spoof or parody of her writing quite convinced. She was serenely and maddeningly herself. Hemingway said she disliked the drudgery of revision and the obligation to make her writing intelligible. And she said often enough that she was unconvinced she would find readers, though she wanted them very much, 'no it is this scribbled and dirty and lined paper that is really to be to me always my receiver, - but anyhow reader'.

In 1930 Alice decided to publish Gertrude's work. Pragmatist that she was, she knew this was the only clear chance of it seeing the light of day. Through Ford Madox Ford, Gertrude had met William Aspenwall Bradley, an American writer and editor who had started a literary agency in Paris. He agreed to act as Gertrude's agent and, in 1929, sent her manuscripts to a number of publishers, including Little Brown, Macaulay, Viking and Harper's, but they all returned them. Stinging from that rejection, Alice took over.

For twenty-three years she had daily typed up Gertrude's work. She believed every word bore the hallmark of genius. But she wanted Gertrude to earn money and to be acclaimed. 'All that I knew about what I would have to do was that I would have to get the book printed, and then to get it distributed, that is sold,' she said. She asked Gertrude to invent a name, and Gertrude laughed and said, 'Plain Edition'. To finance the venture, Gertrude sold Picasso's *Woman with a Fan*, painted in 1905 in his Blue Period. The sale upset Alice, who cried when Gertrude told Picasso.

Gertrude was to be Plain Edition's only author. Alice began with Gertrude's novel *Lucy Church Amiably*. The inspiration for this book was the church, at a hamlet near Bilignin called Lucey, which had a bulbous Russian steeple, brought back from the Napoleonic wars, that looked like a hat. Gertrude wrote the book to the sound of streams and waterfalls, with Alice sitting beside her doing her embroidery: 'Select your song she said and it was done and then she said and it was done with a nod and then she bent her head in the direction of the falling water. Amiably.'

Alice paid the *Union Imprimerie* in Paris to print and bind 1,000 copies of the book. Gertrude wanted the book to look like a child's schoolbook. It was bound in blue and on the cover, in black, it read: *Gertrude Stein A Novel of Romantic beauty and nature and which Looks Like an Engraving Lucy Church Amiably*. On the imprint page were the words 'The Plain Edition an edition of first editions of all the work not yet printed of Gertrude Stein.'

It was published on 5 January 1931. Alice sent advanced notices to all American booksellers. She priced it at $3. She asked Bennett Cerf at Random House to distribute it in the States, but he replied that at the price she was paying for the printing, and the price they could ask for it, it was not interesting. Not many booksellers agreed to stock it, but Alice fared well with English bookstores in Paris. Gertrude took to walking round the city and looking for it in shop windows. This gave her 'a childish delight amounting almost to ecstasy'.

Alice was not satisfied with the quality of the binding of *Lucy Church*. The spine broke easily and the covers did not close. She took the next book, *How To Write*, to the Darantière firm in Dijon – the firm that had printed the Contact edition of *The Making of Americans*. Gertrude said *How To Write* was concerned with equilibration:

> that of course means words as well as things and distribution as
> well as between themselves between the words and themselves
> and the things and themselves, a distribution as distribution. This
> makes what follows what follows and now there is every reason
> why there should be an arrangement made. Distribution is
> interesting and equilibration is interesting when a continuous
> present and a beginning again and again and using everything
> and everthing alike and everything naturally simply different has
> been done.

This time she wanted the book to look like an eighteenth-century copy of a novel by Laurence Sterne she had found in London. Alice had *How To Write* bound in dove-grey and 1,000 copies printed. Darantière then broke from the Dijon firm and set up his own printing works in Paris. He printed two more books for Plain Edition: 500 copies each of *Operas and Plays*, Gertrude's theatre pieces, and her portraits of Matisse and Picasso. He printed these in monotype, which was cheaper, bound them in paper, and put them in canary-yellow slip cases.

In the early years of their summers at Bilignin, Gertrude and Alice were hospitable to the young men – writers and painters – who wanted to curry favour with Gertrude and to improve their own work with her help. Gertrude was particularly sympathetic to the struggles of young Americans who wanted to write and needed money. Paul Bowles ran away from his tyrannical father and went to Paris in the early thirties intent on proving himself as a musician and writer. He described staying in Bilignin in the summer of 1931 in his autobiography, *Without Stopping.*

Gertrude and Alice called him Freddy because they thought that suited him better than Paul. He said they made him feel like a sociological exhibit. Gertrude wanted to know every detail of his home life. She called him a 'manufactured savage'. 'If you were typical it would be the end of our civilisation,' she told him.

Each morning the maid, Thérèse, used to lug a two-foot-high pitcher of cold water up to his room. Bowles was supposed to stand in a small metal tub and pour the water over himself. Then she would bring him a canister of hot water for shaving. Mindful of his father, who made him take cold showers every day as a boy, Bowles left the cold water untouched and splashed about with the hot water and a flannel.

After a few days Gertrude questioned him. 'Thérèse says you don't bathe in the morning.' Bowles explained his aversion. 'It's of no interest whether you like it or not. We're not talking about that. All I'm saying is that you've got to use the water Thérèse brings you,' Gertrude said. She then took to standing outside his bedroom door in the morning calling, 'Freddy. Are you taking your bath?' Paul Bowles would make splashing noises and say that, yes, he was. 'I don't hear anything,' she would pursue. 'Well I am,' he would say. She would wait and listen and then say, 'All right. Basket's waiting for you.'

Basket, Bowles said, was cleaned for an hour in sulphur water every morning by Alice. He squealed and whimpered like a baby throughout the process. If Alice was late, he began squealing at the usual time and went on until he got his wash. After that it was Bowles's job to give him his drying off exercises. Bowles had to run round the garden with Basket chasing him. For this he wore a pair of lederhosen which reached to above his knees. Gertrude called them his 'Faunties', her reference to the trousers Little Lord Fauntleroy wore. 'Ah you've got your Faunties. That's right. Get out there and run Basket.' Basket jumped as he ran and scratched the backs of Bowles's legs. Gertrude leaned from her second-storey bathroom window shouting, 'Faster Freddy, faster.' Bowles would call, 'Isn't that enough?' and Gertrude answered, 'No, keep going.' 'There was no way of doubting that she enjoyed my discomfort,' said Bowles. 'But since such behavior seemed to me a sign of the most personal kind of relationship, I was flattered by the degree of her interest.'

*Gertrude looking from the bathroom window, Bilignin, 1930.*

He said that Gertrude liked goading Alice. Knowing that Alice liked her food hot, Gertrude enjoyed dallying in the garden when lunch was ready so as to observe what she considered Alice's obsessive anxiety about getting inside and sitting down before the meal cooled. They bickered at mealtimes. 'But Lovit I didn't say that,' Alice would say. 'Oh yes you did Pussy.' Neither lost their equanimity though Gertrude's face would colour when she was annoyed. Everyone, including Bowles, said that Alice was invariably right over detail, but then Gertrude would smile wryly as if to imply the absurdity of the rightness or wrongness of trivial matters.

One afternoon, Gertrude asked to look at Bowles's poems. She read them carefully, thought, then said:

'Well the only trouble with all this is that it isn't poetry.'
'What is it?' asked Bowles.
'How should I know what it is? You wrote it. You tell me what it is. It's not poetry. Look at this . . . what do you mean *the heated beetle pants*? Beetles don't pant. Basket pants, don't you Basket. But beetles don't. And here you've got purple clouds. It's false.'
'It was written without conscious intervention,' Bowles told her.
'It's not my fault. I didn't know what I was writing.'
'Yes, yes, but you knew *afterwards* what you'd written and you should have known it was false. It was false and you sent it off to *transition*. Yes, I know they published it. Unfortunately. Because it's not poetry.'

Gertrude was at the time correcting the Plain Edition proofs of *Operas and Plays*. She liked nothing better than for Bowles to read aloud passages of her own prose. She would laugh appreciatively and stop him, saying 'That's wonderful! Read that paragraph again, will you Freddy?'

One afternoon Gertrude announced that they were all going to the market in Aix-les-Bains. Alice shuddered and said, 'O Lovit not by the tunnel!'

'Of course we'll take the tunnel,' Gertrude said. 'We're not going all the way around the Dent du Chat.'

Alice explained to Bowles that the tunnel dripped and that she hated it. 'Of course Gertrude loves them. She'll always take a tunnel if she can.'

They took the tunnel. Alice showed her distress and so did Basket. In the market Gertrude spied an enormous grey eel. Alice protested, but Gertrude insisted on buying it and they took it home through the tunnel. It gave off a stench while being cooked and, when ready, its appearance was far from appetising. Bowles said he only wanted vegetables. 'You eat what you're served,' Gertrude told him. 'It's all good food.' She saw that he had an extra large helping.

Aaron Copland arrived to meet up with Bowles. Gertrude freely discussed Bowles with him. Why did he have so many clothes? Had he any talent as a composer? Did he really work at his music? Copland said he could imagine someone who worked harder. 'That's what I thought,' said Gertrude. 'He's started his life of crime too young.'

Copland told her not to pay attention to what Bowles said, only to what he did. 'I know,' said Gertrude. 'He *says* he bathes every morning.' But there was a shrewdness behind Gertrude's provocation. A clear sense of what suited Bowles best. It was on her recommendation that he went to Tangiers. She told him he would like it because the sun shone there every day. Its louche magic suited him entirely. It was where he chose to live and it was the place that inspired his work.

'We are surrounded by homosexuals,' said Gertrude to another of their young men friends, Sammy Steward:

> They do all the good things in the arts and when I ran down the male ones to Hemingway it was because I thought he was a secret one . . . I like all people who produce and Alice does too and what they do in bed is their own business and what we do is not theirs.

Apart from Bowles's experience of the eel, those who visited took great delight in Alice's food. Samuel Steward particularly remembered a lunch of duck pâté, tiny red crayfish, big tomatoes, partridge, small new potatoes in parsley and butter, white wine and wild strawberries.

Bravig Imbs had only one recollection of staying with them, in the summer of 1930, that was unconnected with food. On his last night Gertrude took him to see a corner of landscape near St Germain les Paroisses, where poplars were planted like trees in a painting and there was a ruined tower. It was a moonlit night and they climbed up to the tower. 'See that road,' said Gertrude. 'It dates back to the Crusaders. They had to pass it to cross the Rhône.' The valley was suffused with moonlight and the Rhône was silver and dark. 'We must be getting back to Alice,' said Gertrude. 'If I'm away from her long I get low in my mind.'

For the rest, Bravig Imbs' memories of Bilignin were of little radishes, seasoned tomatoes, tiny *crévettes*, pickled mushrooms, chilled artichoke hearts, rosy salmon trout, chicken roasted to a turn, cool champagne, salad with pungent chives, Bleur de Gex cheese, steak with herb-flecked spicy sauce, fish from the Lac du Bourget, crumbly goats' cheese, miniature plums. For reasons of food, literature, the beauty of their house and the wonderful magic of the Rhône valley, Gertrude and Alice were never short of visitors.

Gertrude was more interested in writers than painters in the late twenties and early thirties. Her impressive picture collection was built by her and Leo's joint collecting impulse. When they separated, their collecting talent ended too. Gertrude wanted, though, to show her independent aesthetic judgement. She encouraged and bought the work of Picabia, Juan Gris, Pavel Tchelitchew and Christian Bérard. But the young man she most encouraged was an Englishman called Francis Rose. She bought 130 of his paintings during his lifetime. Part of the appeal was that his name was Francis: 'anybody called Francis is elegant unbalanced and intelligent and certain to be right not about everything but about themselves.' It was also propitious that his name was Rose, for she had attained some fame with her tautological assertion, 'Rose is a rose is a rose is a rose.' She and Alice first saw his paintings at Jean Bonjean's gallery in Paris in the late twenties. They had visited the gallery because it was near the vet where they took Basket to be clipped and shampooed. Rose's paintings were facing the wall. Gertrude turned them round, and thought she liked them so she bought first one, then two, then three, then lots. She took days telling Alice how to hang them in the rue de Fleurus. When Francis Rose eventually went to see them in 1930 he went 'quite pink with emotion'. There were three rows of them and they were next to Picasso's pictures. Rose wanted to know what Picasso thought of his work. It seems that Picasso had asked Gertrude how much she paid for them and, when told, said, 'You could have got something quite good for that.'

Rose was in his early twenties when Gertrude and Alice met him. He was living in an all-black room in Montmartre and smoking opium which, he claimed, 'clears the mind, gives peace, removes nervousness and indecision, and destroys neurotic complexes and pain'. He was always having dramas with rather brutal men friends. He stayed at Bilignin, painted a picture of the house, and portraits of Gertrude and Alice and was attacked by gnats which died in his paints.

Gertrude and Alice did not have to make any effort to see anyone. People visited them all the time. When friends fell from grace, or offended, they were banished. 'Miss Stein does not wish to see you again.' 'Miss Stein is not at home.' The rejections were cool, deadly and delivered by Alice. Pavel Tchelitchew was given the chop in 1928, partly because of a painting he did of Alice that made her look like a vulture, and partly because he was having torrid affairs with Edith Sitwell and various men. The painter Eugène Berman was banished from Bilignin in 1929. He was supposed to paint portraits of Gertrude and Alice, but Gertrude did not like his sketches for these. She showed him her word portrait of him, called *More Grammar Genia Berman*, and asked him what he thought of it. His English was not very

*Francis Rose*, Homage to Gertrude, 1932.

good, and he replied that he was not in a position to appreciate it. The next morning Gertrude asked him when he was returning to Paris, as she had other guests arriving and would need his room.

From 1930 to 1931, Gertrude and Alice had 'a hectic one might almost say lurid winter' quarrelling with all their young men, who seemed to be aged twenty-six. 'How did you quarrel with so many all at once?!!!' Carl Van Vechten asked. The first to go was the poet Georges Hugnet. In 1929 he had translated sections of *The Making of Americans* into French. Out of reciprocity, Gertrude offered to do a translation into English of a poem of his, a kind of childhood autobiography called *Enfances*. When he saw her translation, Hugnet said it bore no relation to anything he had written. And he was unimpressed with Gertrude's proposed title for it: *Poem Pritten on the Pfances of Georges Hugnet*. She also wanted her name printed first. He wanted his first and larger, and a cool silence followed. Virgil Thomson tried to intercede. He suggested the title should read

GERTRUDE STEIN 1928
ENFANCES
GEORGES HUGNET 1927

The two poems appeared on opposite pages of the magazine *Pagany*. Hugnet wrote to Virgil Thomson, 'I have friends that are too strong for me'. When Gertrude's version was published in book form, she called it *Before the Flowers of Friendship Faded Friendship Faded*. This title was Alice's idea. She said she had overheard a woman saying it in French in a restaurant.

Then Virgil Thomson was dismissed (though his banishment proved temporary) for his part as failed mediator in Gertrude's translation of Hugnet's poem. Thomson sent Gertrude and Alice an invitation to one of his concerts, which included several pieces written to Gertrude's texts. Gertrude replied on one of her cards engraved 'Miss Stein', under which she wrote 'declines further acquaintance with Mr Thomson'. Alice had anyway never particularly liked him. She thought him frivolous and 'darted little poisoned arrows whenever she could', said Bravig Imbs.

Bravig Imbs wrote about his own banishment. One evening in January 1931, when visiting the rue de Fleurus with his pregnant wife, Valeska, he told Gertrude and Alice that Valeska would be spending the summer quite near Belley, where she had stayed before, and that he would be joining her later when his vacation was due. The next morning he got a phone call from Alice:

Miss Gertrude Stein has asked me to inform you that she thinks your plan of sending Valeska to Belley, considering Valeska's condition, a colossal impertinence and that neither she nor I ever wish to see either you or Valeska again.

Miss Gertrude Stein was polite enough to restrain herself last evening owing to the presence of Valeska, but she thinks your announcement of sending Valeska to Belley without any other friend in the region than ourselves was the coolest piece of cheek she has ever encountered. Your pretension is unpardonable. You must not come to the house or write, for neither visit nor letter will be accepted. We want never to see you again.

And the phone was banged down.

Alice had had enough of all the young men. They ate her food, created work for her, distracted Gertrude from writing. She said that Gertrude was always finding excuses for not working. First it was because Picasso was there, then she hated starting on Mondays, then Carl Van Vechten arrived unexpectedly, then Henry McBride came.

The little court dispersed. The devoted admirers became exiles. Friends of the exiles stayed away out of sympathy. Braving Imbs regretted the parting:

No more hours of gossip, no more recriminating against a common fate with publishers, no more dropping in after dinner, no more little cakes, no more exciting painter discoveries to discuss, no more manuscripts to criticize, no more voyages in the country . . .

I missed Gertrude and Alice very much for a year. Even now, sometimes, I still regret the little cakes.

As for Gertrude and Alice, 'we have been having a nice peaceable time having really quarrelled for keeps with all our young friends,' Gertrude wrote to Carl Van Vechten in January 1931.

That same year Edmund Wilson published *Axel's Castle*. In it, he talked about Gertrude in the same company as Proust, Joyce, Yeats and Eliot. He said that although she wrote nonsense:

One should not talk about 'nonsense' until one has decided what sense consists of . . . Most of us balk at her soporific rigmaroles, her echolaic incantations, her half-witted sounding catalogues of numbers. Most of us read her less and less. Yet remembering especially her early work, we are still always aware of her presence in the background of contemporary literature . . . And whenever we pick up her writings, however unintelligible we may find them, we are aware of a literary personality of unmistakeable originality and distinction.

Gertrude was fifty-seven. She was respected, sought after, quoted, interviewed and lampooned. But, except for contributions to the short-lived, scarcely read literary magazines, she was seldom published. Henry McBride said to her, 'There is a public for you but no publisher.' Juan Gris had died without having achieved the success she felt he deserved. Mildred Aldrich had died with only one flurry of acclaim. In 1929, Claribel Cone had died of pneumonia in Lausanne. Time was running out. Everyone knew of Gertrude, but only a few loyal followers publicised her as the genius she felt herself to be. And though Alice did not swerve from doing all she could to promote Gertrude, she let it be known that she would like her to be rich and successful in a popular way. Picasso and Matisse were rich and famous. Many of the young men whose careers Gertrude had encouraged were doing far better than she was. Fitzgerald and Hemingway had their reputations. Alice believed that if Gertrude wrote a memoir it would almost certainly be a success. Gertrude did not want to write one. 'It does not bother me to delight them,' she said. It was not the prospect of embarrassing others by her revelations that bothered her, but the sense of compromising her own talent. 'Remarks are not literature,' she had said to Hemingway.

Gertrude told Alice that she should write her memoirs. She told her to call them *My Life With The Great*, or *Wives of Geniuses I Have Sat With* or *My Twenty Five Years With Gertrude Stein*. Alice said:

> I am a pretty good housekeeper and a pretty good gardener and a pretty good needlewoman and a pretty good secretary and a pretty good editor and a pretty good vet for dogs and I have to do them all at once and I find it difficult to add being a pretty good author.

There was nothing for it but for Gertrude to do the writing and to make them rich and famous in a popular way.

*At the Palais Idéal at Hautrives, Provence, in 1939.*
*Photograph by Cecil Beaton.*

# 12

## THE AUTOBIOGRAPHY OF ALICE B. TOKLAS

*'She will be me when this you see'*

If there had not been a beautiful and unusually dry October at Bilignin in France in nineteen thirty two followed by an unusually dry and beautiful first two weeks of November would The Autobiography of Alice B. Toklas have been written. Possibly but probably not then.

In autumn 1932, hot weather led Gertrude and Alice to break their usual routine and stay on in Bilignin, instead of returning to Paris. Gertrude said she wrote her bestselling book in six weeks. Friends had often suggested to her that she should write her memoirs. Alice, quite simply, wanted her to write something that made money. She did not like selling their paintings to pay for private publishing. Shove is proof of love, said Gertrude, and reluctantly agreed to go commercial.

The book was written at a time when Gertrude had reason to fear Alice's moods. One evening in April 1932, Gertrude had shown her agent, William Bradley, and the writer, Louis Bromfield, the manuscript of her first novel about her affair with May Bookstaver. Alice read the manuscript too. She had not known of its existence. Gertrude told her she had forgotten about it. Nor had Gertrude ever confided to Alice her feelings about May Bookstaver. Alice became tormented with jealousy. She destroyed all May Bookstaver's letters to Gertrude, and the manuscript was put back in the cupboard.

On the first page of the first exercise book of the manuscript of the autobiography Gertrude wrote, 'Twenty five years [thirty years crossed out] with Gertrude Stein. Autobiography by Alice Babette Toklas.' On the opposite page she wrote, 'If you love a woman you give her money if you need to have a woman you have to wait until you have money to give her.'

It is difficult to imagine that the Gertrude who wrote the *Autobiography* had previously written prose of such convoluted strangeness, that few people knew what she was talking about. In the *Autobiography* Gertrude took Alice's voice, her acerbic, lucid style, her declarative sentences, malicious asides, quirky jokes and regular punctuation. Written in the first person, it sounded so like Alice that friends could hear her and thought she must have played a role in the book's creation - a suggestion Alice denied. Her role was, she led all to believe, that of amanuensis, editor, inspiration and guide.

It was easy for Gertrude to adopt Alice's voice. Alice's remarks, reactions and opinions had entered often enough into her writing. Alice was her pragmatic *alter ego*, cutting through her solipsistic flights, the foundation of her life. All their daily rituals came from her. Gertrude acknowledged the debt. Alice was always 'forethoughtful', which was very nice for Gertrude. Alice freed Gertrude to dwell on a 'higher' plane. The way for Gertrude to anchor her writing to daily experience was through her. And the *alter ego* device gave Gertrude a malicious opportunity. It could be Alice who made the snide remarks and had the equivocal opinions, who called Hemingway 'yellow' and said that Madame Matisse had a mouth like a horse.

None the less, in an early notebook, Gertrude let Alice's self-possessed voice slip and say things in the Gertrude style: 'I was charming I was delicate I was delicious', or 'the result I have had that I have what I have and I always have as I always will had to have that which I have'. All such Gertrudisms were ironed out of the final manuscript.

The book is a light-hearted mixture of facts, opinions and anecdotes. Gertrude said she wanted to write it 'as simply as Defoe did the autobiography of Robinson Crusoe'. The opening section, 'Before I came to Paris', establishes Alice's character, a 'gently bred' young woman of intelligence, poise and wit who had, as a girl, 'some intellectual adventures . . . but very quiet ones'. She was a moderately contented housekeeper for her father and brother. Life 'was reasonably full and I enjoyed it but I was not very ardent in it'.

Then came the San Francisco earthquake, an apocalyptic event equalled only by its consequences: Alice travels to Paris and meets Gertrude Stein! Gertrude is at the centre of 'the heroic age of cubism'. She shows Alice the world of modern art. She takes her to the important art shows, introduces her to everyone of consequence in Paris and allows her to serve The Person at the vanguard of modern taste, modern literature and American cultural identity.

The book quickly moves away from Alice to the main subject of concern - Gertrude. 'In english literature in her time she is the only one. She has always known it and now she says it.' None of the oddness, obliquity or self-doubt that creeps into Gertrude's more hermetic work is present here. She is good-humoured, unpretentious, well-educated, widely travelled, commonsensical and deserving of popular acclaim:

> It has always been rather ridiculous that she who is good friends
> with all the world and can know them and they can know her,
> has always been the admired of the precious.

There is only one language for her and that is English. She does not like
the theatre, she cannot draw and 'Gertrude Stein never had subconscious
reactions'. She artfully distances herself from any suspicions that she might
belong on the margins of literature. She is disarmingly straightforward and
cheerful. An ordinary, middle-class, American lady, educated in Massachusetts
and Maryland, who just happens to be a genius.

Alice is depicted as quiet and compliant, wryly humorous but with no
ambition of her own beyond serving Gertrude. She is the acolyte and cook
and Gertrude is the god. There is no hint of her ambition, temper, sexuality
or coolness.

The *Autobiography*, with Gertrude and Alice at its centre, chronicles a
quarter of a century of Paris life. Picasso, Matisse, Apollinaire, Hemingway,
Scott Fitzgerald - those who became famous are there, but so is the cook
Hélène, Mildred Aldrich, Mabel Dodge, Basket the dog and Auntie the car.
It covers the revolutionary exhibitions of the Fauves and the cubists, the
lively struggle of the little magazines in the twenties, the aspirations of the
expatriate writers after the 1914-18 war. And because, six years after its
publication, Europe was to be wrecked by a war that ended a civilisation,
it came to be seen as an exemplar, a model of its kind.

While she was writing it, Gertrude kept asking Alice if she thought it
would be a bestseller. Alice said she did not think so because it was not
sentimental enough. Nor did Gertrude particularly enjoy working on it.
It was her money-making style and it felt false to her: 'for the first time
in writing I felt something outside me while I was writing, hitherto I had
always had nothing but what was inside me while I was writing.' At night,
to escape from the sense of compromise writing the *Autobiography* gave
her, Gertrude turned to her *Stanzas in Meditation*. In them she wrestled with
the problems of popular writing:

> Believe me it is not for pleasure that I do it.
> Not only for pleasure for pleasure in it that I do it.
> I feel the necessity to do it
> Partly from need
> Partly from pride
> And partly from ambition.

Obliquely she voiced her worry at her merged identity with Alice. Even if Alice was not the literal author, it was her memories and tone of voice not Gertrude's. It gave Gertrude a strange sense of lost identity or multiple personality. 'They are not a simple people They the two of them,' she wrote.

As soon as the *Autobiography* was finished, Gertrude told her Paris agent, William Bradley, that what she had written would 'very likely be commercially successful'. He was immediately enthusiastic. He wrote to her on 13 November 1932:

> Dear Miss Stein
> Of course I shall be *delighted* to see Miss Toklas' Autobiography and hope you will send it to me as soon as it is completely typed. Or, better still, you might send it in two instalments so that I can get on with the reading, as fast as possible . . .

Alice sent the manuscript and Bradley replied at once:

> Dear Miss Stein
> The second part of the ms. has just arrived, and wild horses couldn't keep me from reading it at once!
> I am now looking forward to seeing you both as soon as you return to Paris, next week.

He had no difficulty in selling it to the American publisher, Harcourt Brace. Before the book was brought out, *Atlantic Monthly* serialised it. Gertrude had always wanted her work to appear in that magazine. The editor, Ellery Sedgwick, had turned her down umpteen times. In his previous reject letter he told her:

> We live in different worlds. Yours may hold the good, the beautiful and the true, but if it does their guise is not for us to recognize. Those vedettes who lead the vanguard of picture arts are understood, or partly understood, over here by a reasonably compact following, but that following cannot translate their loyalties into a corresponding literature, and it would really be hopeless for us to set up this new standard.
> I am sorry.

But when he read the *Autobiography* he was positive, if no less condescending. 'What a delightful book it is,' he wrote on 11 February 1933:

> and how glad I am to publish four installments of it! During our long correspondence I think you felt my constant hope that the time would come when the real Miss Stein would pierce the smoke screen with which she has always so mischievously

surrounded herself. The autobiography has just enough of the oblique to give it individuality and character, and readers who care for the things you do will love it . . .

Anything that we can do to help the success of the book, as well as the serial, will certainly be done.

Hail Gertrude Stein about to arrive!

Believe me

Ellery Sedgwick.

The magazine's assistant editor, Edward Aswell, was more fulsome in his praise. The agreement was that the serialisation, in four instalments, could use no more than sixty per cent of the book. He had the job of deciding what to leave out. 'I can tell you that it was no easy thing to decide,' he told Gertrude:

Your autobiography met with such an unusual reception in our office that I think I ought to tell you about it. Mr Bradley addressed the manuscript to me, and sent with it a mysterious letter in which he refused to divulge the identity of the author other than to say that she was a well-known American writer living in Paris. I opened the package about ten o'clock of a very dull morning, rather annoyed by what I took to be a trick of Mr Bradley's to pique my curiosity, and vastly bored by the prospect of having to wade through so many reams of anonymous wood-pulp . . .

In this state of mind I settled down to *Toklas*. I read the first page and right there you had me. I was instantly fascinated and went on reading, turning page after page automatically, not knowing that I turned them, so completely absorbed had I become in your story. At last I was recalled to awareness of the here and now by an increasing darkness in the room. There was hardly light enough for me to see the page before me. I thought a storm had come up and glanced out of the window. There were no clouds, but the sky looked queer. I pulled out my watch. It was after five o'clock and the sun was setting! I could not believe it, but it was so. I had forgotten time, forgotten my lunch, forgotten a dozen things I had meant to do that day, so entirely had I been caught by the spell of your words. I rushed at once to Mr Sedgwick and told him about it. 'Such a thing never happened before in this office,' he exclaimed, and he was right – it never had.

So we accepted the manuscript, and now it is about to be

published. If you could do this to an editor, of all people the least susceptible to the magic of print, what, I wonder, will be the effect of your story on the general public?
Sincerely yours
Edward C. Aswell.

The general public bought the book. The first printing, of 5,400 copies, was sold out by 22 August 1933, nine days before publication. There were four reprints in the next two years. The Literary Guild sold it as a bookclub choice. Gertrude asked her agent to give the English edition to John Lane at the Bodley Head,

> for sentimental reasons, after all John Lane was the only real publisher who had really ever thought of publishing a book for me, and you have to be loyal to every one if you do not quarrel with anyone.

Bernard Faÿ translated the French edition, which was published by Gallimard in 1934, and Cesare Pavese translated the Italian edition in 1938.

Gertrude's friends were so pleased for her. Thrilled. 'It is your year,' wrote Carl Van Vechten. He thought the book divine and said that he was showering copies on happy friends. 'You are a woojums,' he wrote on 1 May 1933, 'and Alice is a woojums and I foresee now that you *must*, soon or late, come to America and then I will photograph you'. Tillie Brown, who had been at school with Gertrude and still lived in Oakland, renewed contact by writing and reminding Gertrude of how rude she had been about Tillie's childhood efforts at authorship - a sermon called *Lighten the Ship*. Miss Mars and Miss Squire wrote from their villa in Venice, where they lived with their Siamese cats, Wow and Min, and their three canaries. They said it was just like reliving those evenings at the rue de Fleurus. But Henry McBride did not want her to be successful. He wrote to her in October 1933: 'I don't like giving you up to the general public and sharing you and Alice with about a million others.' He thought success ruined people. Mildred Aldrich had said of him that he had 'a congenital contempt for successful people'.

For the first time, Gertrude received good and enthusiastic reviews. Edmund Wilson, in a review in the *New Republic*, praised the book's 'wisdom, its distinction and its charm', and said that it showed her influence at the source of literature and art. William Troy wrote in the *Nation* that 'among books of literary reminiscences Miss Stein's is one of the richest, wittiest and most irreverent ever written'. Cyril Connolly called it 'a model of its kind', and said that it stood up to any amount of rereading. And Janet Flanner called it

a complete memoir of that exciting period when Cubism was
being invented in paint and a new manner of writing being
patented in words, an epoch when not everyone had too much to
eat but everyone had lots to say, when everything we now
breathe was already in the air and only a few had the nose for
news to smell it - and with most of the odors of discovery right
under the Toklas–Stein roof.

She said the book was simply written 'in Miss St– that is to say, Miss Toklas's
first, or easiest, literary manner'.

Gertrude offended some of her erstwhile friends by what she had written.
Hemingway seethed with anger and called it a 'damned pitiful book'. Gertrude
had written that she and Sherwood Anderson virtually created Hemingway
and 'they were both a little proud and a little ashamed of the work of their
minds'. She said that he had learned the art of writing from proof-reading
her book *The Making of Americans* and, worst of all, she said that he was yellow.

Hemingway told his friends that Gertrude was menopausal and that all
her former talent had degenerated to 'malice and self-praise . . . *Homme
des lettres*, woman of letters, salon woman. What a lousy stinking life.' He
said she and her feathered friends had decided nobody was any good creatively
unless they were queer, that she thought that all queer people were talented
and that anyone who was any good must be queer. He threatened that one
day he would come out with some memoirs of his own - which he did,
with *A Moveable Feast*. But they were not published until 1964, by which
time both of them were dead. In a veiled way he called Gertrude egomaniacal
and sado-masochistic. When he heard her voice on the radio, in 1934, he
said it was like a distant echo from the tomb of a dead friendship.

The book caused enough offence for the magazine *transition* to publish
a supplement, in February 1935, called 'Testimony Against Gertrude Stein'.
This was a diatribe, with articles by its editors Eugene and Maria Jolas (both
of whom Gertrude disliked because she said they did not pay their
contributors) and, among others, Georges Braque and Henri Matisse. In
a foreword, Eugene Jolas wrote that Gertrude had no real understanding
of what was happening around her, that she was never ideologically intimate
with such movements as Fauvism, Cubism, Dadaism, Surrealism et cetera,
and that

*The Autobiography of Alice B. Toklas* in its hollow, tinsel
bohemianism and egocentric deformations, may very well become
one day the symbol of the decadence that hovers over
contemporary literature.

Matisse was offended by Gertrude's description of his wife. Gertrude wrote she 'was a very straight dark woman with a long face and a firm large loosely hung mouth like a horse'. In his no less equine testimony, Matisse said that his wife 'was a very lovely Toulousaine, erect, with a good carriage and the possessor of beautiful dark hair that grew charmingly, especially at the nape of her neck'. He said that Sarah was the only one of the Steins who understood his work.

Braque, in his testimony, said that Gertrude did not understand her contemporaries, that she never knew French really well, that she entirely misunderstood cubism because she saw it simply in terms of personalities, and that he had felt very uncomfortable when he met Gertrude and Alice during the war at Avignon, and they were wearing boy-scout uniforms, green veils and colonial helmets.

As for Leo, he was beside himself with scorn. 'God what a liar she is!' he wrote to Mabel Weeks:

> If I were not something of a psychopathologist I should be very
> much mystified. Some of her chronology is too wonderful . . .
> Practically everything that she says of our activities before 1911 is
> false both in fact and implication but one of her radical
> complexes, of which I believe you knew something, made it
> necessary practically to eliminate me.

He described her book as 'a case of Adler's deficiency and compensation'. He said, 'It's the first time I ever read an autobiography of which I knew the authentic facts, and to me it seems sheerly incredible.' He called it a farrago of rather clever anecdote, stupid brag and general bosh:

> She tells how we used to buy pictures in pairs so as to satisfy
> both our tastes, which never happened on a single occasion.
> Until Gertrude bought a cubist Picasso, she was never responsible
> for a single picture that was bought, and always said so. She was
> proud of her slow reaction time, and always said she couldn't tell
> whether she liked a picture or not until she had lived with it.

Probably his critical acumen in choosing pictures was sharper than Gertrude's. None the less, they had bought them together and their enthusiasm for collecting ended with the relationship.

He doubted whether there was a single comment or observation in the book that was not stupid. 'I suppose it is a great pleasure, provided one is financially independent, to have so good an opinion of oneself as Gertrude has.' He said it was not surprising that her persistence and social enthusiasm should have got her somewhere, in the trashy values of the day: 'But imagine the stupidity of anyone sixty years of age who makes that remark about learning the qualities of sentences and paragraphs from the rhythm of her dog's drinking.' For Leo, the *Autobiography* showed that Gertrude had become totally unreal, 'and in fact to me she is so far unreal that she doesn't exist as a real person at all'.

Gertrude and Alice loved the money that came with success. 'There is no doubt about it there is no pleasure like it, the sudden splendid spending of money and we spent it.' They had always lived more than comfortably, but simply. Their incomes were not high enough to be taxed. Most of their money went on food, which in France was plentiful and cheap. They ran a car, but as cheaply as possible. In the first year after publication Gertrude received $4,500 from Harcourt Brace, $1,000 from the *Atlantic Monthly* and $3,000 from the Literary Guild.

They had running water piped in at Bilignin and a bathroom and lavatory installed. They got an electric cooker, instead of cooking by coal-fired stove, and in Paris employed two servants instead of one, an Italian couple called Mario and Pia, who began by painting the studio. Gertrude had a telephone put in at Bilignin as well as the one at the rue de Fleurus. 'Now that I was going to be an author whose agent could place something I had of course to have a telephone.' They bought a new eight-cylinder Ford and, for Basket, they bought two collars with studs, and a new coat, fitted by Hermes, the man who made coats for race horses.

The success of the book brought a flurry of social activities. They were invited out all the time. 'Everyone invited me to meet someone and I went,' said Gertrude.

> I always will go anywhere once and I rather liked doing what I had never done before, going visiting and meeting the people who make it pleasant to you to be a lion . . .
> We do not yet use a tiny engagement book and look at it in a nearsighted way the way all the young men used to do as soon as they were successful but we might have.

Though Gertrude liked the money and the good reviews, it bothered her that people were more interested in her personality than her work. Her reasoning was that it was her work that had made them interested in her personality in the first place. She told Bradley to arrange for the publication of her other manuscripts and, soon after the *Autobiography*, Bennett Cerf published in his Modern Library Editions her early works, *Three Lives* and *The Making of Americans*, and a collection of old and new pieces which Gertrude called *Portraits and Prayers*.

Bradley wanted her to go on a lecture tour of America to promote sales of the book. And her American friends wanted her over there too. Gertude did not care that much for lecturing, nor for too much moving around. Bradley brought an agent from an American lecture bureau round to the rue de Fleurus. The agent was a solemn man who published religious books and school textbooks. When Bradley told him Gertrude would be a popular lecturer because of her book he said, 'Interesting if true'.

> And then he said what would I want if I went over. Well I said of course Miss Toklas would have to go over and the two dogs. Oh he said. Yes I said but I said I do not think that any of us will really go over. Oh he said. I decided that if lecture agents were like that that certainly I would not go over and so I told him not to bother.

Gertrude was equivocal about her success. She found it very pleasant to be a lion, but success blocked her ability to write and affected her sense of identity:

> I have always quarreled with a great many young men and one of the principle things that I have quarreled with them about was that once they had made a success they became sterile, they could not go on. And I blamed them. I said it was their fault. I said success is all right but if there is anything in you it ought not to cut off the flow not if there is anything in you. Now I know better. It does cut off your flow and then if you are not too young and you are frightened enough you can begin again . . .
>   What happened to me is this. When the success began and it was a success I got lost completely lost. You know the nursery rhyme, I am I because my little dog knows me. Well you see I did not know myself, I lost my personality. It has always been completely included in myself my personality as any personality naturally is, and here all of a sudden, I was not just I because so many people did know me. It was just the opposite of I am I because my little dog knows me. So many people knowing me I was I no longer and for the first time since I had begun to write I could not write and what was also worse I began to think about how my writing would sound to others, how could I make them understand, I who had always lived within myself and my writing . . . Here all of a sudden I was not just I because so many people did know me.

And they knew her for her merged personality with Alice. As Janet Flanner put it, 'any autobiography of the one must necessarily be a biography of, if not even by, the other'.

The summer of 1933 was strange and dislocated with Gertrude unable to write, disturbed about her identity and having banished many of her friends. Worrying things happened. Gertrude and Alice took their Italian servants, Mario and Pia, from Paris to Bilignin. They arrived in torrential rain and Mario and Pia left immediately, saying the place was too big and that they had been deceived. Gertrude and Alice then went to Lyon and hired a Polish woman and her Czechoslovak husband. The woman was mournful, but turned out to be a very good cook. Her husband was reputed to be a good mechanic. He wanted to do the driving but Gertrude liked to drive her own car.

In July, Janet Scudder said she and her friend Camille Sigard were coming from Paris to stay for a few days. They arrived late, having driven down in one day, and their car needed fixing. The Polish woman was not happy about having to provide a late supper and her husband was not happy about being asked to fix the car so he sabotaged it.

The next day Gertrude had invited two local women for lunch, Madame Caesar and her English friend. Madame Caesar always wore a sort of carpenter's outfit. Her friend always wore trousers, too, and a Basque cap. They raised chickens and ducks in electric incubators. Madame Caesar liked all manner of electrical installations: heaters, stoves and refrigerators, which were rather advanced for that time.

Janet Scudder wanted to drive somewhere and paint, but her car would not even start. Gertrude said she would get Monsieur Humbert, the mechanic from Belley, but the phone would not work, her own car would not start and the servants were behaving in a peculiar manner. Gertrude phoned Monsieur Humbert from the village. When he arrived he found water in the petrol tank in Janet Scudder's car, and a broken spark plug and a rag in the distributor in Gertrude's car. In the middle of all the rumpus, and while the servants were being told to go, Francis Rose arrived with a Californian boyfriend called Carley Mills. Gertrude had quarrelled with both of them, so she did not invite them into the house.

Soon after, there was a scandal with Madame Caesar. Her friend went on holiday to England for a month. While she was away, Madame Steiner, a former friend of Madame Caesar's, moved in with her. The English woman, the day after she came back from holiday, was found dead in a ravine, with two bullets in her head and her Basque hat on a rock beside her. The verdict was suicide, but there was much speculation as to whether she could have shot herself twice. Madame Caesar inherited all the English woman's money and so became very rich. The wife of the electrician moved in with her and Madame Steiner never visited again.

That same summer, Madame Pernollet fell to her death from a window of her hotel on to the cement courtyard. She and her husband owned the hotel in Belley where Gertrude and Alice stayed before they found their home. She was said to have been sleepwalking, but some people wondered if she had killed herself, or even been murdered. Her body was quickly removed from the hotel so as not to disturb the guests.

Gertrude tried, but failed, to write about the strange events of the summer in a book called *Blood On The Dining Room Floor*. 'It was very bothersome. I thought I would try but to try is to die and so I did not really try. I was not doing any writing.'

Her agent, William Bradley, came to stay:

> After a little while I asked him to go away, not because he was
> not a pleasant guest because he was but I do not like any one to
> stay, not because they are in the way but because after a time
> they are part of the way we live every day or they are not and I
> prefer them to be not.

She quarrelled with him because he wanted her to sign up for another autobiography and to go to America to lecture. She stopped meeting him, so they argued over the telephone and in letters instead. She said she did not want to go to America. He said to her surely she wanted to get rich: 'Certainly I said I do want to get rich but I never want to do what there is to get rich . . . There are some things a girl cannot do.'

Then, that winter, her opera with music by Virgil Thomson, *Four Saints in Three Acts*, was put on in New York with its words about pigeons on the grass alas and 'Let Lucy Lily Lily Lucy Lucy let Lucy Lucy Lily Lily Lily Lily Lily let Lily Lucy Lucy let Lily. Let Lucy Lily.' Carl Van Vechten wrote that it was a knockout and a wow, and that it upset New York as nothing else had that winter.

Everybody connected with the production caught some inspiration from it. Frederick Ashton was flown in from London as the choreographer, and the dancing was like a baroque dream. Florine Stettheimer designed the sets and costumes. She was a painter who held a salon in New York. Marcel Duchamp and Carl Van Vechten were two of her salon guests. She used cellophane extensively in the show. There was an extravagant sky, made of a blue cellophane cyclorama, with sunbursts shining through, and palm trees with foliage made of pink taffeta. There were other trees made out of feathers, a sea wall at Barcelona built of shells, and costumes of black chiffon with bunches of black ostrich plumes. St Theresa went on a picnic, in the second act, in a cart drawn by a real white donkey and took a tent with her, made of white gauze with a gold fringe. The use of cellophane contravened the fire regulations and a consequent ruling forbade its further use on a New York stage. On the afternoon of the opening the Fire Department insisted that the cellophane be sprayed with waterglass, which made it wilt, and Florine Stettheimer had to iron it out after they had left. Eventually the donkey was dropped, because it was unpredictable and contravened safety regulations.

John Houseman was the producer. At that time he was an unsuccessful playwright but later, with Orson Welles, he ran the Mercury Theatre. The conductor was Alexander Smallens. The Friends and Enemies of Modern Music gave $10,000 of financial backing to the production. The commercial management did not cope and, at first, nobody got paid. Gala night was 8 February 1934 at the new auditorium of the Wadsworth Atheneum in Hartford.

The gala audience wore evening clothes and tiaras. The streets were icy and there was a taxi strike but that did not keep people away. They arrived in Rolls Royces and private planes. Buckminster Fuller arrived in a bubble-shaped Dymaxion car with Clare Boothe and Dorothy Hale. The New Haven Railroad ran special 'parlor cars' to ferry people to the theatre. When the show moved to the Forty-Fourth Street Theatre, New York, on 21 February, Carl Van Vechten said all New York was agog, and that it was everything Gertrude could ever imagine. 'O I do wish you might have seen this,' he wrote to her. Her name was in electric lights over the theatre. Cecil Beaton was in tears and Jo Davidson said it was the best thing he had ever seen in New York. George Gershwin was there, and Toscanini sat in one of the orchestra chairs and applauded loudly. Paul Bowles heard people talking doubtfully about whether it would be worth even trying to get tickets.

The popularity of the *Autobiography* stirred up interest in the opera. So, too, did Virgil Thomson's decision, after discussion with Carl Van Vechten, to use an all-black cast. Gertrude thought this might be inappropriate to the spirit of her opera, particularly when they did a maypole dance in the second act in transparent costumes. Thomson assured her that it would all be proper and that, if not, petticoats would be ordered immediately.

The show began with a roll of drums and the red velvet curtain opening on Saint Thérèse the First, clad in purple, played by Beatrice Robinson-Wayne, backed by a chorus of angels and saints. The blue cellophane cyclorama dazzled with white lights. From the moment the chorus started with Gertrude's immortal words:

To know to know to love her so.
Four saints prepare for saints.
It makes it well fish.
Four saints it makes it well fish,

*Gertrude's opera,* Four Saints in Three Acts, *New York,* 1934.

the show was a huge success. The favourite part of the libretto was the second of the three scene twos, which came before three of the scene ones, of the first of the two Act threes:

Pigeons on the grass alas.
Pigeons on the grass alas.
Short longer grass short longer longer shorter yellow grass
Pigeons large pigeons on the shorter longer yellow grass alas
pigeons on the grass.
If they were not pigeons what were they.
If they were not pigeons on the grass alas what were they.

There were quite a lot of unrestrained giggles, as at the beginning of one of the Act threes:

Did he did we did we and did he did he did he did did he did
did did he did did he did be categorically and did he did he did
he did he did he did he in interruption interruption interruptedly
leave letting let it be be all to me out and outer and this and
this with in indeed deed and drawn and drawn work.

'A spirit of inspired madness animates the whole piece', wrote the New York Times. The New Republic called it the most important event of the theatre season, and the first pure, free theatre, but Lawrence Gould, a consultant psychiatrist, said, in the New York Evening Post, that Gertrude's passage about Saint Thérèse in a storm at Avila, suggested a form of psychosis known as Echolalia, in which the patient repeats 'ad libitum, with slight variations, a word or phrase that frequently is meaningless except to the trained psychoanalyst.' Carl Van Vechten told Gertrude she was on every tongue, like Greta Garbo. He sent Gertrude and Alice pictures of Gertrude's name in lights and they looked at them all day. The gentlemen's outfitters, Gimbels, put a big sign in their window, 'Four Suits in Two Acts', and Van Vechten sent a picture of that, too.

Gradually, Gertrude and Alice came round to the idea of visiting the States. By July 1934 Gertrude was writing to Carl Van Vechten: 'I am slowly but steadily getting pleased about getting over there and so is Alice, we begin to talk about it quite now as if we were going and even beginning to feel confident about it.' They stopped worrying, and just accepted they were going. As Gertrude put it, 'Worrying is an occupation part of the time but it can not be an occupation all the time.' Alice had been away from America for twenty-seven years and Gertrude for thirty. 'Thirty years are not so much but after all they are thirty years.' Alice was fifty-seven and Gertrude was sixty years old.

Gertrude wrote six lectures to give over there: 'What is English Literature', 'Pictures', 'Plays', 'The Gradual Making of the Making of Americans', 'Portraits and Repetition' and 'Poetry and Grammar'. Bernard Faÿ came to stay for ten days and she read the lectures aloud to him, and when he left it was all more or less decided.

On Faÿ's recommendation and that of the Kiddie, W. G. Rogers, they hired Marvin Chauncey Ross of the Walters Art Gallery in Baltimore to devise the itinerary. Alice instructed him about Gertrude's terms: The audiences were not to exceed five hundred. There were to be no more than three lectures a week. Miss Stein was to be free to do what she wanted for the rest of the time. No one was to introduce Miss Stein at the beginning of her lectures. There were to be no dinners or lunches in her honour – she liked to eat privately with Miss Toklas and friends. Sales of tickets were not to benefit any fund or cause. Miss Stein was to be paid $100 from schools and $250 from clubs. Miss Stein did not want to lecture before audiences of women only.

Gertrude was worried about what the food would be like in America. She thought it sounded very wet, compared to French food: 'Will I like wet food when I eat it when I visit my native land or will I not . . . In the interval of being very busy I meditate a great deal about that.' And William Cook's wife, Jeanne, had told her there would be a shortage of lettuce.

Carl Van Vechten advised them to reserve rooms in the Algonquin Hotel in New York, favoured by artists and writers, and he sent them a menu from the hotel. Gertrude was reassured to read of honeydew melons, soft shell crabs and prime roasts of beef. Alice told her that if they did not like any of it they would just go home. She wrote to Frank Case, manager of the Algonquin, and asked for a double room with two beds and a bath, not higher than the sixth floor. For the same money, Mr Case let them have a suite with a sitting-room too.

They had all their dresses and costumes made in Belley and their shoes made in Chambéry. Gertrude had one outfit made to lecture in in the afternoon, one for lecturing in in the evenings, one to travel in 'and the odd dress or two'. Alice bought endless quantities of lovely gloves. They had a special leather case made for the lecture papers – which fitted exactly, 'and we packed everything we could find to pack'.

Bernard Faÿ got them reduced price tickets for first-class travel on the SS *Champlain*. Neighbours agreed to look after Basket and Pépé because, although they were allowed on the boat, the difficulty, said Alice, would have been in hotels and on planes. Their ship sailed on 17 October 1934. As Gertrude was about to get on the boat train, the button came off one of her new shoes. Trac, their Indochinese servant who was seeing them off, sewed it on again with a needle and some linen thread. 'In this prosaic manner we went off on our great adventure,' said Alice.

*On board the SS* Champlain, *arriving at New York,* 1934.

# 13

---

# AMERICA

*'Having happily had it with a spoon'*

There were flowers for Gertrude and Alice on board the SS *Champlain*. They were from the Duchess of Clermont Tonnerre. Gertrude was a celebrity and their cabin was luxurious. The captain asked them to dine at his table, but they declined. They chose their menus each morning and skipped most of the elaborate courses. The food was the best French cooking and made Alice think of the song, 'Home Will Never Be Like This'.

The deck was covered in glass, like a conservatory and they sat up there in the day talking and reading. They talked to 'a very pleasant doctor and his wife' from New Jersey, a woman who read horoscopes, and the widow of a general who sat at the captain's table and wafted a huge feather fan. On 23 October 1934, the day before they arrived in New York, Carl Van Vechten sent a radiogram to the ship, 'Will you dine with us tomorrow night', and Gertrude sent one back, 'Of course joyfully'.

When the ship docked, reporters came on board to interview Gertrude. Alice dealt with the customs' officials. She wanted to tip them, but Carl Van Vechten told her not even to shake hands. Gertrude was at ease with the men from the Press. When asked if she thought she had introduced anything new into writing she said, 'I have not invented any device, any style, but write in the style that is me.' When asked about her influence on American writers she replied, 'If you can influence yourself it is enough', and when asked about all those repetitions', she replied, 'No, no, no, no, it is not all repetition. I always change the words a little.'

She showed no fright or confusion. She said she was in America 'to tell very plainly and simply and directly as is my fashion, what literature is'. 'Why don't you write the way you talk?' the reporters asked her. 'Why don't you read the way I write,' she replied. Asked about the strange style of *Four Saints* she said,

You see and you hear and you have got to know the difference.
It's very difficult to know how much you hear when you see and
see when you hear. The business of writing is to find the balance
in your own inside.

She avoided politics, saying her business was writing, said Alice was her
secretary and the one 'who makes life comfortable for me', affirmed her
affection for Hemingway, said that Shakespeare, Trollope and Flaubert were
her influences and that she could not understand why she had waited thirty-
one years to revisit her native land.

She posed for photographers, broadcast over a ship-to-shore radio hook-
up and had her passport checked. Bennett Cerf, Carl Van Vechten and the
Kiddie met them at the quayside and they all drove to the Algonquin. They
were pleased with their rooms, except Alice said they were filled with reporters,
cameramen, wires, coils and 'all sorts of impedimenta . . . I could not open
my bag, I could not open my trunk, I could do nothing.'

Gertrude liked the photographers better than the reporters. One came
in and said he had been sent to do a layout of her:

> A layout I said yes he said what is that I said oh he said it is
> four or five pictures of you doing anything. All right I said what
> do you want me to do. Why he said there is your bag supposing
> you unpack it, oh I said Miss Toklas always does that oh no I
> could not do that, well he said there is the telephone suppose
> you telephone well I said yes but I never do Miss Toklas always
> does that, well he said what can you do, well I said I can put my
> hat on and take my hat off and I can put my coat on and I can
> take it off and I like water I can drink a glass of water all right
> he said do that so I did that and he photographed while I did that
> and the next morning there was the layout and I had done it.

Pictures of them were on the front pages of most of the papers. The *Sun,
Post, World-Telegram*, and *Brooklyn Daily Eagle* all began stories about them
on page one. The *New York Times* and *Herald Tribune* both ran long accounts.
There were headlines like 'Gerty Gerty Stein Stein Is Back Home Home
Back.' Gertrude's hat was called a jockey's cap, a deerstalker's cap, tweedy
and mannish, with a visor in front and an upcurl at the back. (In fact Alice
had seen its prototype in the Cluny museum. It had belonged to Louis XIII
and she thought it appropriate for Gertrude so she had it copied.) 'It's just
a hat,' Gertrude said. She was reported to be wearing big men's shoes, her
stockings were thick and woolly, she had a masculine haircut and sturdy
legs, she was stocky, she was plump, she had a large nose, large ears, solid

cheeks, she was a hearty irreverent old lady, a literary eccentric, a grand old expatriate and she was altogether charming.

Alice was described as the Girl Friday, enigmatic bodyguard, typist and constant companion. She was wearing a Cossack hat and black fur coat. She was tiny, thin, mouselike, nervous, dark and small. She was Gertrude's queer, birdlike shadow and twittered when persuaded to speak at all.

Jacques, the head waiter at the Algonquin, did all he could to accommodate their tastes in food and wine. They had T-bone steaks, green-apple pie and 'ineffable ice creams'. Gertrude particularly liked the honeydew melons. Alice, whose taste buds were more refined, thought melons shoud be eaten outside in the sun and anyway she preferred Spanish ones. 'From the beginning the ubiquitous honeydew melon bored me,' she said.

They walked round New York, 'up the avenues and down them and it was wonderful', except that Alice's knees shook because of the skyscrapers, just like they had when Paris had been bombed in 1915. In Times Square they saw in revolving lights 'Gertrude Stein has arrived in New York'. 'As if we did not know it,' said Alice. It upset Gertrude to see her name glittering like that and gave her a strange feeling of recognition and non-recognition.

Everyone seemed to know them – even the taxi drivers. Alice bought some fruit and the storekeeper said to her, 'Miss Toklas are you liking New York?' 'How did he know who I was?' said Alice.

Gertrude suffered stage fright before her first lecture and lost her voice. The nice doctor they had met on the boat, Dr Wood, was a throat specialist so she phoned him up. 'Hearing his voice was already soothing, but having him come and feel my pulse was everything and he was there at the first lecture and so was my voice.' Carl Van Vechten and Fania sent a basket of fruit to the hotel. Before her lecture, Gertrude just ate fruit and oysters. Then she and Alice walked from the Algonquin on West Forty-fourth Street to the Colony Club at Park and Sixty-sixth Street.

Gertrude wore a brown silk dress and a Victorian diamond brooch. The lecture was called 'Pictures'. 'It is natural that I should tell about pictures, that is about paintings,' she said,

> Everybody must like something and I like seeing painted pictures.
> Some people like to eat some people like to drink, some people
> like to make money some like to spend money. I have not
> mentioned games indoor and out and birds and crime and
> politics and photography, but anybody can go on, and I,
> personally I like all these things well enough but they do not
> hold my attention long enough. The only thing, funnily enough,
> that I never get tired of doing is looking at pictures.

She dwelt a little on the problem of the frame - 'the eternal question for painters' - and on the subject matter of painting, and the perplexing relationship between the painting and the thing painted. She was disarmingly straightforward and amiable. 'The truth is', wrote Joseph Alsop for the *Herald Tribune*, 'that with Miss Stein there is never a dull moment.'

Before long, Alice took over the organisation of the whole tour. She fired the official organiser, a young man called Marvin Ross who lived on Long Island, saying that he was a fearful nuisance. She spent a lot of time getting all the papers and correspondence concerning the lectures from him, and then she set about carrying on alone. As ever, she freed Gertrude from any hint of domestic or creative disorder. Alice became her impresario, booking clerk and guard. She knew when to be self-effacing and when to call the tune.

Restricted ticket sales made for excellent publicity and, at Columbia, 1,500 tickets for one of Gertrude's lectures were subscribed. Proof of Ross's mismanagement, said Alice. She told the Dean that if the audience exceeded five hundred there would be no lecture. He hurriedly put out an announcement: 'Miss Stein refuses - adamantly, steadfastly, definitely, unconditionally and absolutely - to address more than 500 people at one time.'

The lecture was on 'Poetry and Grammar'. 'Commas are servile,' Gertrude told her audience:

and they have no life of their own, and their use is not a use, it is a way of replacing one's own interest and I do decidedly like to like my own interest my own interest in what I am doing. A comma by helping you along holding your coat for you and putting on your shoes keeps you from living your life as actively as you should lead it and to me for many years and I still do feel that way about it only now I do not pay as much attention to them, the use of them was positively degrading.

Alice sat next to Mabel Weeks at the lecture 'who said very possessively, Am I not going to see Gertrude?' 'I am sorry but I do not know,' Alice replied, knowing very well that Mabel Weeks was *persona non grata*. So was the mother of Francis Rose's friend, Carley Mills. She phoned and invited Gertrude and Alice to dinner. Alice 'regretted it was not going to be possible'. And Mabel Dodge kept urging Gertrude to meet her, either in Taos, New Mexico, where she had a house, or in Carmel, California. Alice refused.

It was no new thing for Alice to regulate life for Gertrude. As the tour got underway her duties multiplied. She protected Gertrude's every move, fielded off unwanted visitors and made sure the itinerary left plenty of time for lunch, tea and supper, and for having a good time. At one point she lost the diary and lecture schedule, but the manager of the Algonquin told her not to panic, they would turn up again and they did.

Alice briefed reporters, allotted them time with Gertrude and told them when they should go. The reporter from Columbia University's *Spectator* waited for twenty minutes in the foyer of the Algonquin and was then told by Alice that Gertrude would not, as agreed, be available for interview. Alice, who was wearing a feathered hat, said to him, 'You people should have interviewed Miss Stein many years ago when she was not so well known and not so busy.' And she told the reporter from *Art News*, 'Miss Stein has no desire to speak of art or artists, painting or aesthetics. Miss Stein feels she has been occupied with art most of her life and in this time a great deal has been said on the subject.'

Gertrude and Alice stayed in New York a month. 'Have we had a hectic time it is unbelievable,' wrote Gertrude to the Kiddie:

> You know I did a news reel for the Pathe people, I think it goes
> on today, and everybody knows us on the street, and they are all
> so sweet and kind it is unimaginable and you go into a store
> anywhere to buy anything and they say how do you do Miss Stein
> and Alice goes anywhere they say how do you do Miss Toklas
> and they so pleasantly speak to us on the street, its unbelievable,
> to-day and that was funny one man said to the woman who was
> with him, there goes your friend Gertrude Stein as if he had had
> enough and more than enough. I too thought I might be news
> but not like that . . . This afternoon we took off, saw nobody
> xcept the reporter from the American, and we just sat around
> with everything disconnected and it was necessary . . . and good-
> night, and after doing nothing all afternoon we are going to bed
> which is again very necessary.

They were thrilled at their reception. But Gertrude sharply pointed out to her publisher Alfred Harcourt, of Harcourt Brace, 'Remember this extraordinary welcome that I am having does not come from the books of mine that they do understand like the Autobiography but the books of mine that they did not understand.'

Alice got used to the skyscrapers and she and Gertrude liked wandering around the streets. Neither of them was keen on the radio and thought that nothing came out of it but crooning. Gertrude was disappointed in the ten-cent stores: 'there was nothing that I wanted and what was there was not for ten cents . . . The ten cent stores did disappoint me but the nut stores did not.' She liked the drug stores, too: 'I was always going in to buy a detective novel just to watch the people sitting on the stools.' It was, she said, like a piece of provincial life in a real city.

Carl Van Vechten did all he could to make their stay a success. He, Gertrude and Alice called each other Woojums all the time and formed the Woojums family. Dozens of Woojums letters passed between them and the Woojums roles were defined. Carl Van Vechten was Papa Woojums, and the one who made things happen. Alice was Mama Woojums, the lesser parent who did all the tedious work and had on her hands Baby Woojums, variously described as he or it, who got into tempers, was provocative but delightful, needed constant attention and liked to get up late. Fania was not a Woojums at all, though sometimes she was called Madame Bottoms or the Empress.

'6587 white orchids dabbled with yellow butterflies to my two pretty woojums,' wrote Papa Woojums to his wife and child. Or 'long drooping branches of yellow mimosa to you'. 'Dearest love to Papa Woojums from lonesome lonesome Baby and Mama Woojums,' Gertrude and Alice replied.

He arranged lots of dinner parties and visits for them. At one, he introduced them to George Gershwin who played tunes on the piano from the musical he was working on, which was *Porgy and Bess*. Mary Pickford suggested that photographers take a picture of her and Gertrude shaking hands but, when Gertrude seemed to like the idea, Mary Pickford melted away saying 'No, no, I think I had better not'. She feared the publicity would do Gertrude more good than herself. At another party, Blanche Knopf, wife of the publisher Alfred Knopf, said she wanted a manuscript of Gertrude's to publish, but when Gertrude gave her one, 'the boys in the office said it would not do'.

Gertrude and Alice went to the Yale-Dartmouth football game in New Haven, and football fans asked Gertrude to sign their programmes. A very drunk man kept saying to her that he had to see her, he just had to see her. 'And I just had to see him,' said Gertrude. 'I did see him and he did see me.'

*Four Saints* was scheduled for a week's run in Chicago in November. Gertrude wanted to interrupt her lectures and fly there to see it - Curtis Air offered them free tickets - but neither she nor Alice had ever been in an aeroplane. They were apprehensive, and only agreed to fly if Papa Woojums went with them. They had never even seen a plane up close before and were unsure how people got in them. Up in the air, Alice asked anxiously how Gertrude was feeling. 'Do not interrupt my pleasure,' Gertrude replied. She was thinking about art:

> ... when I looked at the earth I saw all the lines of cubism
> made at a time when not any painter had ever gone up in an
> airplane. I saw there on the earth the mingling lines of Picasso,
> coming and going, developing and destroying themselves, I saw
> the simple solutions of Braque, I saw the wandering lines of
> Masson, yes I saw and once more I knew that a creator is
> contemporary, he understands what is contemporary.

*The Woojums family. From left to right, Baby Woojums, Papa Woojums and Mama Woojums, 1934.*

They spent two weeks in Chicago and thought everything was wonderful. Gertrude wrote to the Kiddie, 'We have a wonderful time, the opera was wonderful everything was wonderful. Everything has been wonderful, we are making plans for a leisurely tour of the whole country, by air of course . . . I want to stay in the USA for ever.' Gertrude lectured at Chicago University about what an epic is and about organisation and inside and outside. She signed autographs and copies of her books. She always asked for a reciprocal exchange of signatures. Her lectures were a success and she was invited to do a teaching seminar. She wrote four lectures on 'Narration' for this.

Most evenings they went to see *Four Saints*. Most nights Alice dreamed she was being run over by a locomotive. Gertrude was interested in gangsters, so late one evening the police took them in a squad car to look for a homicide, but it was raining, nobody was doing any murdering, and all they saw was a walking marathon. Gertrude hired a drive-yourself car with flat tyres. She had problems with the traffic signs and a policeman told her, when she was driving the wrong way down a one-way street, that she and Alice would most likely get killed before they left town.

They met Thornton Wilder, who taught at the University and wrote introductions to *Narration*, *The Geographical History of America*, and the posthumously published *Four in America*. He let Gertrude and Alice use his apartment which was close to the University. The apartment was designed for convenience. Meat, butter, milk and eggs were delivered from a hatch outside straight into the refrigerator. Everything could be ordered by phone. Alice described it as her 'ideal of happy housekeeping'.

In her lectures on 'Narration', Gertrude described English and American writing as 'two nations having the same words telling things that have nothing whatever in common'. She thought Americans should adapt language to their lives, 'pressure being put upon words to make them move in an entirely different way'. She explained her ideas about getting away from narrative progression in writing. 'Knowledge is not succession but an immediate existing,' she said. She told her audience that she saw some American soldiers in France, during the 1914-18 war, 'standing standing and doing nothing standing for a long time not even talking but just standing and being watched by the whole French population'. She said that symbolized narrative as it is now.

In one lecture she said that narrative was anything anybody ever said:

Anyway anybody everybody can say anything about narrative their own or anybody else's narrative but one thing is certain and sure that anybody telling everything even if it is nothing that they are telling or is either telling what they want to tell what they have to tell what they like to tell or what they will tell they tell a narrative.

*Flying to Chicago, 7 November 1934.*

She also talked about journalism and said that newspapers offered real life with the reality left out and gave people the assurance that they existed, because if nothing happens 'that makes anybody feel you cannot call a day a day'. Everything she said went down very well.

They went to Wisconsin, then on to Minnesota in a little moth plane, just the two of them and the pilot, flying low over the snow. 'It was unbelievably beautiful,' wrote Gertrude to the Kiddie:

> and the symmetry of the roads and farms and turns make
> something that fills me . . . and the shadows of the trees on the
> wooded hills, well the more I see the more I do see what I like,
> I cannot tell you how much we like it, last night my eyes were
> all full of it.

Then they went on to Michigan, in mid-December, in a big new Douglas plane. Gertrude wanted all three Woojumses to buy their own second-hand plane and pilot it themselves. Papa Woojums thought it a wonderful idea, but Alice's views are not on record. She did not always enter easily into the Woojums game. She tended to misspell it as Woojams and to sound like a serious person trying to be silly. Papa Woojums and Gertrude thought the Woojums family should have a crest of a tub of champagne and a corset, and the legend 'We do what we do which is a pleasure!'

Their trip took them to universities in Wisconsin, Iowa and Ohio, to audiences in Richmond, Charlottesville, New Orleans, St Louis, Cleveland, St Paul, Detroit, Ann Arbor, Indianapolis, Toledo, Washington, Baltimore, Columbus, Houston, San Francisco, Pittsburgh. Wonderful, wonderful, wonderful, was the refrain of both their letters. All the years of rejection were swept away and Gertrude, to her delight, was famous:

> I cannot say that we don't like it we do like it wonderfully every
> minute and everything has worked out so beautifully . . . I am
> delighted really delighted with the way all the audiences take the
> lectures and it makes me happier than I can say.

'Greetings for the merriest Xmas ever,' wrote Alice to the Kiddie. 'Which it is,' she added. They spent it with Gertrude's cousin, Julian Stein, in Baltimore. On Christmas Eve, Gertrude visited Scott and Zelda Fitzgerald. It was the last time they were to meet. He was drunk when she arrived. Zelda was out of mental hospital for the holiday. As was her practice, Gertrude talked normally to Scott Fitzgerald, ignoring the fact of his drunkenness. Zelda showed her paintings she had done in hospital. Gertrude genuinely admired them and Zelda asked her to choose two. Fitzgerald wrote to Gertrude:

It meant so much to Zelda, giving her a tangible sense of her own existence, for you to have liked two of her paintings enough to want to own them ... everyone felt their Christmas eve was well spent in the company of your handsome face and wise mind and sentences 'that never leak'.

Gertrude and Alice loved the colour and light in New England in January. They met up with the Kiddie, who edited a paper in Springfield, Massachusetts. He drove them all round New England in the snow, with tyre-chains on his car that were always breaking. They went sleigh-riding in a real sleigh with a black horse. They were taken to the White House, in Washington, where they mistook the cabinet ministers for plumbers and labourers. Mrs Roosevelt told them the President was indisposed and unable to meet them.

Mrs Roosevelt was there and gave us tea, she talked about something and we sat next to someone. Then later two men came through from somewhere going to somewhere, one quite an old one and the other one younger. Mrs Roosevelt asked them if they would have some tea and they said no.

At the Brooklyn Museum a dignitary shut Gertrude's finger in a taxi door and she had to go to a dirty drugstore to get it fixed. 'One of the few things really dirty in America are the drug stores.'

Gertrude liked Virginia, but not Massachusetts or Connecticut. At least, 'I like it all but you have to like something better than other things even so.' At the Choate School, Wallington, Connecticut, she delivered the lecture 'How Writing is Written', on 12 January 1935, and it was published in the *Choate Literary Magazine* in February. Alice wrote to Papa Woojums:

I hope they won't suppress Baby's lovely little personality a bit, they will help him to develop his literary aspirations, he will charm them and be the joy of the headmaster, but - will he really be happy at any school. It would be best for him. And how will we ever bear it? Ah me.

They went south to Carolina. Alice said she would have adored Charleston, only Gertrude caught an awful cold when they spent the day on a plantation and were rowed for hours on a swamp with hanging gardens, in a torrential downpour.

In New Orleans, they stayed in the Roosevelt Hotel and visited the last of the Creoles in her original house, that had not changed for a hundred years. Sherwood Anderson met up with them and took them to a restaurant where they had Oysters Rockefeller - oysters in their shells put in deep

*Gertrude surrounded by students, Williamsburg, Virginia, 1935.*

sand-filled dishes and the oysters covered with spinach, tarragon, chervil, parsley, spinach, breadcrumbs, salt, pepper and flecks of butter.

In Minneapolis they dined with a friend of Papa Woojums in a room filled with blue orchids and bowls of grapes, while the snow fell outside. They ate lobster cooked in eggs, brandy, port wine, whisky, cream, lemon and butter. 'This dish has an illusive flavour,' said Alice, who collected recipes throughout the tour.

Gertrude liked the advertisements on hoardings. Changing planes at Atlanta, she saw the sign 'Buy Your Meat and Wheat in Georgia', and the words stuck in her mind. She also liked the advertisement for a razor that read

Grand dad's beard was harsh and coarse
That was the reason for his fifth divorce.

For the last month of their tour, in March 1935, they headed west, back to California and the places of their youth. In Los Angeles they went to a party in Beverly Hills given by Lillian May Ehrman, a socialite friend of Papa Woojums. They met Charlie Chaplin, Dashiell Hammett, Lillian Hellman and Anita Loos. Gertrude had particularly asked for Dashiell Hammett to be there, because he was her favourite writer. She was asked how she had managed to get so much publicity for her tour, and she said it was by having a small audience.

She had the idea that she would like Hollywood to do a film of the *Autobiography*, with the real characters acting in it. Papa Woojums said that no actors could play Gertrude and Alice, not even Greta Garbo and Lillian Gish.

Gertrude took a driving test in Los Angeles:

... they asked some twenty questions and nothing had anything to do with how you drive or with machines, it all had to do with your health and your mother's and father's health and with what you would do if anything happened and what the rules of the road are, well I answered them all and they were mostly right after all those things are just ordinary common sense and I said afterward but Alice Toklas who cannot drive at all could have answered just as well ...

Then they hired another drive-yourself car to go to San Francisco – an eight-cylinder Ford, with automatic gear change. 'Through acres of orchards and artichokes we made our way north to Monterey,' said Alice. It was where she went, when young, to escape from the oppression of the Levinsky household. They stayed at the same Del Monte hotel. They ate abalone in cream sauce, grilled chicken, spring lamb cooked on a spit, basted by brushing with a bunch of fresh mint, and served with gooseberry jelly, followed by an iced soufflé made with egg yolks and sugar and flavoured with Kirsch.

Mabel Dodge phoned the hotel. Alice dealt with her:

> She said, Hello when am I going to see Gertrude? and I
> answered, I don't think you are going to. What? said she. No,
> said I, she's going to rest. Robinson Jeffers wants to meet her,
> said she. Well, I said, he will have to do without.

Gertrude and Alice went to the Sequoia Park and into the Yosemite Valley
and took the Seventeen-Mile Drive. In San Francisco their hotel had a
sweeping view of the Bay. 'We indulged in gastronomic orgies,' said Alice.
They had sand dabs *meunière*, rainbow trout in aspic, *paupiettes* of roast
fillets of pork, eggs Rossini and *tarte Chambord*. At Fisherman's Wharf they
waited for two enormous crabs to be cooked in a cauldron on the sidewalk,
then ate them while they were warm for a picnic lunch.

The mayor of San Francisco gave Gertrude a large, gold-coloured, wooden
key to the city, 'it was all very lovely and very grand,' said Gertrude. 'Coming
back to my native town was exciting and disturbing,' wrote Alice. 'It was
all so different and still quite like it had been.' Work had begun on the
construction of the Golden Gate Bridge and she thought it would destroy
the landscape.

She briefly met with Harriet Levy, who sent a telegram to Gertrude:

> Have been following your triumphal tour with awe. Cannot
> discover what is to be the length of your visit here but hope at
> the shortest that you will preserve an hour for me.

Alice made no mention of any meeting with her brother Clarence. They
had quarrelled years before over inherited land and did not write to each
other. He killed himself in 1937, two years after Alice's visit to the States.

Gertrude felt uncomfortable in California, with all its reminders of her
childhood and adolescence. Though she was patriotic about America, she
did not feel right in her home town:

> Roots are so small and dry when you have them and they are
> opposed to you. You have seen them on a plant and sometimes
> they seem to deny the plant if it is vigorous . . . Well we're not
> like that really. Our roots can be anywhere and we can survive,
> because if you think about it we take our roots with us. I always
> knew that a little and now I know it wholly. I know because you
> can go back to where they are and they can be less real to you
> than they were three thousand, six thousand miles away. Don't
> worry about your roots so long as you worry about them. The

essential feeling is to have the feeling that they exist, that they are somewhere. They will take care of themselves and they will take care of you, too, though you may never know how it has happened. To think of only going back for them is to confess that the plant is dying.

They both visited the places where the houses of their childhood had been, but it meant very little.

The big house and the big garden and the eucalyptus trees and the rose hedge naturally were not any longer existing ... What was the use of my having come from Oakland it was not natural to have come from there yes write about it if I like or anything if I like but not there, there is no there, there.

At the end of April they went back to New York, were reunited with Papa Woojums and stayed again at the Algonquin. The tour had been a grand success. And Gertrude was now rich. *Cosmopolitan* paid her $1,500 for an article, 'I came and here I am'. The *New York Herald Tribune* commissioned six articles from her - on American colleges and education, American newspapers, American crimes, American cities, American houses, and American food. She wrote in her 'money style' - discursive, easy, patriotic and flattering. She knew for sure that she had an audience and that the audience was fond. 'There are lots of kinds of soups and all very good ones', she told them, 'and there are really no new kinds of pie.' The articles were enormously liked, said the editor, by the readers he cared for most. Her naïvety, common sense and eccentricity won them round. She was patriotic, libertarian and funny. Do what you want to do, she told her readers. America is the land of the free.

Gertrude heard the gramophone records she had made of readings of her work and saw the Pathe newsreel of herself. Alice had proved her marketing, promotion and publicity skills. Before the trip, Alice had written wistfully to Papa Woojums, 'Will there be any one over there who will say there goes Gertrude Stein I have heard of their doing that and I would love it to happen.' Her wish came true. They left America with a triumphant promise to come back soon. Bennett Cerf of Random House promised Gertrude he would publish a book of hers each year. They sailed on the SS *Champlain* for Paris on 4 May 1935. 'Oh dear oh dear we do not want to go we love it so and we do,' said Gertrude. But go they did and they were never to return.

*With Bernard Faÿ in the gardens at Bilignin.*
*Photograph by Cecil Beaton.*

# 14

ANOTHER WAR

*'It is queer the world is so small
and so knocked about'*

In Gertrude's view, the only ones really grateful for the 1939-45 war were the wild ducks that lived in the marshes of the Rhône. All hunting guns were requisitioned, so no one could shoot at them. 'They act as if they had never been shot at, never, it is so easy to form old habits again, so very easy.' She hoped war would go out of fashion, like duelling. She thought the quickest way to stop it would be to ban the salute. 'That is what goes to everybody's head. No saluting no war.'

After their return from America, Gertrude and Alice tried to settle into their old routine of summer in Bilignin and winter in Paris. For Alice, the peacefulness of the Rhône valley, and her gardens, were a consolation for having to leave America. Above everything else she enjoyed working in them. The Kiddie sent American corn to plant and told them not to give it to any fascists. 'Why not,' said Gertrude, 'if the fascists like it and we like the fascists, so I said please send us unpolitical corn.'

Alice planted the vegetables and American corn for the spring and toiled away. 'I commenced to gather the *fraises des bois*, a never ending task.' Gertrude acquired a pedometer - she called it a speedometer - and noted the twelve or sixteen kilometres a day she walked with Basket. She picked mushrooms and hazelnuts, talked to neighbours, wrote to friends, read detective stories and at some point in the day did her writing. She even took to gardening:

> it was a great pleasure I cut all the box hedges and we have a great many and I cleared the paths more or less well, the box hedges I did very well and then the weeds came up in the garden.

But life was not quite the same. There were 2,500 reservists stationed in Belley and 600 in Bilignin. Thirty of them and their machine guns were in Gertrude and Alice's barn. They stayed a month or so. Gertrude said they used anything they could lay their hands on and that they did not remind her of war, but they did not remind her of peace. She wrote to Papa Woojums that she and Alice would spend their next war in America. Alice felt edgy enough to want to lodge a copy of everything Gertrude had ever written in the Yale University library. She began to type extra copies of everything:

> Mama Woojums has decided because if there is a revolution it
> would be best that the complete works unedited of Baby W.
> should be in the hands of papa W. the safe hands of papa W. she
> is going to do them and to send them to you.

wrote Gertrude to Papa Woojums. 'All summer I cooked and now I'm typing,' said Alice.

Gertrude continued to worry about identity, being a genius, memory and eternity. She meditated

> about how to yourself you were yourself at any moment that you
> were there to you inside you but that any moment back you
> could only remember yourself you could not feel yourself and I
> therefore began to think that insofar as you were yourself to
> yourself there was no feeling of time inside you you only had the
> sense of time when you remembered yourself and so I said what
> is the use of being a little boy if you are to be a man what is the
> use . . . And so I began to be more and more absorbed in the question
> of the feeling of past and present and future inside in one

She wrote *The Geographical History of America or the Relation of Human Nature to the Human Mind*, in which she wondered whether she was who she was because her little dog knew her, or whether 'that only proved the dog was he and not that I was I'. Papa Woojums said the book was SUBLIME STEIN. He thought it was more her than anything she had ever done and her conjunction of TEARS and Human Nature and WRITING and Human Mind 'slayed' him.

In February 1936, Gertrude and Alice flew to England and Gertrude lectured to audiences of American students at Oxford and Cambridge universities. 'What Are Masterpieces' and 'An American and France' were her subjects. Alice said she was a marvellous success. They stayed with the composer and author, Lord Berners, at his home, Faringdon House, in Berkshire. Gertrude said he was very amusing and what a cook! He wanted to set one of her plays to music. They also stayed with Sir Robert Abdy, known as Bertie – whom Gertrude said was gentle and sweet but decidedly peculiar – and his wife Diana, at their homes in London and Cornwall, and had dinner with Lady Cunard and lunch with the editor Alan Lane and Havelock Ellis.

Berners composed a ballet using a revised version of Gertrude's play *They Must. Be Wedded. To Their Wife.* Called *A Wedding Bouquet*, it was first produced at Sadlers Wells on 27 April, and on 4, 8 and 17 May 1937. Berners designed the costumes and décor, Frederick Ashton was the choreographer, Ninette de Valois, Margot Fonteyn and Robert Helpmann danced in it. The part of Pépé the Chihuahua was played by Joyce Farron. The Sadlers Wells Opera Company sang the text and Constant Lambert was the musical director. There were calls for the author at the end and Gertrude went on stage and bowed, 'in the best Baby Woojums fashion'. She could not sleep the nights before or after the show. Alice said she behaved very satisfactorily. Gertrude thought Frederick Ashton was a genius but Alice had not heard bells. 'We met everyone,' said Gertrude, 'and I always do like to be a lion, I like it again and again, and it is a peaceful thing to be one succeeding.'

She wrote another book of memoirs called *Everybody's Autobiography*. She described it as a noble book and hoped it would make lots of money. Papa Woojums said it was not as amusing or gossipy as the Alice B. Toklas *opus*, but more of a work of art and in line with the rest of her work. It was to be illustrated with his photographs. Gertrude thought he was going to print a separate set for each book. 'Why my wonderful Baby Woojums,' he replied:

How did I ever give you that idea? I must have written some
very clumsy English. It would be marvellous if we could do it,
but I would have to print night and day for eight or nine months
and I would have to print over 40,000 photographs and it would
cost thousands and thousands!

W. G. Rogers, The Kiddie, whom they had met in the First World War, stayed at Bilignin in the summer of 1937. His wife was a poet, Mildred Weston. They had entertained Gertrude and Alice in the States and this was to be a reciprocal visit. 'Mildred will write a little poem about Bilignin', Gertrude wrote to the Kiddie, 'and I will write a portrait of the Kiddies and Pépé will bark and Alice will do the rest'.

They planned a sentimental journey to the places they had visited when the Kiddie was a doughboy in the 1914-18 war. Gertrude wrote to him:

Do you know what we are going to do. We are going to drive
ourselves to Avignon Arles St Remy Les Baux and then sleep at
Nimes and go to Uzes and St Gilles and Aiguesmortes and
Vienne and back to Bilignin and all the way Mrs Kiddy will listen
to the remembering of all of us and the very best time will be
had by all.

*Gertrude singing her favourite song, 'The Trail of the Lonesome Pine',*
*on the garden wall at Bilignin, 1937.*

On holiday with them, Rogers described Gertrude and Alice as 'dear enemies'. Gertrude goaded Alice. If Alice hinted they must start at nine, Gertrude would be ready at ten-thirty. If Alice suggested that Gertrude should not serve Pépé bread soaked in a fishy sauce, Gertrude would give him another piece. If Alice voiced her apprehension at driving down a road forbidden to vehicles, Gertrude would go down it. Alice, he said, was Gertrude's *alter ego*. She never gave direct instructions but hinted at what must be.

In 1937 Gertrude and Alice lost their Paris home of twenty-five years. At one o'clock on 25 November, the landlord of 27 rue de Fleurus told them that they must move because he wanted the place for his son. They went straight to a friend, Meraud Guevara, who had a dalmatian dog called Poncho, who was a friend of Basket. Meraud Guevara had been looking at apartments in the area and she took them to see 5 rue Christine. So by three in the afternoon, as Gertrude told Papa Woojums:

> we had found a lovely apartment seventeenth century pannelling,
> in the rue Christine ancient home of the Queen Christine
> daughter of Gustavus Adolphus and it costs the same as this and it
> has a terrace roof in front of it, oh well we will be in it the 15 of
> January, and its address is 5 rue Christine, and we are so xcited.

The apartment was over a bookbinder's workshop and the outside staircase was in his yard. 'When we saw the little street we were dubious but when we saw the apartment we were thrilled,' said Alice. They hired carpenters, painters and plumbers and wondered about curtains and what to put on the bathroom floor. They ordered a wallpaper they had seen in New York of white pigeons on a blue background for the 'bedroom and boudoir' and accepted all offers of help. They found 'a nice English boy' to move their books.

The new apartment still had Queen Christine's boiseries, reading cabinet and parquet floors. Gertrude was optimistic and ready to let go of the past. 'I guess 27 got so historical it just could not hold us any longer,' she told Sherwood Anderson.

Alice worked so hard she 'did not know any longer that she could sit she lost the habit and just went on being on her feet,' Gertrude told the Kiddie. Natalie Barney wrote to Romaine Brooks, 'Alice T. is withering away under the stress of moving into a new flat . . . I am afraid the bigger one who gets fatter and fatter, will sooner or later devour her. She looks so thin.'

Janet Flanner viewed the move as good because it made Gertrude take an inventory of her paintings for the moving men which she had never done before. She arrived on moving day with a pot of white flowers for the new apartment. Gertrude gave her a paper and pencil and said, 'Put the pot anywhere and make me an inventory of my art here.' She counted up 131 paintings, including five Picassos that had been put away in the china closet.

Gertrude and Alice had a refrigerator installed and friends sent them gadgets, as presents, of the sort Alice loved: an egg whisk, a garlic crusher, a meat thermometer, a lid opener. For some days the hot water would not work and Alice thought Queen Christine had a jinx against hot water, but it was soon sorted out. 'Our home oh papa papa Woojums it is so lovely and we are so pleased we just can't believe it', wrote Gertrude.

Gertrude wrote five articles about money, which were published in the *Saturday Evening Post*, and was accused of being reactionary. She wrote a libretto, *Dr Faustus Lights The Lights*, in the hope that Gerald Berners would set it to music. In it Dr Faustus, the inventor of electric lights, is accompanied by a dog who does not bay at the moon because there are so many artificial lights. Because of the prospect of war, Lord Berners could not produce it.

Gertrude's most successful book at this time, following *Everybody's Autobiography*, was *Picasso*. She wrote it in French - after thirty-five years in France, her French had improved. 'Never did I think anything could be so difficult never,' she told the Kiddie. Alice 'reduced tenses grammar spelling and genders into some kind of order'. It was published by the Librairie Floury in 1938. The American version was published by Scribner's. Bennett Cerf, of Random House, was put out that the book went to a rival publisher. He had kept the promise he made to Gertrude when she left America - of publishing a book of hers each year. Gertrude offered him *Dr Faustus* instead. 'We have endeavored - and I think succeeded,' he replied,

> in creating the impression that we were your exclusive publishers in America. Now, to have another firm bringing out so important a book as this one breaks down, in one stroke, the whole structure that we were building so carefully . . . Just how this other offer developed is a mystery to me . . . At the moment I cannot see any point in publishing the Faustus play. If it is ever produced on Broadway, that will be the time to bring it out in book form. Simply to publish it without an actual stage production to back it up would be a mistake in my opinion.

In *Picasso*, Gertrude drew together ideas she had often expressed: about the need of the artist to be contemporary, how in the twentieth century everything cracks and is destroyed, how Picasso perceived and portrayed this. She made clear his debt to her:

> I was alone at this time [1909] in understanding him perhaps because I was expressing the same thing in literature perhaps because I was an American and as I say Spaniards and Americans have a kind of understanding of things which is the same.

Tragedy struck in November 1938. Basket died, aged ten. Gertrude and Alice cried and cried. Papa Woojums knew how they felt:

> I am awfully upset about Basket. It seemed to me he was an immortal dog and would be eternal. I always love animals so much more than people and I have a pang whenever I recall any of my dead cats. When they die it is agony and anguish for months. That is why I don't have them any more. There are people who take these things more lightly and get a new dog every time one dies and of course it IS possible to love a new animal, though it never takes the place of an old animal. I am so very sorry, sweet Baby Woojums and I know what a heartbreak it is . . . Love to you and Mama Woojums.

Other friends commiserated too. Mme Pierlot had lost her Jimmie, who was the same age as Basket. Picasso said never get the same kind of dog again. He told them to get an Afghan hound, like his. Gertrude thought them sad dogs, which was all right for a Spaniard, but not for her and Alice. Both the vet and a friend in Belley, a writer called Henri Daniel-Rops, advised them to get another dog like Basket and to call him by the same name. Daniel-Rops had done that twice with his Claudine, 'and gradually there will be confusion and you will not know which Basket it is'.

This was in line with Gertrude's thinking. She thought le roi est mort: vive le roi, a normal attitude of mind. They went to Bordeaux and got a new white poodle right away: 'and he is a beauty and came straight from the kennel and was scared of everything including stairways . . . Baby Basket has lovely eyes so we feel he is Basket's baby and we feel so much better.'

People in Bilignin and Belley spent a lot of time discussing whether he was more beautiful or sweeter than the last Basket. He could leap up in the air higher than Gertrude's head. He had an indefinable way of standing, but the children did not call him Monsieur Basket as they had Basket the First. Gertrude and Alice sat with him while he gnawed his bone so that he did not take it on the bed or the couch. They stopped him eating Alice's wool and Gertrude's best shoes. Pépé felt neglected and got an attack of rheumatism and had to be fussed. Gertrude sent the details to Papa Woojums:

> The new Basket eats our handkerchiefs and then races madly around the terrace to have them come out at the other end they get stuck and sometimes there has to be a pull of all of which intimate family life we tell Papa Woojums.

Gertrude maintained, through to the summer of 1939, that there would not be another European war. Her friend Eric Sevareid, an American news

*With Basket the Second at Bilignin. Photograph by Cecil Beaton.*

correspondent for CBS, said she could not think politically, but only in terms of the human individual: 'She did not understand that the moods and imperatives of great mass movements are far stronger and more important than the individuals involved in them.' Gertrude regarded the Second World War as a plunge back into medievalism. It showed, in her view, that the world had the mental development of a seven-year-old boy. She thought the war began with the abdication of Edward VIII and jew baiting.

Cecil Beaton and Francis Rose were staying in Bilignin in the summer of 1939. Cecil Beaton called Gertrude the General and took many photographs of her and Alice. He was alarmed by her optimism:

> She will not hear of war talk. It is almost a breach of etiquette
> to mention the fact that events look black or the prospect
> horrifying. 'Oh no, no. War isn't logical, no one wants a war.' . . .
> almost in defiance of the 'General' we buy newspapers with
> portentous headlines: 'Situation plus grave'. By degrees the peace-
> ful existence we've enjoyed these last weeks has been shattered.

The General faced reality on the morning the butcher phoned to tell Alice she could not have the joint she had ordered because the soldiers had requisitioned all the meat. Gertrude and Alice became panic stricken. Gertrude told Beaton and Rose that she could not take responsibility for their staying on and that they must leave.

His nerves awry, Cecil Beaton went for a walk by himself that evening: 'I'd been closeted in this small house, or in the small car overrun with dogs all day. I decided to go for a walk by myself for half an hour before dinner.' He got grandly lost. It rained, the sky was pitch black and small lanes forked in all directions. He terrified the inhabitants of a simple cottage by banging on their door while they were listening to news of the imminence of war.

Back at the house they were panicking about him too. The cook and Trac, the Chinese servant, had gone out to reconnoitre. Francis Rose was beside himself with anxiety. A neighbour called in to give the latest news about the war. 'War?' said Gertrude. 'Who cares about war. We've lost Cecil Beaton.' She and Alice went driving down the lanes sounding the horn and calling his name until they found him. 'Never have I enjoyed a hot bath and fish more,' said Cecil Beaton.

Gertrude and Alice were with their neighbours, Madeleine and Daniel Rops, when Germany invaded Poland. The phone rang and Daniel Rops was gone some time. The others worried, because the Rops had a soldier son:

> He came back. We said what is it. He said the quenelles that
> Mère Mollard was making for us have gone soft.

Quenelles, well quenelles are the special dish of this country made of flour and eggs and shredded fish or chicken . . . and cooked in a sauce and they are good.

When France joined the war Gertrude panicked and made 'quite a scene'. She kept saying 'they shouldn't, they shouldn't'. Her friend, the Baroness Pierlot, comforted her. 'I had been so sure there was not going to be war and here it was, it was war.' Gertrude said she did not care about Poland, but it frightened her about France. Then when Italy joined in they thought they were in everybody's path.

Everyone was in a flurry. Gertrude and Alice got passes to use the roads and drove hurriedly to the rue Christine. Alice said:

We commenced to take down the pictures to protect them from concussion from the bombs. But we found that there was less room on the floor than on the walls so the idea was abandoned.

They packed their winter clothing, Picasso's portrait of Gertrude, Cézanne's portrait of Mme Cézanne and settled their affairs. They could not find their passports, but they found Basket's pedigree which allowed them to get rations for him throughout the war. When they arrived back in Bilignin the American Consul at Lyon phoned and told them to leave the country while it was still possible. They drove to Lyon to get new passports. The Consulate was so crowded they decided to return the next day and not to wait. On the way home they met their neighbours, Dr and Mme Chaboux, and told them where they had been. 'Oh don't think of leaving,' said Dr Chaboux. 'One is always better where one belongs than hunting a refuge. Everybody knows you here. Everybody likes you. We all would help you in every way. Why risk yourself among strangers?'

That kind of fatalism appealed to Gertrude. So they unpacked their bags and Alice buried the spare gasoline in the garden, to protect it from bombs and the German army. Even when private cars were no longer allowed, and the Germans said all gasoline had to be turned in, she would not relinquish it. 'I wasn't going to give it to the Germans - not I.' Gertrude went for a walk and said to one of the farmers, 'We are staying.'

'Vous faites bien,' he said. We all said Why should these ladies leave? In this quiet corner they are as safe as anywhere. And we have cows and milk and chicken and flour . . . Here in this little corner we are en famille, and if you left, to go where? - aller où. And they all said to me aller où and I said You are right - aller où. We stayed and dear me I would have hated to have left.

As Gertrude put it, 'We always pass our wars in France.' They stayed despite the fact that they were Jewish and could have found security and fame in the States. Frenchmen do like peace and their regular daily life, said Gertrude, who could identify with that. With all the difficulties and the isolation from friends, she said the war years were the happiest of her life. She felt she came close to ordinary French people and learned more about them than in all her previous thirty-five years in France. She said the most discussed issues in Bilignin were the absence of butter and gasoline.

One of the big troubles of Alice's war was that she could not get cigarettes. 'She has to she has to she just has to if not well anyway she just has to.' Ration cards were introduced for tobacco and they were only given to men. Gertrude came to an agreement with the tobacconist in Belley that, as the cards made no reference to gender, she and Alice would only put their initials. That worked for a year with a little back-up help from friends. The next year the cards were more elaborate and initials only would not do. They could not wangle it. Alice thought it quite wrong that boys of eighteen had a right to chocolate and cigarettes, while seasoned smokers like herself were denied. Friends helped. Sylvia Beach and Bryher sent them in from Switzerland and someone found a sergeant in the French army who sold his rations. When the Italian army came to Belley, they had tons of very nice little cigarettes they were prepared to sell. Then everybody started growing tobacco in their gardens and Alice learned to do roll ups on a machine. The tobacco was not properly dried, or treated, and tasted dreadful and not at all like her much loved Pall Mall, but 'Alice Toklas was happy again'.

They had not spent a winter at Bilignin before. They hired a wireless and listened to the news three times a day. Gertrude liked the snow and the moonlight, sawing wood and walking with Basket in the blackout. She bought quantities of detective and adventure stories every week from Aix and Chambéry. Each night she consulted a book of astrological predictions called *The Last Year of the War - and After*, by Leonardo Blake. She called it the Bible and said its predictions were right.

They were in the mountains, there was snow, it was very cold and there was no way of heating the house except by open fires. They had enough coal for the kitchen stove and for one grate fire that they kept burning night and day. And there was plenty of wood. Gertrude said that Alice and Pépé sat in the fire - he in his coat and she in her shawl. And they had a cat with a moustache called Hitler. Local people called and sat for three-hour stints to get warm. Hospitality at teatime consisted of two cups of tea without sugar, milk or lemon, and one cigarette.

Alice took to 'passionately reading' the most elaborate recipes while huddled by the fire. Gertrude always gave her a cookbook at Christmas. During the

Occupation she gave her *The Great Book of the Kitchen* by Montagne and Salle. Not one of the ingredients was obtainable, but Alice cooked in her mind: tornadoes of beef with truffles and cream sauce, and lobster cooked with turkey, partridges and capers and served with the best dry champagne – very cold, but not iced.

Throughout the war Alice had a recurring dream of a long silver dish floating through the air on which were three slices of ham.

One of Gertrude's prime considerations for staying put in Bilignin was that she was fussy about her food. 'In the beginning like camels we lived on our past,' said Alice. Before requisitioning was enforced, she stored up dried fruits, gelatine, chicory to replace coffee, sardines, spices, corn meal and cleaning materials. She made vast quantities of raspberry jam. She preserved tomatoes by skinning them, mixing them with salicylic acid, heating them and then storing them in jars with half an inch of oil at the top to stop air entering. She set aside two large glass jars filled with dried fruit: candied orange and lemon peel, pineapple, cherries and raisins. When the war was over she intended to bake a liberation fruit cake.

They were allowed a quarter-of-a-pound of meat each for a week. Until fishing was forbidden, the Rhône supplied them with salmon trout and the Lac-de-Bourget with carp, trout and perch. From the gardens, they had all Alice's vegetables and fresh fruit and, from the wine cellars, plenty of 'delicious dry white wine'. Milk, butter and eggs were scarce. By the time the German army had requisitioned supplies, there was little left for the local inhabitants.

The woman who sold them their butter and cheese used to deliver it in a wagon drawn by a white horse called Kiki Vincent. He was twenty years old, but she had no proof of this and he did not look his age, so he was requisitioned and given the number 73726. The woman went to see the captain of the occupying regiment, who said if he had known in time he could have saved Kiki, but Kiki had gone. She called at Gertrude and Alice's house in a car and cried into what butter she had.

When the Germans forbade fishing, the butcher supplied Gertrude and Alice with crawfish. He caught them live in an open umbrella, with bait attached to the ends of the ribs. Alice kept them in a tank covered with planks and the butcher gave her scraps of meat to feed them. Guests were given crawfish cooked in cognac, wine, carrots and shallots, or crawfish cooked in walnut oil, tomato paste, onions and wine. It was, said Alice, a monotonous diet – 'a protracted indeed a perpetual Lent'.

After about six months, the 'blessed black market' was organised. Baroness Pierlot introduced them to it. She said, 'It is not a matter of money, it is a matter of personality. One buys on the black market with one's personality.'

flour, some butter. She and Alice found a restaurant in Artemare where the chef cooked for his favoured clients - trout in a crêpe, braised pigeon, spring lamb with carrots and onions and asparagus tips, truffle salad and wild strawberry tart. A neighbour would call and tell Alice that a farmer was clandestinely killing two lambs, would she like half of one. Alice learned butchery and Basket ate the head.

Madame Peycru, the baker, kept cakes under the counter. What was on show was for the occupying forces. 'Not good enough for you,' she said to Alice as she handed her chocolate truffles, brioche and cakes wrapped in a newspaper.

There would always be someone knocking on the kitchen door wanting to sell a quarter of a pound of butter, a sausage, sweetbreads, or brains. 'For some time we had strange and varied food,' said Alice. But the black market was expensive, and funds were not coming through from America. In 1942 they packed Cézanne's *Portrait of Madame Cézanne* into the car, crossed the border to Switzerland and sold it to a dealer. 'We ate the Cézanne,' said Alice.

Friends wondered why, as American Jews, they did not stay in Switzerland. They had made other arrangements for their protection. Bernard Faÿ, who in 1940 became head of the Bibiliothèque Nationale, asked Marshall Pétain to ensure their safety. Pétain wrote to the *sous-préfet* at Belley and told him to look after them. Faÿ also helped them get extra bread and petrol. In 1944 he was arrested for collaborating with the Germans and sentenced to twenty years hard labour.

The war cut off Gertrude's enjoyment of her fame, but she went on writing. *Paris France* was published in 1940 with illustrations by Francis Rose, Picasso and the Baroness Pierlot. It was seventy pages long and extolled the solid virtues of provincial French people. It was not really about Paris at all, though Papa Woojums said he could smell and hear Paris when he read it. She wrote a children's book called *The World Is Round* and a diary account of the war called *Wars I Have Seen*. Alice did not type this up, in case the Germans searched the house. She figured they would not be able to read Gertrude's writing, so there was nothing to fear with the book in manuscript.

In the winter of 1942 Pépé refused to go out because of the cold. Alice took him to the vet in a Spanish basket. The vet said, 'There is no saving him I shall have to give him an injection.' Alice kissed Pépé and shook the vet's hand. She said she could not see where she was walking through her tears. 'We will sit somewhere for a moment,' said Gertrude, 'and then have lunch and go back to Bilignin.'

That same winter they had to move from Bilignin. The owners of the house, Captain and Madame Putz, said they wanted it for themselves. It was a deep blow for Gertrude and Alice. Their garden was their larder, they were in their sixties, it was too far into the war for them to leave France and they were dependent on their neighbours in Bilignin and Belley. Gertrude took out a lawsuit. It went against her, but she was granted an extension of the lease. When the Americans joined the war, Captain Putz tried again to reclaim the house. A second lawsuit was begun but then Gertrude and Alice found another house. It was a chateau called Le Clos Poncet at Le Colombier in the mountains just outside Culoz, a railway town fifteen kilometres from Belley. Alice said it was a large and rather pretentious house and she had to start a new vegetable garden from scratch.

Gertrude sold their car to a friend who was in the Red Cross and whose own had been bombed. 'I was sad to see it go but nevertheless there will sometime be lots of others'. She walked a great deal, and had the bicycle turned into a tricycle for Alice. The gendarme at Culoz helped them to get around and to get a goat, which they called Bizerte.

Gertrude got to like trains. She liked the dark stations, the sociability, the uncertainty of whether the trains would run. She and Alice always arrived at the station ahead of time and with all their papers in order. Basket liked trains, too, because everyone fed and admired him.

One day they were going on the train to Chambéry to buy a jar of jam. Gertrude was talking to a young woman about Paris and Lyon, and about the woman being a coiffeuse and some day having a studio in Paris, when suddenly the landscape ceased to be familiar:

and I said dear me this does not look like Chambréy, why no
they said it goes to Annecy, oh dear we said what can we do and
we all talked and everybody gave advice and a German officer
looked as if he wanted to join in but naturally nobody paid any
attention to him nobody ever does which makes them quite timid
in a train.

They got off at the next station and found there was a train to Aix-les-Bains in two hours, then one to Culoz at eight that night. Everyone talked to them and told them where they could eat. Gertrude loved the unexpectedness of it all. They sat in a little café. A German officer at the bar looked like Hemingway and, like Hemingway, he was drinking. He had a brandy, then an *eau de vie*, then a glass of sparkling white wine, then an Amer Picon, then another glass of sparkling white wine. When he left, he insisted on shaking hands with the woman who owned the café, which everybody felt should not have happened.

At Aix, they bought real silk scarves and wool stockings from Pierre Balmain's mother, who had a specialty shop there. Then they found a tea place and drank hot chocolate. When the shops closed they went to wait for two hours for the train. Alice sat on a bench near the ticket office, because there were so many people sleeping in the waiting room. Gertrude walked up and down with the dog. On the news-stand she saw a copy of *The Autobiography of Alice B. Toklas* in French. She was very excited and went to tell Alice. The woman ticket-seller got excited too, put on her headscarf, bought the book and asked Gertrude to sign it. Gertrude asked her name and wrote it in the front of the book as a dedication and everybody was very pleased.

In Culoz they were more aware of the war than in Bilignin. They saw an armoured train, a train full of prisoners, freight trains with names of Polish and East Prussian towns, like Breslau and Koenigsberg, and a train with the flag of the Italian Fascist republic. They were listening to the cook telling them that the way to cure diarrhoea was to beat the white of an egg in a cup of water, when they heard that the German army was going to blow up the railway stations. 'Are we to be frightened or not, we have not quite made up our minds,' said Gertrude.

They had an enormous dislike of Germans. 'The only thing human about them is that they like to eat pork,' wrote Gertrude in her book *Wars I Have Seen*:

> they are a people who always choose some one who will lead
> them in a direction which they do not want to go, it is their
> instinct for suicide, the twilight of the gods, they are always
> going to pieces and when that happens they have neither pride
> nor courage ...

They felt the war went on too long. They could see no end to it. They wore shoes with wooden soles for about a year and they had to burn peat. Alice darned their clothes. She darned the darns, and then darned the darned darns. Pierre Balmain used to cycle over with darning needles and cottons. He was still an unknown student and he made Gertrude and Alice's clothes. After the war they helped to launch his first collection in Paris.

Propaganda came out of the wireless all the time. 'One thing is very certain nobody seems to be loving any more. Do you love one another is not at all true now,' said Gertrude. She liked to hear the German propagandists talking English on the wireless, saying how the English advocated birth-control by killing unborn children, respected men like Malthus and could not be called human. The French radio stations interfered with the broadcasts and Gertrude thought the whole thing, in the midst of all the misery, very small-boyish. 'And so the world is medieval just as medieval as it can be.'

On a day when German soldiers were rounding up the French resistance fighters, the Maquis, from the mountains, Alice got lemons from the grocer

- someone had brought them from a wedding in Tunis. 'We who live in the midst of you salute you,' wrote Gertrude of the Maquis. The Maquis were practically unarmed when they first attacked the German transport system by cutting railroad lines, blocking tunnels and blowing up bridges.

Civilians were told by the Germans that if they walked in the mountains they would be shot. At the worst stage of the war there was no news, no newspapers, no trains, no telephone links and twenty-three barricades between Culoz and Belley, a distance of fifteen kilometres. 'This kind of war is funny it is awful but it does make it all unreal, really unreal,' wrote Gertrude.

Curfew was enforced at six in the evening and all windows that faced the street had to be blacked out until seven in the morning. Gertrude cleaned the weeds off the terrace so that when the American army arrived it could sit there comfortably. Alice thought the weeds would have time to grow again. Gertrude had never worn a watch before, but she bought one now because they shot you if you were out after six. It was a Swiss sports watch for men or women: 'I wear it with immense pride and joy and it seems to keep time and I get home in time and do not get shot by the Germans.'

One day in July 1944 she arrived home and found a hundred German soldiers billeted in the house. Basket was so horrified he could not even bark. 'Gertrude Stein with her manuscript and the poodle were whisked upstairs to the bedroom,' said Alice. 'It was a hideous confusion.' One of the soldiers who had accidentally killed his adjutant was kept locked in a room. He cried all the time and said he wanted to commit suicide. The officers' dogs roamed round the house and their horses and donkeys trampled on Alice's flowerbeds. The soldiers killed a calf on the terrace, cooked it on an improvised spit, helped themselves to supplies and souvenirs, took the door keys and left the following day. Alice hid her jars of candied fruits in the linen cupboard and they went undetected. 'That meant a lot to me,' she said. 'They were a symbol of the happier days soon to come.'

Gradually the Germans became bedraggled. They stopped paying for things in the shops, because they had no money, and then they seemed to drift away. Gertrude could call Basket at ten in the evening and she heard a man whistling in the road in the night. 'What a sense of freedom to hear some one at midnight go down the street whistling.'

> Now at half-past twelve to-day on the radio a voice said attention attention attention and the Frenchman's voice cracked with excitement and he said Paris is free. Glory hallelujah Paris is free.

For Gertrude and Alice it was like the fourth of July in their youth in the San Joaquin valley. They heard that the American allies were only twenty-five kilometres away at Aix-les-Bains. Gertrude took Basket to the local barber and said, 'I want you to shave him and make him elegant. It is not right when the Americans come along and when Paris is free that the only French poodle in Culoz and owned by Americans should not be elegant.' Basket had his paws and muzzle shaved. The vet perspired with the effort and so did Basket.

Alice found American-flag ribbon in the local store and gave it to the little boys, as she had in the previous war. She wondered if it was the same ribbon left over from then. Then they went to put flowers on the soldiers' monument, in Culoz, in honour of the Maquis. French and American flags were flying from the windows of all the houses. The number of Stars and Stripes varied, depending on how much dye could be found. Some of the girls managed whole dresses made out of tricolour ribbons. The Maquis marched down the main street and everyone stood to attention and sang the Marseillaise. Basket tried to run away because of the trumpets and had to be tied with a handkerchief.

The local people shaved the heads of the girls who kept company with the German soldiers during the occupation and called it the coiffure of 1944. 'Naturally it is terrible because the shaving is done publicly, it is being done today. It is as I have often said life in the middle ages,' said Gertrude.

On 31 August 1944 they went to Belley, by taxi, to go shopping and to the bank. When they got out of the car people told them, 'The Americans are here.' 'Lead me to them,' said Gertrude. The watchmaker, who was a 'violent pro-ally', told his son to do just that. They went into a hotel room filled with the Maquis and the mayor of Belley. Gertrude said, in a loud voice, 'Are there any Americans here,' and three men stood up. They were Lieutenant Walter E. Oleson of the 120th Engineers and Privates Edward Landry and Walter Hartze of the Thunderbirds:

> We held each other's hands and we patted each other and we sat down together and I told them who we were and they knew. I always take it for granted that people will know who I am and at the same time at the last moment I kind of doubt, but they knew of course they knew.

Gertrude and Alice went for a ride in the soldiers' jeep, did their shopping and became even more excited, because the town was full of French soldiers in American cars. They saw two more men who looked like Americans and 'flew over to them'. They were Lieutenant Colonel William O. Perry, Headquarters 47th Infantry Division, and his driver, Private John Schmaltz. Alice 'at once requisitioned them for dinner and the night – as they would have to dine and sleep somewhere why not at our house.' 'Alice Toklas got into the car with the driver and the colonel came with me,' said Gertrude.

'We had a triumphant entry at Culoz and at the house,' said Alice:

> The servants cried and curtsied and hailed them as *nos liberateurs*.
> Impossible to calm the cook. Finally she agreed to go back to the
> kitchen to prepare a dinner . . . saying, Do not worry, madam,
> now I can cook even if there is no cream and not enough butter
> and eggs.

The liberation menu was trout in aspic, chicken in tarragon, tomato and
lettuce salad, chocolate soufflé, wild strawberries and coffee. Neighbours
provided the chicken, eggs and butter. The American colonel and his driver
provided the chocolate and the coffee. They all sat up much of the night
talking. The soldiers came from Colorado, and brought America to Gertrude
and Alice. The cook worked until midnight, making quantities of little
American and French flags, which she used to decorate a big cake filled
with frangipani cream.

The soldiers talked more to Gertrude and Alice at breakfast the next day.
They all patted and kissed each other, and then the soldiers went away. As
Alice and Gertrude were sitting down for lunch, four more Americans arrived.
They were war correspondents and one of them was Gertrude's friend, Eric
Sevareid. They wanted Gertrude to go to the Press camp at Voiron the next
day and broadcast to America. 'The eyes of these two elderly women shone
like the eyes of children on a picnic,' Sevareid said. Voiron was further than
either of them had travelled from Culoz in two years.

They caused something of a sensation in the Press camp and they ate
ham and eggs, tinned corn, sweet pickles, biscuits, tinned peaches and coffee
with evaporated milk. Alice smoked lots of American cigarettes and called
it 'a memorable lunch with our liberators'.

Gertrude broadcast live to the American nation:

> What a day is today that is what a day it was the day before
> yesterday, what a day! I can tell everybody that none of you know
> what this native land business is until you have been cut off from
> that same native land completely for years. This native land
> business gets you all right. Day before yesterday was a wonderful
> day. First we saw three Americans in a military car and we said
> are you Americans and they said yes and we choked and we
> talked, and they took us driving in their car these long-awaited
> Americans, how long we have waited for them and there they
> were Lieutenant Olsen and Privates Landry and Hartze and then
> we saw another car of them and these two came home with us, I
> had said can't you come home with us we have to have some

Americans in our house and they said they guessed the war
could get along with them for a few hours and they were
Colonel Perry and Private Schmaltz and we talked and patted
each other in that pleasant American way and everybody in the
village cried out the Americans have come the Americans have
come and indeed the Americans have come, they have come, they
are here God bless them. Of course I asked each one of them
what place they came from and the words New Hampshire and
Chicago and Detroit and Denver and Delta Colorado were music
in our ears. And then four newspaper men turned up, naturally
you don't count newspaper men but how they and we talked we
and they and they asked me to come to Voiron with them to
broadcast and here I am . . .

You know I thought I really knew France through and through
but I did not realize what it could do and what it did in these
glorious days. I can never be thankful enough that I stayed with
them all these dark days, when we had to walk miles to get a
little extra butter a little extra flour when everybody somehow
managed to free themselves, when the Maquis under the eyes of
the Germans received transported and hid the arms dropped to
them by parachutes, we always wanted some of the parachute
cloth as a souvenir, one girl in the village made herself a blouse
of it.

It was a wonderful time it was long and it was heart-breaking
but every day made it longer and shorter and now thanks to the
land of my birth and the land of my adoption we are free, long
live France, long live America, long live the United Nations and
above all long live liberty, I can tell you that liberty is the most
important thing in the world more important than food and
clothes more important than anything on this mortal earth, I who
spent four years with the French under the German yoke will tell
you so.

I am so happy to be talking to America today so happy.

When they got home, Alice baked her liberation fruit cake, spread it with
almond paste and icing, and sent it to the general whose army had liberated
the region of the Ain. He was General Patch, who commanded the Seventh
Army. Then she started on the manuscript of Gertrude's book, *Wars I Have
Seen*, typing it up 'like mad'.

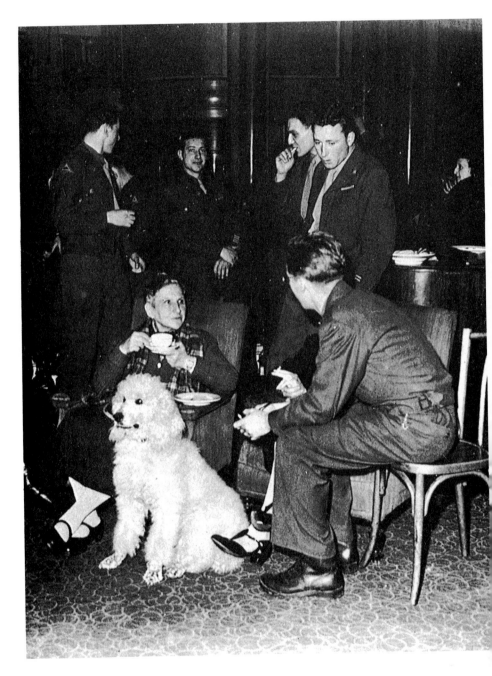

*With GIs, 1945.*

# 15

---

# PEACE

*'Dead is dead yes dead is really dead*
*yes to be dead is to be really dead yes to be dead*
*is to be really dead'*

In the darkest days of the occupation Gertrude had been homesick for the quays of Paris and for a roast chicken in a restaurant. She felt a superstitious fear about the apartment at the rue Christine and did not like talking about it. She and Alice were told that the Gestapo had broken into it in August 1944 and waved a photograph of Gertrude in the air saying they would find her. The concierge called the French police who ordered them out. Bernard Faÿ ensured that the Gestapo did not confiscate the pictures:

> Picasso called and said 'The Germans are preparing to move the collection of my pictures owned by Gertrude Stein, do something.' I got in touch with Count Metternich (in charge of protecting works of art in occupied areas) and asked him to act quickly, which he did. The collection of Gertrude Stein was in the custody of the German Administration of Jewish Properties. Metternich told the Administration of Enemy Property to put its seals on Stein's door. The two administrations had a bureaucratic battle and it was impossible for them to move the property. The collection was saved.

None the less, the Gestapo took the keys to the apartment, returned the next day, stole silver and valuables and damaged the place, so a friend arranged for a Russian workman, called Svidko, to do repairs.

Gertrude and Alice stayed on in Culoz through autumn 1944. They watched the arrival of the troop trains, greeted the GIs, chatted with them and signed autographs. They heard conflicting reports about the state of Paris. Some said there was no food, gas or electricity. Gradually letters got through again, though these were still censored. 'Papa and Mama Woojums', was changed to 'Father and Mother Woojums'. Carl Van Vechten had tried to explain the relationship to the authorities, but without success.

In the middle of December, Gertrude and Alice headed back to Paris. They hired a truck and packed all they had accumulated in their five years in the country. Neither of them ever returned to the Rhône Valley. On the journey, there was heavy snow, the tyres burst, the car broke down and the driver had to reverse down a winding lane for three kilometres in the snow in the dark. Peace is stranger than war, thought Gertrude. They were stopped by armed resistance fighters who thought they were Germans. Not we, said Gertrude indignantly, showing her papers. Alice explained that the bundles were meat, butter and eggs and that the big thing was a Picasso painting of Gertrude. Don't touch it, she said.

When finally they arrived in Paris, it was the same as when they had left it. 'So much more beautiful but the same,' said Gertrude.

> All the pictures were there, the apartment was all there, and it was all clean and beautiful. We just looked and then everybody came running in, the concierge, the husband of the laundress downstairs, the secretary of our landlord, the bookbinder, they all came rushing in to say how do you do and to tell us about the visit of the Gestapo; their stamp was still on the door.
>
> I did not want to know, because knowing is frightening, but I had to know and it is interesting.

The next day Picasso called and they all embraced and kept saying 'It is a miracle, all the treasures which made our youth, the pictures, the drawings, the objects, all there.' Alice was angry that the Gestapo had taken their porcelain, crystal and linen. Gertrude said to her, 'Don't talk to me about it. Let them go. We got out scot free really - don't let us talk about those things.'

Gertrude walked round Paris with Basket. She began to think that the war had been a nightmare and that they had simply been away for their summer vacation. Paris impressed her more than ever before:

> Every little shop was there with its same proprietor, the shops that had been dirty were still dirty, the shops that had been clean before the war were still clean, all the little antiquity shops were still there, each with the same kind of things in it that there used to be . . . It was a miracle, it was a miracle . . . How lovely it all was, and the quays of the Seine . . . And so we are back in Paris, yes, back in Paris.

Friends resurfaced. Francis Rose came to Paris for an exhibition of his paintings. Cecil Beaton returned from the Far East, Sylvia Beach from

*35 rue Christine. Photograph by Cecil Beaton.*

Switzerland and Natalie Barney from Italy. She and Romaine Brooks spent the war years in the Villa Sant'Agnese on the outskirts of Florence. Kahnweiler had been in hiding under a false name. There was even a brief reconciliation between Gertrude and Hemingway, who had worked as a war correspondent.

Bernard Faÿ was imprisoned on charges of collaboration with the enemy. Gertrude and Alice thought that his conviction took no account of his patriotism, or of the problems of living in an occupied country. They sent him sweets, letters and vitamins, and tried very hard to secure his release.

Gertrude returned to the limelight. *Wars I Have Seen* sold more than 10,000 copies and Bennett Cerf sent them the good reviews it received. Papa Woojums wrote, 'I have sent the whole American army so far as I know it STRAIGHT TO 5 rue Christine!' Gertrude held GI salons. She became one of the sights of Paris for the American army, like the Place Pigalle, or the Eiffel Tower. Alice said the American invasion was at times just too much.

Gertrude told Cecil Beaton:

> It's quite ex-tra-ordinary the way these boys come to see us. They
> come to see Pablo and they come to see me. They don't go to
> anybody else and I don't believe they come to see us because
> we're celebrities, but because we're rebels. They know Pablo and
> I have had to put up a fight in our time and we've won.

She liked being the Forces Sweetheart and was sentimental about the soldiers, whom she saw as having a special American innocence, decency and good-heartedness. 'Write about us,' the GIs said and write about them she did in *Brewsie and Willie*. Her style was the conversational idiom of two ordinary soldiers preoccupied with what life would be like back in America, after the war was over. Gertrude thought it a 'kind of handsome' book. 'I think I really got them as they were, it was pretty wonderful and I got them,' she wrote to Papa Woojums.

Gertrude accepted, with Alice who had gone rather deaf, invitations to speak at army camps, at GI schools, at lectures organised by the Red Cross. The GIs all wanted to be photographed with her, Alice and Basket. After one meeting fifty GIs walked them home, to the puzzlement of the gendarmerie. 'The door bell rings all day long, one soldier and then another, I must say I do like them all,' Gertrude told Papa Woojums. They were invited to hear the Glenn Miller band with the troops. Gertrude 'gave them a little address', then ten of the band went over to the rue Christine one afternoon with their instruments, including drums and double bass, and gave a concert. Alice made them chocolate ice-cream.

Gertrude wrote patriotic articles for the *New York Times Magazine* and *Life*. In June 1945, the US Army invited her to tour their bases in occupied

Germany. 'It was in an American bomber that we went,' wrote Alice. *Life* magazine commissioned a piece about the trip and Gertrude called it 'Off We All Went To See Germany.' They were escorted by twelve soldiers. They had their photographs taken with all the GIs and they ate from mess tins. They went to Salzburg in Austria and were photographed on the terrace of the Berghof, Hitler's home at Berchtesgaden:

> There we were in that big window where Hitler dominated the
> world a bunch of GI's just gay and happy . . . just being foolish
> kids, climbing up and around and on top, while Miss Toklas and
> I sat comfortably and at home on garden chairs on Hitler's
> balcony.

They inspected the art treasures plundered by Goering from all the conquered countries of Europe. Gertrude thought the works showed no personal taste for collecting.

Wandering through a bombed area in Frankfurt, Gertrude noticed that all the German people stared at her and Alice. She realised that the two of them were the first foreign civilian women the people had seen. 'Some went quite pale and others looked furious.'

'Teach them disobedience,' she said of the Germans on her tour:

> Make every German child know that it is its duty at least once
> every day to do its good deed and not believe something its
> father or its teacher tells them, confuse their minds . . . and
> perhaps they will be disobedient and the world will be at peace.

Some said that the best way to confuse the minds of German children would be to issue her works in their classrooms.

Papa Woojums said it was marvellous, in *Brewsie and Willie*, how Gertrude got the ATMOSPHERE and the VERNACULAR. At the end of the book she became rather oratorical and fervent, and gave a sermon 'To Americans':

> GIs and GIs and GIs and they have made me come all over
> patriotic. I was always patriotic, I was always in my way a Civil
> War veteran, but in between, there were other things, but now
> there are no other things. And I am sure that this particular
> moment in our history is more important than anything since the
> Civil War. We are there where we have to have to fight a spiritual
> pioneer fight or we will go poor as England and other industrial
> countries have gone poor, and dont think that communism or
> socialism will save you, you just have to find a new way, you
> have to find out how you can go ahead without running away

with yourselves, you have to learn to produce without exhausting your country's wealth, you have to learn to be individual and not just mass job workers, you have to get courage enough to know what you feel and not just all be yes or no men, but you have to really learn to express complication, go easy and if you cant go easy go as easy as you can. Remember the depression, dont be afraid to look it in the face and find out the reason why, dont be afraid of the reason why, if you dont find out the reason why you'll go poor and my God how I would hate to have my native land go poor. Find out the reason why, look facts in the face, not just what they all say, the leaders, but every darn one of you so that a government by the people for the people shall not perish from the face of the earth, it wont somebody else will do it if we lie down on the job, but of all things dont stop, find out the reason why of the depression, find it out each and every one of you and then look the facts in the face. We are Americans.

Gertrude wrote articles about the American army for *Life* and the *New York Times*, and gave lectures. Natalie Barney said of her and the American soldiers, 'She led them as a sort of *vivandière de l'esprit*, from war into peace, and to realize their own, instead of their collective, existence.'

The American army were good customers for Gertrude's work. Alice managed to sell to them the many remaining copies of the five books published in the Plain Edition in the early thirties. Papa Woojums made sure that the soldiers took packages from America, for Gertrude and Alice, of coffee, tea, cakes, cookies, newspapers, rice, flints for Alice's cigarette lighter, dish cloths and anything else that could not be found in France. Marie Laurençin painted a portrait of Basket the Second, because he was now a famous dog.

Virgil Thomson wanted to do another opera with Gertrude. She began the libretto in October 1945 and took, as her heroine, Susan B. Anthony, America's leading nineteenth-century suffragette. The title was *The Mother of Us All* and the heroine was fierce about men:

> Men said Susan B. are so conservative, so selfish, so boresome
> and said Susan B. they are so ugly, and said Susan B. they are
> gullible, anybody can convince them ... they are poor things,
> they are poor things ... men are conservative, dull, monotonous,
> deceived, stupid, unchanging and bullies ... they know how to
> drink and get drunk.
>
> Men can not count, they do not know that two and two make
> four if women do not tell them so. There is a devil creeps into
> men when their hands are strengthened. Men want to be half

slave half free. Women want to be all slave or all free therefore men govern and women know ...

Papa Woojums said the opera was BETTER than *Four Saints* and that he talked to Virgil Thomson AT LENGTH about it over the telephone and 'sensational' was the word Virgil Thomson used.

The editor of the *Yale Poetry Journal* asked Gertrude what she thought of the atomic bomb, as America had just dropped two on Hiroshima and Nagasaki. Gertrude wrote a piece *Reflections on the Atomic Bomb* in 1945:

> I said I had not been able to take any interest in it. I like to read detective and mystery stories, I never get enough of them, but whenever one of them is or was about death rays and atomic bombs I never could read them. And really way down that is the way everybody feels about it. They think they are interested about the atomic bomb but they really are not any more than I am. Really not. They may be a little scared, I am not so scared, there is so much to be scared of, what is the use of bothering to be scared, and if you are not scared, the atomic bomb is not interesting. Everybody gets so much information all day long that they lose their common sense. They listen so much that they forget to be natural. This is a nice story.

As well as her new successes Gertrude wanted past books republished. 'You see I think some of my books should be treated like classics and left on sale,' she told Bennett Cerf in September 1945. By November she was angry with him for not complying with this idea. 'Keep your pants on letter that will delight you is on way,' he cabled back to her. He told her that he was going to publish a one-volume edition called *Selected Writings of Gertrude Stein*. Papa Woojums wrote the introduction, which Gertrude thought marvellously balanced and said made her very happy.

In December 1945 Gertrude went with Alice by car to Brussels to talk to soldiers stationed there. She felt tired on the trip. She said she would not travel about so much and that they would see fewer people. 'It had been too exhausting - the occupation and seeing nearly the whole American army', Alice wrote to Papa Woojums. Gertrude had also lost weight, and complained of colitis. She had had abdominal pains in Culoz, but she disliked doctors and taking medicines. The local doctor told her to wear her corset differently, and she thought that it alleviated the pain to some degree.

In April 1946 her doctor told her she needed to build herself up and have an operation. She refused this. Everything became a great effort for her.

She agreed to go away for a holiday. She bought a new Simca car and on 19 July she, Alice and Basket left Paris for Luçeaux, in the Sarthe. Bernard Faÿ, who was in prison, offered them the use of his country house there, a Priory at St Martin. It was about 200 kilometres from Paris and a GI, Joseph Barry, drove them down.

They settled in at St Martin, then went for a drive to Azay-le-Rideau, where Gertrude and Alice had once thought of buying a house. Gertrude became very ill and they booked in at a hotel. A local doctor said she needed to see a specialist at once. The next day Gertrude, Alice and Jo Barry took a train back to Paris. Alice had called Allan Stein, Gertrude's nephew, and told him to arrange for an ambulance to meet the train.

Gertude was taken to the American Hospital at Neuilly. Both she and Alice were optimistic that they would return to the Sarthe in September. Doctors examined her, then refused to operate. They said she had cancer that was too far advanced for surgery. Alice said:

> Tired suffering Baby dismissed them all and said she never
> wanted to see any of them again. She was furious and frightening
> and impressive like she was thirty years and more ago when her
> work was attacked. And then we got Valerie-Radot [sic] and
> Leriche and they consented because she implored them to.

Valery-Radot was a member of the Académie de Médicin and head of the French Red Cross. He delayed the operation for some days. On 22 July, Gertrude was cheered by receiving copies of *Brewsie and Willie*, the day it was published in New York.

Before her operation Gertrude made her will. Alice and Allan Stein were to be her executors. She bequeathed her portrait by Picasso to the Metropolitan Museum in New York. She left all her manuscripts, correspondence and photographs to the library of Yale University and instructed her executors to pay Carl Van Vechten whatever sums of money he 'in his own absolute discretion, deems necessary for the publication of my unpublished manuscripts'. The rest of her estate, 'of whatever kind and wheresoever situated', she left

> to my friend Alice B. Toklas, of 5 rue Christine, Paris, to use for
> her life and, in so far as it may become necessary for her proper
> maintenance and support, I authorize my Executors to make
> payments to her from the principal of my Estate, and, for that
> purpose, to reduce to cash any paintings or other personal
> property belonging to my estate.

After Alice's death the estate was to pass to Allan Stein, Gertrude's nephew, and after his death, to his children. The estate was to be administered by a lawyer in Baltimore named Edgar Allan Poe. To save French inheritance taxes, Gertrude bequeathed her entire collection of paintings to Allan Stein, trusting him to carry out her intentions. This was to create problems which she could not foresee.

The surgeons operated on Saturday 27 July. Alice said:

> By this time Gertrude Stein was in a sad state of indecision and worry. I sat next to her and she said to me early in the afternoon, What is the answer? I was silent. In that case, she said, what is the question? Then the whole afternoon was troubled, confused and very uncertain, and later in the afternoon they took her away on a wheeled stretcher to the operating room and I never saw her again.

'We cannot retrace our steps,' wrote Gertrude in *The Mother Of Us All*:

> going forward may be the same as going backwards. We cannot retrace our steps, retrace our steps, all my long life but. (A silence a long silence)
> But - we do not retrace our steps, all my long life, and here, here we are here, in marble and gold, did I say gold, yes I said gold, in marble and gold and where -
> (A silence)
> Where is where . . .

'And oh Baby was so beautiful,' wrote Alice to Papa Woojums four days later,

> - in between the pain - like nothing before. And now she is in the vault of the American cathedral on the Quai d'Orsay - and I'm here alone. And nothing more - only what was. You will know that nothing is very clear with me - everything is empty and blurred.

*Alice after Gertrude's death.*

# 16

---

## CARRYING ON FOR
## GERTRUDE

*'I am nothing but the memory of her'*

Alice's memory worsened after Gertrude's death:

> Oh you should have known what it was. I could have begun with
> the beginning and given you everything connected with every day
> along the line, until Gertrude died. I lost my memory then,
> because I think I was upset and my head, when it came back,
> just wasn't clear.

She allowed herself little time for displays of grief. On her return from the
funeral she burned all personal notes they had written to each other. Within
days she was insisting to Papa Woojums that *everything* Gertrude had written
must be published and that he must see to this, and that *every* publication
with an article by or about Gertrude must be sent to the Yale library. She
chivvied Virgil Thomson to get on with the production of *The Mother of
Us All*. She sent out review copies of *Brewsie and Willie* and chased Saxe
Commins, an editor at Random House, for advance copies of Gertrude's
*Selected Writings*. When the book arrived she carried it around with her.
'It is so beautiful - so perfect - it has completely upset me,' she wrote to
Papa Woojums on 19 November 1946.

Gertrude had made no arrangements about death. It was not something
they discussed. As ever, it was up to Alice to sort things out. Jo Barry drove
her down to the Sarthe to collect their holiday trunks and Basket. The landlady
at the rue Christine agreed that Alice and Basket could stay on there. Alice
tried to take Basket on the sort of walks round Paris he had enjoyed with
Gertrude.

She bought a double plot at the Père Lachaise Cemetery, where the great
French dead lie buried. She asked Francis Rose to design a grave. His design
was modelled on the gardens at Bilignin. Gertrude's body lay in the vault

at the American Cathedral for nearly three months while Alice negotiated the purchase of the plot. Gertrude was buried on 22 October 1946. It was a mild morning with an overcast sky. A dozen friends stood round the grave. A Dean Beekman read three psalms and 'such parts of the service from the Book of Common Prayer as Baby would have subscribed to'. There were lots of flowers, 'and now Basket and I are more alone than ever,' wrote Alice to Papa Woojums.

The lettering on the headstone was in gold. The name of Gertrude's birthplace was misspelled: Allfghany Pennsylvania instead of Allegheny, and the date of her death wrongly inscribed as the 29th, not 27 July. The 29th was the day of Leo's death a year later – also of cancer. No one told Leo of Gertrude's death. He mentioned it in a postscript in a letter to a friend, Howard Gans, written in August 1946:

> I just saw in *Newsweek* that Gertrude was dead of cancer. It surprised me, for she seemed of late to be exceedingly alive. I can't say it touches me. I had lost not only all regard, but all respect, for her.

To his cousin, Fred Stein, Leo wrote that same month:

> It is strange. I always expected that Mike and Gertrude, both of whom had apparently better constitutions than I, and who took much better care of themselves would outlive me. I have spent myself recklessly and after the terrific strain of the neurosis underwent the greater strain of curing it and now am the only one left.

A week or so later he wrote again to Howard Gans mentioning his haemorrhoids which were bleeding and were a nuisance. He felt weak, tired and without appetite. Radium treatment was advised. Cancer was diagnosed and he was told he should have an operation. He did not want this, thinking he would not survive. He said he was not afraid. He could not leave the subject of Gertrude alone. He continued to tell whoever would listen that her work was utter bosh and commonplace, expressed in jargon. But he wanted to see anything about her that was printed in the papers and any of her publications.

A few days before he died, he outlined for the umpteenth time the profound difference in their characters: that she had no critical interest, was basically stupid, that their private lives were independent, that there was never any quarrel between them, that anything he said about her was not a consequence of personal relationship or feeling. He wrote of her in the present as if she were still alive:

She is in my opinion one of the fake intellectuals like Picasso who write in Jargon because they can't get enough effect with decent English. Gertrude simply doesn't know the language, she has no ideas and is entirely incapable of them. She has a hearty humanity though this has no universality. She sees no contradiction between assertions of possibility and assertion of the most unlimited assurance about matters of which she knows nothing – which includes everything except individual character which she had observed closely. She rejoices in publicity in which I take no interest at all. I like it when people really understand me and if their understanding is not real admiration says nothing to me . . .

Gertrude like Picasso seems to have had far reaching effect because now every one can write as every one can paint. Gertrude's style seems to me at its best when it's a baby style perfected, as in the Wars Book. It often reminded me of Around the World in Eleven Years.

The 'family romance', and the coldness of her rejection, shadowed him to his grave. As for Alice, she was stunned by her loss. 'Oh Carlo,' she wrote to Papa Woojums, 'could such perfection such happiness and such beauty have been and here and now be gone away.' But she soon came to believe that Gertrude was only round the corner in Père Lachaise, waiting. There was much to do before joining her there. She dedicated herself to furthering Gertrude's reputation.

Friends had not had the faintest idea of Gertrude's illness. 'It is a most shocking thing to think of her as deprived of life,' Bernard Faÿ wrote to Alice from prison. He hoped Gertrude was with God and said that he could still hear her voice and would hear it as long as he lived.

Francis Rose wrote to Alice exhorting her to 'carry on for Gertrude', and to see that all Gertrude's work was put in perfect order for the world to love. Alice needed little nudging. She told Papa Woojums he had *carte blanche* to draw on the funds in the Baltimore bank for publishing everything Gertrude had ever written. Donald Gallup, Curator of the Collection of American Literature at Yale, sent Carl Van Vechten a list of Gertrude's unpublished work. Van Vechten was staggered and overwhelmed at the prospect before him:

My initial feeling was that Gertrude had bitten off more than I could easily chew, a feeling greatly intensified after I had inquired of certain publishing friends of mine how much it would cost to print and bind the vast pile of manuscript still unpublished. The sums mentioned were so enormous that my heart sank at the thought of the project ahead of me.

*With Papa Woojums.*

The task took him eight years. The Yale University Press published a volume a year, with introductions written by friends. Papa Woojums wanted Alice to write the first of these, but she panicked. 'Gertrude would have despised and hated the idea,' she said. She let him know, as ever, that Gertrude was the writer and she, merely the maidservant. Her refusal and self-denigration soured their subsequent relationship. None the less, Carl Van Vechten said the whole publishing enterprise was 'a labor of love for all those concerned', and even a little more than that for him. 'Now I will quote for you what she herself says about *A Novel of Thank You*,' he wrote, with a hint of desperation, in his preface to the final volume:

A Novel of Thank You means that at any time they are as much when it it is widened by its being worn out worn and less worn then and everybody can say should it be what they came to do.

Alice believed it was her mission to see all Gertrude's work printed. But she did not want intimacies revealed. She kept back Gertrude's first novel, about her love for May Bookstaver. She wrote to Donald Gallup at Yale in 1947:

I have the manuscript. It is a subject I havent known how to handle nor known from what point to act upon. It was something I knew I'd have to meet some day . . . and to cover my cowardice I kept saying - well when every thing else is accomplished. But you are the *only* person who ever asked . . . Now what shall I do about it? I am asking you and Carl . . . you two must decide. The only thing I know is I wouldnt want it read - that is therefore not published - during my life. Gertrude would have understood this perfectly though of course it was never mentioned. Is there not some way of sending it to you or Carl or both of you under this condition. Of course it must not be found here someday when Allan comes and takes over.

In the end she left Carl Van Vechten and Donald Gallup to decide what to do. They changed some of the personal details and, in 1950, the Banyan Press published 516 copies, with the title *Things As They Are*. The significance of the book meant more to Alice than to readers. It did not attract much notice and Alice, who had dreaded hearing anything about it, felt agitated by the silence.

She became very frugal. She wanted to keep the paintings together as the Gertrude Stein Collection, and determined not to sell any of them unless she absolutely had to. She drew $400 a month from the Stein estate, from which she paid all household and personal expenses. The money was often slow in coming through and she had to get her lawyer to intermediate. She felt that her numerous little economies put her 'in the banal majority' of ordinary people. She soon fell out with Allan Stein, the co-executor of Gertrude's will, and said he 'commenced to assert himself with cold aggression.' She said that he was a horror, that he refused to cooperate with her, made everything as difficult as possible and obstructed her wherever he could. 'We dont meet any more frequently than necessary - and then I dont listen to him.' She regarded him as a victim of his 'exaggeratedly cultivated home', said that he had been denied a proper childhood, had no inner resources and cared only for business and horse racing. Nor would she have anything to do with Sarah Stein who, after Michael Stein's death in 1938, lived with a Christian Science woman-friend called Gabrielle de Monzie.

Occasionally, Alice saw Allan Stein's wife Roubina, who took a legal separation from her husband in 1950, ran the perfume business he had started and brought up their two children. 'I dont happen to care for her,' wrote Alice, 'and wont be seeing her any more than strictly necessary.' This personal animosity led to economic hardship. It was in Allan and Roubina Stein's power to obstruct the sale of paintings to provide funds for Alice or the private publishing of Gertrude's work - and this they did, out of financial self-interest. For her part, Alice worried that they would seek to sell some of the paintings for their own gain, so she stamped the back of each canvas: 'This picture belongs to the estate of Gertrude Stein'.

Winter electricity bills left her aghast. To save money she permanently closed the dining room. She kept one room - the salon - comparatively warm and she and Basket stayed near the radiator. The kitchen and bedroom were tepid, the other rooms glacial. 'We ate Madame Cézanne but I dont want - figuratively - to burn a Picasso,' she wrote to Papa Woojums, on Christmas Day, 1946. She ate her meals on a tray by the heater. The concierge turned the water off at 8.15 every evening to prevent the pipes freezing and did not turn it on again until eight in the morning. Alice said the apartment was not hot enough for germs to breed, so she never caught colds.

She and Gertrude had always gone by car to the shops. Now Alice said the winter queues were beyond her endurance. It was, she felt, out of the question 'to walk to the central markets and return with my baskets'. Her maid, Gabrielle, who infuriated her, brought in the shopping. Alice said the shops were now full of things like soya beans, water chestnuts and salted coconut chips at prohibitive prices. She ate simply - coffee when she got up, a plate of cooked fruit in the evening and one meal in the middle of the day - a little meat or fish, two vegetables and bread. When she had guests, 'as rarely as possible', she spent two days cooking and chopping. Nor were all her guests at ease over her culinary efforts. A young writer, Otto Friedrich, experienced a difficult lunch:

Miss Toklas asked a few questions, but before she had finished her own shrimp, she was off to the kitchen again, leaving us to contemplate the works of Sir Francis Rose. Then she returned with a chicken, with Gabrielle lurking behind with a plate of zucchini. . . . Miss Toklas carved with skill, but she was so tiny that she could barely reach across the high table to get at the animal . . . Once she had served three helpings she vanished again, and we sat in silence for several minutes until she returned with the orange sauce. Once again desultory questions, compliments on the sauce, gossip about a new novel, and then Miss Toklas slipped out of her high chair again and was off to supervise the dessert, a complicated custard. The dessert was delicious, but it was a relief to have the struggle ended, the meal over with.

She was alone at Christmas 1946. She cleaned all the wood panelling and the pictures, put DDT over the carpets and blankets, and in her woollen combinations, to keep out the moths and lit candles for Baby. Basket rolled on the carpet and made great white clouds of toxic dust. On New Year's Eve, Alice went to bed an hour before midnight 'so as not to know anything about it'. And she suffered at the thought of spring as she wrote to Donald Gallup: 'Do you remember how you suddenly can see everything way down the street - that's the first week in May - and the buds on the chestnuts are out. Thirty eight times we saw it together.'

It grieved her when Picasso's portrait of Gertrude went to the Metropolitan Museum of Art. Picasso came to say goodbye to it and said, 'ni vous ni moi le reverra jamais'. Lawyers wanted him to sign a paper guaranteeing the portrait was by him, but Alice refused to ask him. 'Good God,' she wrote to the Kiddie. 'Dont they know it's Gertrude by Picasso.' Alice hung Picasso's *Man with a Guitar* in the space where Gertrude's portrait had been, but she found the room emptier than ever. 'I cant bear to think of its not being here,' she wrote to Gertrude's American friend, Bobsie Goodspeed, on 10 February 1947:

> Gertrude always sat on the sofa and the picture hung over the
> fireplace opposite and I used to say in the old happy days that
> they looked at each other and that possibly when they were
> alone they talked to each other.

Alice took up letter writing after Gertrude's death and called it her work. Her handwriting was tiny, written with the 'eyelash of a fly'. She experimented with different pens and, as one of her economies, wrote on both sides of tissue thin airmail paper. She sewed and embroidered, and wore her thimble out every couple of years. A dozen or so people who used be Gertrude's friends continued to be hers. In the spring and autumn she went with them, occasionally, to a concert or to the theatre. In the winter 'I keep to the radiator,' she said. Students came to talk to her about Gertrude. 'Sometimes there is a question I can answer or a deduction I can change.' A few people came to see the pictures.

Supplies continued to be scarce for some years after the war. The Kiddies - William Rogers and his wife, Mildred - sent her cigarettes, sugar, dusters, Kleenex, woollen underwear and kitchen gadgets which she loved. She said she wanted a gadget for prising Gabrielle out of the house. Friends worried about her finances. She explained that she had the right to sell pictures, but 'that does not happen to be a thing I care to do'. Allan Stein would not let her sell the collection as a whole to a museum. Nor would he easily let her sell individual paintings to pay for publishing Gertrude. Though Gertrude had made clear that Alice was her beneficiary, as the value of the pictures rose, so did his interest in keeping them. He made Alice draw up an inventory of everything in the apartment that had belonged to Gertrude and everything that was hers.

Alice became even more possessive of Baby's life and work. Biographers were given short shrift unless they gave unequivocal adulation to Gertrude's work and steered clear of all things personal. She wrote to Julian Sawyer, an American lecturer who wanted to explain the sexual references in Gertrude's work:

> You will understand I hope my objection to your repeated
> references to the subject of sexuality as an approach to the
> understanding of Gertrude's work. She would have emphatically
> denied it - she considered it the least characteristic of all
> expressions of character - her actual references to sexuality are
> so rare . . .

She told Donald Sutherland that Sawyer was ignorant, unintelligent, insensitive and pretentious. In contrast, she was very pleased with Sutherland's biography of Gertrude. He kept away from personal matters, put Gertrude in the company of Proust, Joyce and Henry James, and thought her work as exciting as anything America had produced in the twentieth century. 'It is deeply satisfying and a great comfort to me to know that the important - the authoritative thing for this generation will be said in my time and by you,' Alice told him.

She was mightily unhelpful to the biographer, John Malcolm Brinnin, when he visited her in September 1950. She was put off by his romanticism about being in Gertrude's house and thought his questions superficial, futile 'and not helpful to any understanding of Baby's work or even of her character'. She made him make a 'solemn promise' not to mention Leo's attacks on Gertrude and to exclude all mention of herself from his book. She wrote and told him she would have nothing to do with an anecdotal history and that the atmosphere of Gertrude's home was a private matter, and that if her own existence had ever made the slightest difference to Gertrude's work, it was of nothing to equal the effect on Gertrude of landscape.

She was equally frosty to Elizabeth Sprigge, who wrote a biography of Gertrude in the mid-1950s. Alice thought her 'colossally unworthy' and told Annette Rosenshine, 'she had read very little of Gertrude's work'. She called her manuscript hateful, and it took a visit to a midnight mass for the Resurrection and 'ineffably beautiful and elevating chanting' to 'wash out' Elizabeth Sprigge's 'vulgarities and insinuations'.

Nor were close friends, who tried their hand at recreating Gertrude, any better received. Alice liked the idea when the Kiddie mooted writing a memoir of his friendship with Gertrude, though she cautioned him to leave out everything that was not to do with literature and to omit all references to her. She thought the finished thing littered with fabrications and errors and with 'the acidity that taints New England cooking'. She said it would be a book club selection if it was about someone else and that the Kiddie could not have had any genuine feeling for Gertrude to have written such a thing.

She thought Francis Rose's memoir full of endless lies, though she did not mind gossip about *his* private life. Rose tried to claim that his valet, who was also his lover, was his illegitimate son. Rose tried legally to adopt him, so that the valet could inherit Rose's title. And in the summer of 1957, Alice got a call from the British military hospital at Levallois because Rose had been beaten up by the lover he had brought with him from London. 'The doctors say there is nothing the matter with him but his character. It is too sad,' said Alice.

Soon after Gertrude's death, Alice began to express her belief in God and the 'hereafter' and the prospect of reunion. 'Without it one just plods on and now without Baby there is no direction to anything – it's just milling around in the dark – back to where one was before one was grown up', she wrote to Fania Marinoff. But Alice did plod on, in her indomitable way. In the summer of 1948 she went on holiday to the country with Basket. She stayed in the Hôtel du Cheval Blanc, in Thouars, in Deux Sèvres. It was the first time in forty years that she had travelled alone. The weather was bad and so was the food, but she found a good bookshop and liked the Romanesque architecture in the town. She had to sit on her bags in the corridor of the train on the journey back. 'Not unless there's a possibility of a reserved seat will I get on a train again - not I,' she said.

As time passed, her letters became more cheerful. At first they were all about Gertrude and Gertrude's work, but after a while she wrote about friends and acquaintances and her own news. Like many a widow, she began to serve herself rather than her master. Papa Woojums and Donald Gallup were impressed enough by the wit and liveliness of her letters to suggest that she should write a 'Biography of Gertrude Stein' as a companion to Gertrude's *Autobiography of Alice B. Toklas*. Alice emphatically opposed the idea:

> It seems so strange that you should think I could possibly write any thing about Gertrude that would add to what she so completely so perfectly said herself . . . Surely Gertrude would never have thought of anything like that –

Carl Van Vechten thought Gertrude had made Alice scared even of writing a long letter. He told Donald Gallup he saw two scenes where Gertrude ridiculed her about writing a cookbook. Alice had long wanted to do this and had collected recipes since she was a child. She was so upset, after one of these scenes, she would not speak to Gertrude for two days. The result was that Alice was terrified at putting pen to paper, if the subject was Gertrude.

In January 1950 she sold a cookery article to *Vogue*. And magazines like *House Beautiful* commissioned well-paid pieces from her on 'How to Cook with Cognac', 'Secrets of French Cooking', 'Cooking with Champagne' and 'Blessed Blender in the Home'. Isabel Wilder, Thornton Wilder's sister, sent Alice glass bowls for her Mixmaster, she developed her passion for gadgets like eggbeaters and knife sharpeners, and she tried new recipes and exchanged them with friends.

Alice carried on for Gertrude, guarding Gertrude's privacy, promoting her genius, encouraging publication and translation of all that she had written. But she began to allow herself more ground. Her acerbic manner resurfaced. She was frightful to the maid and cutting in her comments to those she disliked. She had extravagant lapses from her frugality and bought expensive perfume, gloves, muffs and tocques. She went to the opening of the Dior autumn collection in 1950 and thought there was 'a far too generous use of commonplace buttons and pockets'.

She went to Picabia's fifty-year retrospective exhibition, read William Faulkner's latest novel, *Intruder in the Dust*, and Elisabeth Bowen's *The Heat of the Day*. She thought Truman Capote's success overrated and his characters' sex lives 'boresome'. She was 'mad about *A Streetcar Named Desire*', thought Jane Bowles's *Two Serious Ladies* the most delightful novel to come her way in years and years, and wrote to Paul Bowles about his book *The Sheltering*

*Sky,* telling him that she greatly appreciated, enjoyed and admired it. 'No novel since *The Great Gatsby* has impressed me as having the force-precision-delicacy that the best of Fitzgerald has until yours.'

She became quite deaf - and so did Basket. In November 1951, Cecil Beaton and Greta Garbo rang the bell at rue Christine several times, but neither Alice nor Basket heard. So Beaton and Garbo phoned and arranged to call. 'The French papers say they are to marry,' Alice wrote to Papa Woojums, 'but she doesn't look as if she would do anything as crassly innocent as that. *Expliquez moi* as Pablo used to say to Baby.' Alice said she had heard that Cecil Beaton was in love with Greta Garbo and that the Duchess of Kent was in love with him.

Bernard Faÿ's sentence was commuted from life to twenty years, Basket got sick with an abscess, the maid, Gabrielle, had 'more things wrong with her than it was possible to enumerate', the hoover went on the blink and the rent went up. Alice's arthritis fatigued her, but she did not want to spend money on doctors. She suffered various accidents in the flat. She took the cover off the largest radiator to wash the woodwork behind it, dropped the cover on her foot and ankle and had to wait forty minutes for Gabrielle to come and rescue her. She could not walk for days after that, and she had done all her sewing and mending so she embroidered handkerchiefs.

A collection of Leo's letters, papers and journals was published in 1950. Alice was scornful of his criticisms of Gertrude. 'He was amongst the majority - the commonplace majority as Gertrude called him - of the sad and mistaken' she said to Donald Gallup.

She made friends with an American couple called Virginia and Harold Knapik. He was a musician, she worked at the American Embassy and Alice thought her 'ever so good looking' and refreshing, 'like a strong wind off the lake'. Virginia Knapik told the embassy that Alice was her aunt - that way, Alice got tax free cigarettes.

In August 1950 the Knapiks gave Alice and Basket a lift down to the Cher. Alice stayed as the paying guest of Madame Debar, who grew tobacco and farmed rabbits, chickens and pigeons. She took pillow slips to sew, Balzac to read and letters to answer. The house was rambling and old with a twelfth-century chapel and walled garden, and very good food. The only other guest was 'a young Swedish girl who has seen eighteen aurora borealises but not remarked them - she is deadly dull but as she speaks no French and very little English she does not have to be noticed.'

Allan Stein died in January 1951. Alice was pleased and regretted her previous efforts to be provident and forethoughtful for his sake. She hoped his death would allow her to see through her 'long cherished little dream' of selling Gertrude's pictures *en bloc* to a museum. But Roubina Stein, whom Alice

*Alone with Basket.*

referred to as 'the Armenian widow of Allan Stein', blocked everything Alice wanted to do concerning Gertrude's estate. 'She is neither an easy nor pleasant person to deal with,' Alice said. Neither was Alice easy and pleasant with her. Roubina Stein asked Alice to sell one of Gertrude's pictures for her because she was in debt. Alice refused, saying, 'I live frugally so as not to have to do so myself'. When, in 1954, Alice sold about forty Picasso drawings, not listed in any inventory, in order to finance publishing Gertrude, Roubina Stein made a great fuss.

Gabrielle left the rue Christine at the end of September 1951. Alice called her departure a liberation and an economy. She said that Gabrielle was disorderly, collected empty tins and bits of string, had put her through months of mental anguish and frightened Basket. She claimed she could easily manage the extra work herself and she hired a *femme de ménage* to help her, but the *femme de ménage* soon left.

Basket went blind in 1952 and fell twelve feet off the terrace in the dark on to the roof below. Alice could not find him and the concierge rescued him. Basket was cut and had lost his confidence. He died on 24 November 1952. 'He ate his usual three meals a day then collapsed', Alice wrote to Papa Woojums:

His going has stunned me. For some time I have realised how much I depended upon him and so it is the beginning of living for the rest of my days without anyone who is dependent upon me for anything.

Fortunately Dora Maar (Picasso was her lover in the 1930s) had painted a portrait of Alice and Basket the previous April. Alice was very pleased with it. She did not contemplate getting a dog to succeed Basket:

Paris is no place for a big dog unless one has a car to take him several times a week for runs in the woods and a small dog would have had to be the same kind as the wholly adorable devilish little Pépé - a Chihuahua - and naturally they are not found here.

Later that year, Gertrude's opera, *Four Saints In Three Acts*, was given a performance in Paris, which was a consolation. Leontyne Price sang Saint Theresa. Alice gave a party for the cast at the rue Christine. She made four very large cakes and served *petits pains au paté* and punch and tea.

More for money than love, Alice turned to a writing career of her own. Harpers asked her to write a cookbook. They wanted 70,000 words and gave her an advance and a contract when she had finished 30,000 words. Alice was seventy-six and found the work 'tormenting and very unsatisfactory'.

Despite an attack of jaundice, she finished the book in three months, between February and May 1953. She worked with no telephone calls and no door bells answered. Written in her sharp and witty style, she mixed recipes, anecdotes and reminiscences. Francis Rose did the illustrations and it was all a great success. She included chapters on the vegetable gardens at Bilignin, the food she and Gertrude ate on their American tour, the restaurants and hotels they found when touring in Aunt Pauline and Lady Godiva, the food in Belley and Culoz during the German Occupation. She called one chapter 'Murder in the Kitchen'. It was all about assassinating carp, smothering pigeons, and stuffing Blanchette the Barbary duck with oranges.

Another chapter she called 'Recipes From Friends'. 'Undoubtedly the only thing of merit in the deadly dull offering' she said, in her self-effacing way. Cecil Beaton offered iced apples; Papa Woojums, garlic ice-cream; Natalie Barney, stuffed egg plant; Virgil Thomson, shad-roe mousse. Pierre Balmain, Marie Laurençin, Dora Maar, Isabel Wilder and Virginia and Harold Knapik all contributed. Brion Gysin, a painter and writer who lived in Morocco, who was a close friend of Paul and Jane Bowles and Papa Woojums and who first met Gertrude and Alice in the thirties, offered hashish fudge. Alice innocently included the recipe. Gysin wrote that anyone could whip up hashish fudge on a rainy day, and that it would provoke euphoria, brilliant storms of laughter, ecstatic reveries and extensions of personality on several simultaneous planes. He said that you could get cannabis from American window-boxes or most places in Europe, that the fudge would be good for Ladies' Bridge Clubs and that anything Saint Theresa did could be done better after it.

Reviewers wondered whether they had a new insight into Gertrude's work. Alice was shocked and furious. Harper's sent a telegram to the Attorney General to see if they were in trouble and should stop printing further copies. Thornton Wilder said that no one would believe Alice's innocence and that she had pulled off the best publicity stunt of the year.

The book was also published in London and translated into French and Italian. Alice used the royalties to pay for more electricity. She went off happily in the summer of 1953 for a month in Spain with the Knapiks. She bought paper, string, ink, needles, cotton and a new thimble for the trip. She read George Orwell's *Homage to Catalonia*, Graham Greene's *The Power and the Glory* and the Kinsey Report while she was there, but thought American sex hopelessly dull. 'Sex is perhaps like culture – a luxury that only becomes an art after generations of leisurely acquaintance,' she wrote to her friend Mercedes de Acosta, who was a playwright, poet, and friend of Greta Garbo, on 26 September 1953.

At home, in Paris, Alice saw very few people. The apartment at rue Christine became faded, the carpets and curtains beyond repair. 'It will have to see me through as it is,' she wrote to an English friend. 'Do you remember how pretty it was all new and clean.' She bought a new Parker pen for writing her letters and recipes, started walking with a cane, 'It helps to get about quicker and with more security', was too hot in July, and too cold in January, and dined on a cup of broth and a baked apple. Janet Flanner took her to *Oklahoma*, and Natalie Barney and Francis Rose took her to lunch. Alice said that Natalie Barney, who was eighty, was the one bright spot left in a fairly cheerless world. 'She looks wonderfully flourishing - she has they say a new love affair - isn't it a miracle?' A volume of Gertrude's called *Painted Lace and Other Pieces* was published by Yale in 1955 with an introduction by Kahnweiler. Alice told Papa Woojums it made her ecstatic: 'It's a beauty physically and Baby at her most adorable perfection - of course the contents are a lovely transporting surprise to me.'

Around her life faded. Marie Laurençin died in June 1956. 'Marie was part of my happy early life in Paris - forty eight years ago now,' wrote Alice:

> She was enchanting - quite legendary . . . Her disappearance is
> another break with my past. It makes me feel more alone. If
> there were not still things to do for Gertrude there would be no
> reason for me to live on.

No one on earth could equal Gertrude. In the summer of 1957 Alice spent two-and-a-half months in the country. At the church in Germigny-des-Prés, 'conversion came over me almost completely', she wrote to a friend:

> Will Saint Anthony find a ray to show me the way to God. Yes I
> was baptised a Catholic as a small child with my mother's
> knowledge - then I wandered - only the saints remained. Of my
> few friends half are Catholics - three recent converts.

Though there are no church records of Alice's baptism in San Francisco or Seattle, and the Toklases and Levinskys sometimes went to synagogue, she saw a priest in Paris on 9 December. He said the baptism counted. Alice confessed, received Holy Communion, was given a missal, a rosary and some cards. 'Now I have everything to learn to live in the peace of our Lord Jesus Christ,' she wrote.

She thought that this was the only way to get together with Gertrude again. She feared that Gertrude's atheism and Judaism had not entertained the idea of a future life:

> About Gertrude's place. In the begining there was the undeniable
> knowledge that she had no conviction of a future life. The good
> Father Taylor - who heard my first communion [*sic*] - and
> Bernard [Faÿ] both told me that she was in Heaven and that I
> should pray to her there. Of course this is a great comfort.
> Bernard says he has known this a long time and was waiting
> always for me to come back to Holy Church.

Alice read the works of St Francis in the evenings, lit candles and prayed.
She now believed that the past was not gone and nor was Gertrude. 'It
left me in a dither when suddenly it came to me - where was Gertrude.
She is there waiting for us.' She talked of her comfort in 'the peopled heaven
- not only God and Jesus but the angels and saints'. Gertrude was there,
beatified.

Encouraged by the American publisher, John Schaffner, Alice began writing
her memoirs in spring 1958, when she was nearly eighty. She fancied calling
them *Things I Have Seen*. It was agreed that she should collaborate on them
with the writer Max White, whom she had first met in 1935 and who had
then corresponded with Gertrude. Like Alice, he too had converted to
Catholicism.

Alice did not want her memoirs to reveal anything about herself. 'We
are agreed that the reminiscences should be centered on Baby and her work,'
she wrote to Papa Woojums. 'That mine be discarded . . . You agree - dont
you? I am nothing but the memory of her.'

For weeks, Max White went six days a week for four or five hours each
day to the rue Christine. Then in June 1958 he vanished. Alice wrote to
John Schaffner on 17 June:

> It is indeed very strange news that I have to tell you. Three days
> ago I had a letter from Max White announcing quite inexplicably
> that he was giving up the collaboration - destroying the notes he
> had taken - the work on them he had done (he had shown me
> three excellent typewritten pages) returning to Holt at once one
> half the advance royalties (the rest later) - and was leaving Paris
> in a few days. He is no longer at his hotel - his present address
> is unknown.
>
>     All this has left me stunned. The time - about four hours a day
> six days a week - and the effort have been wasted. I have no
> idea what prompted him to take this decision. Since it was I who
> suggested his collaboration I feel guilty - to you and to Holt who
> have been so kind and patient - re Harper as well as Max White.

Have you anything to suggest.
Please have a solution to the present difficulty.
With warmest greetings.
Ever cordially
Alice Toklas.

While Alice had been telling friends that the project was going swimmingly, and advancing rapidly, White had been getting more and more disaffected. 'All she can do is lie and deny it and contradict herself. If this were amusing stuff I'd have been able to make something of it,' he said. He felt Alice manipulated every piece of information. When it came to recounting Gertrude's death, Alice got the much cited last words in the wrong order. 'It was washed of all emotion and turned to legend,' he said. His dissatisfaction made her respond with 'deep animosity'. He left.

> I went the three short blocks from the rue Christine to my hotel
> in Git-le-Coeur where I tore my notes into tangled strips and
> stuffed them into a linen mail sack and took them the few steps
> that brought me to a public trash receptacle on the boulevard
> des Grands Augustins. I made sure no last piece of paper clung
> to the inside of my mail sack. The dustmen would empty the
> S.V.P. before dawn.

He then went to Madrid and wrote his letter to Alice ending the collaboration. To friends, Alice presented herself as the bewildered injured party, saying how flabbergasted she was that he just disappeared and destroyed her notes. Max White wrote to his lawyer on 29 June 1958:

> I'm not going to talk about it to anyone else except to explain
> that Miss Toklas couldn't remember her memories. I've given her
> an opportunity to blame me and save her face (a life-long
> preoccupation of hers) but everything is anecdote beside the real
> fact that there was no basis for a book. Hoping against hope I
> discovered this slowly. I'm the only one capable of judging just
> how incapable Alice is of any sort of collaboration. She's
> completely incapable.

Alice looked for another collaborator, then decided to write the memoirs herself. It was slow, joyless work for her. She had left it too late. She was old, tired and arthritic and her sight was going. She began writing in 1958 and the 50,000 words took her more than two years. The book was published in the spring of 1963 with the title *What Is Remembered*. Her style was droll and laconic, but it was another act of service. Alice was the acolyte, Gertrude the saint. *Time*'s reviewer called it the 'book of a woman who all her life has looked in a mirror and seen someone else'.

In spring 1959, when Alice was eighty-two, she ordered a new hat from her milliners, which she said was a wow, 'put on plenty of feathers I had told her', bought a bottle of Jicki at Guerlain and a new scarf, and went off to have 'lava baths' at Aqui for her arthritis. In October she was paid $35 for reviewing Sylvia Beach's book, *Shakespeare and Company*. 'That will mend the springs and recover the armchair – the horsehair has worn out.' She wanted to buy a new chair, but thought the price staggering. She did a four-minute BBC broadcast on Pierre Balmain's collection which paid for a pair of 'winter sandals'. Her feet had become so deformed by arthritis that she could no longer wear shoes. And she became quite blind. For a time she dictated letters to a secretary, 'but she was a great nuisance and it was a relief to be rid of her'.

Money was a nagging problem. The landlady of the apartment block at the rue Christine sold the block to a company, who then sold the flats. All the tenants bought theirs, except Alice, who could not afford to buy without selling a picture. She thought French law would protect her and give her security of tenure because she was old. Nor could she find the premium needed adequately to insure Gertrude's pictures. By 1960 these were extremely valuable. Alice's insurance was based on the valuation at the time of Gertrude's death. The highest valuation on any picture was $2,500. Roubina Stein wanted a new inventory drawn up and the insurance revised. Alice disliked all dealings with her and saw her as grasping and avaricious. The pictures did not represent money to Alice. They were symbols of Gertrude and the life they had shared.

In August 1960, when she was eighty-three, Alice went to stay in a convent in Rome. Before she left Paris she, as always, made sure that the concierge would visit the apartment regularly. She told him never to let anyone know that she was out of Paris. She stayed with a Canadian order of cloistered nuns at the Monastery of the Precious Blood. 'Here I am with the good sisters,' she wrote to Virginia Knapik:

> comfortable and very happy – my little room (very convent) is hot
> but will be appreciated next month – the nights are cold – the
> air blows in from the sea fifteen miles away. Dawn comes slowly
> but dusk is rapid – so I have time to dress for mass in the chapel
> at six-thirty – then coffee at seven-forty – bath when the water is
> hot later . . . the food is simple and nourishing and there are
> vegetables. There is wonderful soup – but I am waiting for winter

for that. If winter isnt going to be perfect what is? The arthritis
is better. I walk down one flight and a half to chapel and back to
my room and down two flights and back for lunch without a
stick and there is an elevator.

She stayed with the sisters from August 1960 to summer 1961. She worked
on her memoirs. She liked the sunrise and eating Italian food, out of doors.
She went to a Papal audience in November and found it 'momentous and
moving'. 'His Holiness is small. His gestures precise - descriptive.' The Pope
spoke to her in Italian and blessed her in Latin, and when it was over she
felt weak.

She had to ask her friends to write dark and large on white paper, her
eyes were so poor. It took her three-quarters of an hour to write a page
of a letter under a strong lamp. Blessings were in her epistles, along with
descriptions of the marrons glacés.

While she was at the convent, her allowance from the Stein estate was
three months late in coming through. She was advised by her lawyer to
sell a painting to cover her monthly allowance, doctor's bills and insurance
of the pictures. She sold Picasso's *Green Still Life* to Henri Kahnweiler for
$60,000. Roubina Stein made a fuss, insisting that she and her children should
have determined a minimum price.

Alice returned from Rome to Paris in June 1961. She had been away ten
months:

Now you must know the shocking news that greeted my entrance
to the flat. The walls were bare - not one Picasso left - the
children of Allan Stein want them loaned to a museum where
they would be adequately insured which of course I could not
do. Two good lawyers are defending the case. Isnt it a bore?

While Alice was away, Roubina Stein got into her apartment and, using
the inventory drawn up at the time of Gertrude's death, found certain drawings
to be missing. Alice had sold these to pay to publish Gertrude. Roubina
Stein did not try to get in touch with Alice. Instead she went to court and
had the pictures declared 'endangered' by Alice's absence from the apartment.
She said Alice had no bars on her windows and left the place unguarded.
The day before Alice returned from Rome, all the paintings, including those
that belonged to her and were not part of Gertrude's estate, were taken
from her apartment and stored in the vault of the Chase Manhattan Bank
in Paris. Then they were sent to London.

A visitor, the writer James Lord, described the apartment without the
pictures:

The apartment had not been repainted for more than fifteen years, with the result that where each picture had hung a discolored area of its exact size now remained. Like drab and disconsolate ghosts, these shapes were far more insistent and inexorable presences than the paintings themselves had been, because they never for a moment allowed one to forget that what had been was now no more.

Alice was eighty-four and she tried to show a brave face. 'The pictures are gone permanently,' she wrote. 'My dim sight could not see them now. Happily a vivid memory does.' Roubina Stein did not want to consider the paintings as Gertrude's collection, or as part of Alice's life, but as her own capital. She kept them locked away until after Alice's death, then sold them to a New York consortium for $6 million. They were soon dispersed.

Alice sent the two little chairs she had tapestried in Picasso's designs to the Stein Collection at Yale. She would have liked to have kept them with her, but told Donald Gallup, 'the descendants of Allan Stein will confiscate them if I don't get them to you'.

Two months after her return from Rome, Alice fell and broke her kneecap. 'Don't worry about me,' she wrote to a friend. 'All old people fall - an aunt skating on the ice - a granduncle jumping off a streetcar.' She was sent to a nursing home and thought the place a fit subject for a novelette: 'There are ten people on the staff and they all hate each other.' She recovered, and went on her stalwart way. Her editor, 'who is a darling - he and his handsome young wife', came to talk to her about the manuscript of her memoirs. She had completed 215 pages. He promised to get her a secretary so that she could dictate the rest - to be paid for from advanced royalties. A 'nice young Englishman' read aloud to her, 'he's just finished Synge's *Playboy of the Western World* - tremendous! I haven't read it for nearly fifty years! What a genius he was.' Pierre Balmain visited too, 'accompanied by an utterly charming young Chinaman whom he met in Peking'. She went to his winter show and sat between Princess Isabelle of France and the American ambassador.

At Christmas, she returned to the Sisters of the Precious Blood. The Stein estate again withheld her remittance and she lived only on the royalty advance from her publisher. She wrote of her financial troubles to her lawyer:

> I am shocked and surprised at not having received a remittance for so long a time . . . It is urgent that he sends me the money by wire at once - for I am down to bedrock. It has not been easy for me to write these things to you. Gertrude Stein - in her generosity to me - did not foresee that such an occasion could arise.

While Alice was in Rome, her landlady sued for possession of 5 rue Christine. Under French law no rented apartment could stay empty for more than four months in a year. Roubina Stein had already let the authorities know that Alice spent time out of the country. Friends intervened to help Alice. Virgil Thomson, Thornton Wilder, Janet Flanner, Jo Barry, Donald Sutherland – and she thought it would all be sorted out in her favour. But, on 15 May 1963, the landlady sent a bailiff round at 7.30 in the morning to read an eviction order to her. Alice was in bed with a broken hip. She was eighty-six and almost blind. 'I was born in 1877,' she said to the bailiff. 'If I leave this apartment it will be to go to Père Lachaise.'

Friends did all they could and campaigned in the press. But the officials said that if Alice needed to go to Rome for her health, she should move there permanently, and so she was evicted in 1964 when she was eighty-seven. Janet Flanner found her a new apartment on the Left Bank, near the Eiffel Tower, a few miles from the rue Christine at 16 rue de la Convention: 'Well here I am at my age in a new home – very modern – but with no right to drive nails in the walls – in a country of painting!'

She missed the old apartment that was filled with memories of Gertrude. She took nearly all Gertrude's furniture to the new place, but the only picture, propped against a wall, was a riverscape of the Seine by Dora Maar. It was the last picture Gertrude had acquired for her collection. Alice gave that, too, to Yale. The new apartment was modern and convenient, with underfloor heating, but without character, or a sense of home:

> I dont think I'm ever going to become attached to it. The walls
> are so thin one hears everything. A neighbor sneezed the other
> day and I heard it distinctly. That is why you can't drive nails in
> the wall. An earthquake would bring us all into the court five
> flights below and I don't promise to survive.

But survive she did, for a couple more years. 'I've taken to filter-tipped cigarettes as a step to not smoking. I think,' she wrote in April 1965. She had the cataract on her eyes removed, was bed-ridden, lucid and broke. Donald Gallup recorded trying to visit her in 1965. The maid was away and Alice heard the doorbell, but could not answer it. He left the flowers he had brought outside the door.

'I dont know what is to become of me,' Alice wrote to her friends, Harold and Virginia Knapik, on 9 January 1966:

> For the present moment I'm living on the proceeds of the bank –
> the Armenian's lawyer is trying to make some sort of settlement
> without selling any of the pictures - but how he's going to

manage it I'm sure I don't know.
Do come back soon. I shan't last forever.

To commemorate her ninetieth birthday, which would have been on 30 April 1967, Gil Harrison, editor of *New Republic*, had planned to present her with a bound volume of tributes from friends and passages from her letters. But she died early in the morning of 7 March 1967, less than two months before her birthday. In her will, written in French, she left the royalties from her books to her priest, and small bequests to friends. She said that she was to be buried 'in the same tomb as Gertrude Stein in the Père Lachaise Cemetery' and that the tomb 'must be consecrated to the Holy Catholic Religion'. She asked for her own name, birth-date and date of death to be placed on the back of the stone. Even in death, she did not want to encroach on Gertrude's fame and reputation. The back of the headstone is not visible from the cemetery path and only those who know will step over other graves and find proof, engraved in gold, that Alice is there too - with Gertrude and behind her to the end.

# REFERENCES

All titles appear in full in the Select Bibliography.
A key to book abbreviations appears there.

Bancroft Library, University of California, Berkeley
YCAL   Yale Collection of American Literature
NYPL   New York Public Library

## 2 GERTRUDE'S EARLY YEARS

p.17    *I guess you know*: Gertrude Stein to
        Harriet Levy, undated. YCAL
p.17    *One should always be*: WIHS
p.17    *If anyone is the youngest*: 'The
        Superstitions of Fred Anneday, Annday,
        Anday', *Nassau Lit.*, XCIV [December
        1935], 6
p.18    *a man of brilliant ideas*: Duncan
p.18    *he liked to buy things*: MOA
p.20    *a natural figure*: WIHS
p.20    *Oh God send him a safe return*: 'The Diary
        of Amelia Stein', 1878. Bancroft Library,
        University of Berkeley, California
p.20    *Our little Gertie*: Brinnin
p.21    *She was never important*: MOA
p.21    *emotions began to feel themselves*: WIHS
p.22    *In the winter*: MOA
p.23    *Come on papa*: ibid
p.23    *His children never could lose*: ibid
p.24    *And then he would be full up*: ibid
p.24    *You have to take care*: ibid
p.25    *father Mussolini*: EA
p.25    *He always liked to think*: MOA
p.25    *Sometimes their father*: ibid
p.26    *It is better*: EA

p.26    *There was nothing there*: WIHS
p.26    *out of doors*: Paris France
p.27    *The pariah is one*: JIS
p.27    *All sex expression*: ibid
p.27    *I still recall*: ibid
p.27    *she was not a pleasant person*: EA
p.28    *a very good nose*: EA
p.28    *Dear Simon*: Daniel Stein to Simon Stein,
        13 June 1890. YCAL
p.28    *I must have the mony*: Simon Stein to
        Michael Stein, 3 December 1909. YCAL.
p.29    *My dear Allan, Mike, Sara*: ibid
p.29    *to be sure most of the time*: EA
p.31    *We were heartless youngsters*: Miller. (These
        college themes have been printed in
        *Form and Intelligibility*.)
p.31    *In other lands*: MOA
p.32    *was more a bother*: EA
p.32    *Mediaeval means*: WIHS
p.32    *I was shocked*: Duncan
p.32    *naturally was not satisfied*: EA
p.33    *I remember going to court*: ibid
p.33    *He saw not any one of them*: Duncan
p.33    *There were so many debts*: EA

# 3 ALICE'S EARLY YEARS

# 4 FIRST LOVE FOR GERTRUDE

## 5 THE RUE DE FLEURUS

## 6 ALICE MEETS GERTRUDE

# 7 OUSTING THE OTHERS

# 8 MARRIAGE

# 9 THE FIRST WAR

## 10 FAMOUS MEN, AND WOMEN

## 14 ANOTHER WAR

## 15 PEACE

public relations director for *Newsweek* in Paris. Gertrude modelled the character of Jo the Loiterer, in her opera *The Mother of Us All*, on him. When he was a student at Michigan University, he was arrested for picketing at a pre-war political rally. As picketing was not a crime, he was charged with loitering

p.248  *Tired suffering Baby*: ABT to Carl Van Vechten, 31 July 1946. YCAL
p.249  *By this time Gertrude*: WIR
p.249  *And oh Baby was so beautiful*: ABT to Carl Van Vechten, 31 July 1946. YCAL

# 16 CARRYING ON FOR GERTRUDE

(Alice's letters are collected in *Staying on Alone*)

p.251  *Oh you should have known*: Duncan
p.252  *such parts of the service*: ABT to Carl Van Vechten, 22 October, 1946. YCAL
p.252  *I just saw in Newsweek*: JIS
p.253  *She is in my opinion*: Leo Stein to Hiram Haydn, 21 July 1946. YCAL
p.253  *Oh Carlo*: ABT to Carl Van Vechten, 3 September 1946. YCAL
p.253  *It is a most shocking thing*: Gallup, *Flowers*
p.253  *My initial feeling*: Introduction to *Unpublished Writings*, vol. 8
p.255  *I have the manuscript*: ABT to Donald Gallup, 19 April, 1947. YCAL
p.256  *commenced to assert*: ABT to Donald Gallup, 23 March 1948. YCAL
p.256  *We dont meet*: ABT to Louise Taylor, 11 February 1951
p.256  *I dont happen to care*: ibid
p.257  *Miss Toklas asked*: Otto Friedrich, 'The Grave of Alice B. Toklas', *Esquire*, January 1968
p.257  *so as not to know*: ABT to Samuel Steward, 31 December 1946
p.257  *Do you remember how you suddenly*: ABT to Donald Gallup, 21 December 1946
p.257  *Good God*: ABT to W. G. Rogers, 17 February 1950
p.258  *Sometimes there is a question*: ABT to Annette Rosenshine. Bancroft Library
p.258  *You will understand*: ABT to Julian Sawyer, 12 June 1947
p.258  *It is deeply satisfying*: ABT to Donald Sutherland, 19 October 1947
p.259  *and not helpful*: ABT to Carl Van Vechten, 27 February 1950
p.259  *she had read very little*: ABT to Annette Rosenshine, 2 February 1955. Bancroft Library, C-H 161
p.259  *Without it one just plods*: ABT to Fania Marinoff, 21 February 1948. YCAL
p.259  *Not unless there's a possibility*: ABT to

Louise Taylor, 15 September 1948
p.260  *It seems so strange*: quoted in Gallup, *Pigeons*
p.261  *The French papers say*: ABT to Carl Van Vechten, 27 November 1951. YCAL
p.261  *He was amongst the majority*: ABT to Donald Gallup, 31 July 1950. YCAL
p.261  *A young Swedish girl*: ABT to Ellen Alix Taylor Daniel, 6 August 1950. YCAL
p.262  *She is neither*: ABT to Ralph W. Church, 23 January 1955. Bancroft Library, 71/79C
p.263  *His going has stunned*: ABT to Carl Van Vechten, 24 November 1952. YCAL
p.263  *Paris is no place*: ABT to Lawrence Strauss, 11 July 1953. Bancroft Library, C-H 76
p.265  *It will have to see me*: ABT to Louise Taylor, 19 September 1954
p.265  *It's a beauty*: ABT to Carl Van Vechten, 13 November 1955
p.265  *Marie was part*: ABT to Mercedes de Acosta, 28 June 1956
p.265  *Will St Anthony*: ABT to William Alfred, 10 October 1957. Harvard
p.265  *Now I have everything*: ibid, December 1957.
p.266  *About Gertrude's place*: ibid, 26 August 1958
p.266  *It left me in a dither*: ABT to Sammy Steward, 7 August 1958. Bancroft Library, 72/133C
p.266  *We are agreed*: ABT to Carl Van Vechten, 21 May 1958. YCAL
p.267  *It is indeed*: MS, Columbia University Library, New York
p.267  *All she can do is lie*: quoted in Simon, *The Biography of Alice B. Toklas*
p.267  *I went the three short blocks*: ibid
p.268  *That will mend the springs*: ABT to Princess Dilkusha de Rohan, 18 October 1959
p.268  *Here I am*: ABT to Virginia Knapik, 9 August 1960

p.269     *Now you must know*: ABT to Fernando Pivano, 9 June 1961

p.270     *The apartment had not been repainted*: James Lord, 'Where the pictures were: a memoir', *Prose*, no. 7, 1973

p.270     *Dont worry about me*: ABT to Princess Dilkusha de Rohan, 23 August 1961

p.270     *he's just finished Synge's*: ABT to Princess Dilkusha, 20 March 1963

p.270     *I am shocked and surprised*: ABT to Russell Porter, 28 December 1961

p.271     *I don't think I'm ever*: ABT to Harold and Virginia Knapik, 9 June 1965

p.271     *Donald Gallup recorded*: Gallup, *Pigeons.*

# SELECT BIBLIOGRAPHY

# GERTRUDE STEIN

A & B   *Alphabets and Birthdays* Introduction
        by Donald Gallup (Yale University
        Press, New Haven, 1957)

AFAM    *As Fine As Melanctha* Foreword by
        Natalie Clifford Barney (Yale
        University Press, New Haven,
        1954)

AABT    *The Autobiography of Alice B. Toklas*
        (Bodley Head, London, 1933)

BTV     *Bee Time Vine and Other Pieces* Preface
        by Virgil Thomson (Yale
        University Press, New Haven,
        1953)

        *Before the Flowers of Friendship Faded
        Friendship Faded* (Plain Edition,
        Paris, 1931)

        *Blood On The Dining-Room Floor*
        Foreword by Donald Gallup
        (Banyan Press, Pawlet, Vermont,
        1948)

        *Brewsie and Willie* (Random House,
        New York, 1946)

        *Composition As Explanation* (Hogarth
        Press, London, 1926)

EA      *Everybody's Autobiography* (William
        Heinemann, London, 1938)

        *Fernhurst, QED and Other Early
        Writings* Edited and with
        introduction by Leon Katz (Peter
        Owen, London, 1972)

        *The Geographical History of America or
        The Relation of Human Nature to
        the Human Mind* Introduction by
        Thornton Wilder (Random House,
        New York, 1936)

G & P   *Geography and Plays* (Four Seas,
        Boston, 1922)

GSoP    *Gertrude Stein on Picasso* Edited by
        Edward Burns (Liveright, New
        York, 1970)

HTW     *How To Write* (Plain Edition, Paris,
        1931)

        *Lectures in America* (Random House,
        New York, 1935)

        *Lucy Church Amiably* (Something Else
        Press, New York, 1969)

MOA     *The Making of Americans* (Something
        Else Press, New York, 1966)

        *Matisse, Picasso and Gertrude Stein with
        Two Shorter Stories* (Plain Edition,
        Paris, 1933)

        *Narration: Four Lectures by Gertrude
        Stein* Introduction by Thornton
        Wilder (University of Chicago
        Press, Chicago, 1935)

        *A Novel of Thank You* Introduction by
        Carl Van Vechten (Yale University
        Press, New Haven, 1958)

O & P   *Operas and Plays* (Plain Edition, Paris,
        1932)

PL      *Painted Lace and Other Pieces*
        Introduction by Daniel-Henry
        Kahnweiler (Yale University Press,
        New Haven, 1955)

        *Paris France* (Batsford, London, 1940)

        *Picasso* (Batsford, London, 1938)

P & P   *Portraits and Prayers* (Random House,
        New York, 1934)

SW   Selected Writings of Gertrude Stein    WIHS   Wars I Have Seen (Batsford, London,
        Edited by Carl Van Vechten                    1945)
        (Random House, New York, 1946).          What Are Masterpieces. Foreword by
        Includes The Autobiography of Alice          Robert Bartlett Haas (Conference
        B. Toklas, Tender Buttons,                    Press, Los Angeles, 1940)
        Composition As Explanation, Portrait     The Yale Edition of the Unpublished
        of Mabel Dodge at the Villa                   Writings of Gertrude Stein (Yale
        Curonia, As A Wife Has A Cow: A               University Press, New Haven,
        Love Story, Four Saints in Three Acts         1951-8), includes Alphabets and
        Tender Buttons (Claire Marie, New             Birthdays (1957), As Fine As
        York, 1914)                                   Melanctha (1954), Bee Time Vine
        Three Lives (Bodley Head, London,             and Other Pieces (1953), Mrs
        1915)                                         Reynolds and Five Earlier Novelettes
        Two: Gertrude Stein and Her Brother           (1952), A Novel of Thank You (1958),
        and Other Early Portraits Foreword            Painted Lace and Other Pieces (1955),
        by Janet Flanner (Yale University             Stanzas in Meditation and Other
        Press, New Haven, 1951)                       Poems (1956), Two: Gertrude Stein
UK   Useful Knowledge (Bodley Head,                   and Her Brother and Other Early
        London, 1929)                                 Portraits (1951)

## LEO STEIN

        The ABC of Aesthetics (Boni &        JIS   Journey into the Self: Being the Letters,
        Liveright, New York, 1927)                   Papers and Journals of Leo Stein.
        Appreciation: Painting, Poetry and Prose     Edited by Edmund Fuller (Crown
        (Crown Publishers, New York,                 Publishers, New York, 1950)
        1947)

## ALICE B. TOKLAS

ABTC   The Alice B. Toklas Cookbook (Anchor          California at Berkeley, C-H 33
          Books, New York, 1960)             SOA   Staying on Alone: Letters of Alice B.
          Aromas and Flavours of Past and Present     Toklas Edited by Edward Burns
          Introduction by Poppy Cannon              (Angus & Robertson, London,
          (Harper & Bros, New York, 1958)           1974)
Duncan   Interview by Roland E. Duncan (1952),  WIR   What Is Remembered (Holt, Rinehart
          for the Oral History Department,          & Winston, New York, 1963)
          the Bancroft Library, University of

## GENERAL

Acosta, Mercedes de, Here Lies the Heart (Reynal      New York, 1942)
   & Co., New York, 1960)                          — Sherwood Anderson's Notebooks (Boni &
Acton, Harold, Memoirs of an Aesthete (Methuen,         Liveright, New York, 1926)
   London, 1948)                                   Baker, Carlos, Ernest Hemingway: A Life Story
— More Memoirs of an Aesthete (Methuen, London          (Collins, London, 1969)
   1970)                                           Balmain, Pierre, My Years and Seasons (Doubleday,
Ackroyd, Peter, Ezra Pound and His World               New York, 1965)
   (Thames and Hudson, London, 1980)              Beach, Sylvia, Shakespeare and Company (Faber
Aldrich, Mildred, A Hilltop on the Marne                and Faber, London, 1960)
   (Constable, London, 1915)                       Beaton, Cecil, Photobiography (Doubleday, New
Anderson, Sherwood, Gertrude Stein:                    York, 1951)
   Correspondence and Personal Essays (University  — The Wandering Years: Diaries: 1922-39
   of North Carolina Press, Chapel Hill, 1972)        (Weidenfeld and Nicolson, 1961)
— Sherwood Anderson's Memoirs (Harcourt Brace,     Bodart, Anne, The Blue Dog and Other Fables for

the French Translated by Alice B. Toklas
(Houghton Mifflin, Boston, 1956)

Bowles, Paul, *Without Stopping* (Peter Owen,
London, 1972)

Boyle, Kay and McAlmon, Robert, *Being Geniuses
Together* (Doubleday, New York, 1968)

Bridgman, Richard, *Gertrude Stein in Pieces*
(Oxford University Press, New York, 1970)

Brinnin, John Malcolm, *The Third Rose: Gertrude
Stein and Her World* (Little, Brown and Co.,
Boston, 1959)

Bryher, *The Heart to Artemis: A Writer's Memoirs*
(Harcourt Brace, New York, 1962)

Burns, Edward (ed.), *The Letters of Gertrude Stein
and Carl Van Vechten, 1913-46* (Columbia
University Press, New York, 1986) (two vols.)

Connolly, Cyril, *Previous Convictions* (New York,
1963)

Cooper, Emmanuel, *The Sexual Perspective:
Homosexuality and Art in the Last 100 Years in
the West* (Routledge and Kegan Paul,
London, 1986)

Edstrom, David, *The Testament of Caliban* (Robert
Hale, London 1938)

Faÿ, Bernard, *Les Précieux* (Librairie Académique
Perrin, Paris, 1966)

Field, Andrew, *The Formidable Miss Barnes* (Secker
& Warburg, London, 1983)

Fitch, Noel Riley, *Sylvia Beach and the Lost
Generation* (Souvenir Press, London, 1984)

Fitzgerald, F. Scott, *The Letters of F. Scott
Fitzgerald* Edited by Andrew Turnbull
(Bodley Head, London, 1964)

Flanner, Janet (Genet), *An American in Paris*
(Hamish Hamilton, London, 1940)

— *Paris Was Yesterday 1925-39* (Angus and
Robertson, London, 1972)

Gallup, Donald (ed.), *The Flowers of Friendship:
Letters Written to Gertrude Stein* (Alfred A.
Knopf, New York, 1953)

— *Pigeons on the Granite* (Yale University, New
Haven, 1988)

Haas, Robert Bartlett and Gallup, Donald, *A
Catalogue of the Published and Unpublished
Writings of Gertrude Stein* (Yale University
Library, New Haven, 1941)

Haas, Robert Bartlett, 'Gertrude Stein Talking -
A Transatlantic Interview' (1945), *Uclan Review*
(Summer 1962), (Spring 1963), (Winter 1964)

Halpert, Stephen and Johns, Richard (eds.), *A
Return to Pagany 1929-32* (Beacon Press,
Boston)

Hanscombe, Gillian and Smyers, Virginia L.,
*Writing for Their Lives* (The Women's Press,
London, 1987)

Hemingway, Ernest, *Ernest Hemingway: Selected
Letters, 1917-61* Edited Carlos Baker (Scribner's
& Sons, New York, 1981)

— *A Moveable Feast* (Bantam, London, 1969)

Hobhouse, Janet *Everybody Who Was Anybody*
(Weidenfeld and Nicolson, London, 1975)

Imbs, Bravig, *Confessions of Another Young Man*
(Henkle-Yewdale House Inc, New York, 1936)

James, William, *Psychology* (Henry Holt, New
York, 1913)

Jolas, Eugene (ed.), *Testimony Against Gertrude
Stein* (Servire Press, The Hague, 1935)

Jones, Howard Mumford (ed.), *Letters of Sherwood
Anderson* (Little, Brown and Company, Boston,
1953)

Kahnweiler, Daniel-Henry, *Letters of Juan Gris*
(Percy Lund, Humphries, London, 1956)

Lachman, Arthur, 'Gertrude Stein As I Knew
Her', typescript (Beinecke Library, Yale)

Levy, Harriet Lane, *920 O'Farrell Street*
(Doubleday, New York, 1947)

— 'Recollections', typescript, C-H II (Bancroft
Library, University of Berkeley)

Luhan, Mabel Dodge, *Intimate Memories*
(Harcourt, Brace and Co., New York, 1933-7)
Vol I: *Background* (1933), Vol 2: *European
Experiences* (1935); Vol. 3: *Movers and Shakers*
(1936); Vol. 4: *Edge of the Taos Desert* (1937)

Mellow, James R., *Charmed Circle: Gertrude Stein
and Company* (Phaidon Press, London, 1974)

Miller, Rosalind S., *Gertrude Stein: Form and
Intelligibility* (Exposition Press, New York,
1949)

Museum of Modern Art, New York, *Four
Americans in Paris: The Collections of Gertrude
Stein and Her Family* (1970)

Nichols, Beverley, *All I Could Never Be* (Cape,
London, 1949)

Olivier, Fernande, *Picasso and His Friends*
(Heinemann, London, 1964)

Pollack, Barbara, *The Collectors: Dr Claribel and
Miss Etta Cone* (Bobbs-Merrill Co. Inc., New
York, 1962)

Rogers, W. G., *When This You See Remember Me.
Gertrude Stein in Person* (Rinehart, New York,
1948)

Rose, Francis, *Saying Life* (Cassell, London, 1961)

— *Gertrude Stein and Painting* (Book Collecting
and Library Monthly, London, 1968)

Rosenshine, Annette, 'Life's Not A Paragraph',
typescript, 68/154C (Bancroft Library,
University of Berkeley, 1964)

Saarinen, Aline B., *The Proud Possessors* (Random
House, New York, 1958)

Sawyer-Lauçanno, Christopher, *The Invisible*

*Spectator: Autobiography of Paul Bowles*
(Bloomsbury, London, 1989)

Scudder, Janet, *Modeling My Life* (Harcourt Brace,
New York, 1925)

Secrest, Meryle, *Between Me and Life: A Biography
of Romaine Brooks* (Macdonald and Jane's,
London, 1976)

Sevareid, Eric, *Not So Wild A Dream* (Alfred
Knopf, New York 1946)

Shattuck, Roger, *The Banquet Years* (Harcourt
Brace, New York, 1955)

Simon, Linda, *The Biography of Alice B. Toklas*
(Peter Owen, London, 1978)

Sprigge, Elizabeth, *Gertrude Stein: Her Life and
Work* (Harper and Bros., New York, 1957)

Stein, Amelia, 'The Diary of Amelia Stein',
(Bancroft Library, ms C-H 136, University of
Berkeley, California, 1878)

Steward, Samuel M. (ed.), *Dear Sammy: Letters
from Gertrude Stein and Alice B. Toklas*
(Houghton Mifflin, Boston, 1977)

Sutherland, Donald, *Gertrude Stein: A Biography of
Her Work* (Yale University Press, New Haven,
1951)

*Testimony Against Gertrude Stein.* Supplement to
*transition* (February, 1935)

Thomson, Virgil, *Virgil Thomson* (Weidenfeld &
Nicolson, London, 1967)

Vollard, Ambroise, *Souvenirs d'un marchand de
tableaux* (Albin Michel, Paris, 1937)

Weininger, Otto, *Sex and Character* (Putnam, New
York, 1906)

Wickes, George, *The Amazon of Letters: The Life
and Loves of Natalie Barney* (W. H. Allen,
London, 1977)

Williams, William Carlos, *The Autobiography of
William Carlos Williams* (Random House, New
York, 1951)

Wilson, Edmund, *Axel's Castle* (Scribner's, New
York, 1952)

— *The Shores of Light* (Farrar, New York, 1952)

— *The Twenties* (Macmillan, London, 1975).

# CREDITS

The author and publishers would like to acknowledge the
following for permission to include material:

The Collection of American Literature, Beinecke Rare
Book and Manuscript Library, Yale University, for
extracts from letters and writings of Gertrude Stein,
Daniel Stein, Simon Stein, Michael Stein, Leo Stein,
Daniel Stein, Mabel Weeks, Carl Van Vechten, Mildrid
Aldrich, Howard Gans, Sylvia Beach, Ernest
Hemingway, Edith Sitwell, Ellery Sedgwick, Edward
Aswell, Alice B. Toklas and Bennett Cerf; the extracts
from *What is Remembered* by Alice B. Toklas, copyright
© 1963 by Alice B. Toklas, reprinted by permission
of Henry Holt and Company, Inc and A.M. Heath;
extracts by Gertrude Stein from *Wars I have Seen*
(Batsford), *The Making of Americans* (Something Else
Press), *Fernhurst, QED and Other Writings* (Peter Owen),
*Geography and Plays* (Four Seas), *Picasso* (Batsford), *Paris
France* (Batsford), *Composition as Explanation* (Hogarth
Press), *The Mother of Us All, Brewsie and Willie* (Random
House), *Bee Time Vine and Other Pieces* (Yale), *Two:
Gertrude Stein and Her Brother and Other Portraits* (Yale),
*As Fine as Melanctha* (Yale), Painted Lace and Other
Pieces (Yale), *How to Write* (Plain Edition), *Stanzas in
Meditation* (Yale), *Lucy Church Amiably, Natural
Phenomena, Rich and Poor in English, Accents in Alsace:
A Reasonable Tragedy, Alphabets and Birthdays* (Yale),
*Useful Knowledge* (Bodley Head), *Waterpipoe, Turkey
Bones and We Liked It: A Play, Tender Buttons* (Claire
Marie), *Coal and Wood, All Sunday, A Lyrical Opera,
Gertrude Stein on Picasso* (Liveright) and *Matisse, Picasso
and Gertrude Stein* (Plain Edition) reproduced courtesy
of the Estate of Gertrude Stein and David Higham
Associates; extract from *The Third Rose* by John
Malcolm Brinnin (Little Brown, Inc) © 1959, ©
renewed 1987, by John Malcolm Brinnin; extracts
from *Shakespeare and Company* by Sylvia Beach, ©
1959 by Sylvia Beach and renewed in 1987 by Frederic
Beach Dennis, reprinted by permission of Harcourt
Brace Jovanovich, Inc; extract from *Movers and Shakers*
volume 3 of *Intimate Memories* (4 volumes) by Mabel

Dodge Luhan (Harcourt Brace Jovanovich) by
permission of Curtis Brown Ltd © 1935, 1963 by
Mabel Dodge Luhan; extracts from *Ada: A Portrait*
by Gertrude Stein, *Four Saints and Three Acts* by
Gertrude Stein, *Selected Writings of Gertrude Stein, The
Autobiography of Alice B. Toklas* by Gertrude Stein, ©
1933, renewed 1961 Alice B. Toklas, *Everybody's
Autobiography* by Gertrude Stein, © 1937, renewed
1965 Alice B. Toklas, *Lectures From America* by
Gertrude Stein, © 1935, renewed 1963 Alice B. Toklas,
all by permission of the Estate of Gertrude Stein,
Random House, Inc and David Higham Associates;
extract from *Journey into the Self* by Edmund Fuller
© 1950 by the Estate of Leo Stein, by permission
Crown Publishers, Inc; extract from *The Flowers of
Friendship: Letters Written to Gertrude Stein* by Donald
C. Gallup (Editor), © 1953 by Donald C. Gallup, by
permission of Alfred A. Knopf, Inc; extracts from
*Portraits and Prayers* by Gertrude Stein, courtesy of
the Estate of Gertrude Stein and David Higham
Associates; extracts from *Staying on Alone: Letters of
Alice B. Toklas* edited by Edward Burns, courtesy of
Liveright and Angus & Robertson, London and Sydney;
extracts from *The Alice B. Toklas Cookbook* by Alice
B. Toklas (Anchor, 1960), © 1954 Alice B. Toklas, ©
renewed 1982 Edward M. Burns, reprinted by
permission of HarperCollins*Publishers*.

Photographs credited to the Cone Collection at the
Baltimore Museum of Art are part of the collection
formed by Dr Claribel Cone and Miss Etta Cone of
Baltimore, Maryland.

Every effort has been made to trace the copyright
holders of the material reprinted in this book. The
author and publishers would be glad to hear from
copyright holders they have not been able to contact
and print due acknowledgement in the next
edition.

# INDEX